"A valuable contribution to studies of the allotment era in particular and to studies of U.S.-American I--1:- ------ nialism in general."

—John R. Gram, *Southwest*

D0851525

"Ellinghaus's work shines a light ᴏ.. ᴀ ᴄɪᴜᴄɪᴀʟ component of federal Indian policy."

—Christopher Steinke, *Nebraska History*

"Ellinghaus utilizes an impressive amount of archival research and specific case studies to show how the concept of blood permeated the policies of the Office of Indian Affairs during [the late nineteenth and early twentieth century]."

—Paul Spruhan, *Canadian Journal of Native Studies*

"Ellinghaus offers this book as a means for critiquing and analyzing the phenomenon of settler colonialism which allowed for tropes of authenticity to persist today. It also adds to the story of Native Americans' unrelenting resistance with racial science and white structures. In light of the semi-recent events at Standing Rock, Native American persistence throughout history is again highlighted by their ability to resist and act against their oppressors."

—Hannah Blubaugh, *Origins*

"Katherine Ellinghaus brilliantly traces the uneven practices that produced a powerful discourse of American Indian blood quantum. With sure hand and subtle interpretation, *Blood Will Tell* offers a compelling new reading of a technology of identity at once complicated and crude."

—Philip J. Deloria, Carroll Smith-Rosenberg Collegiate Professor at the University of Michigan–Ann Arbor and author of *Indians in Unexpected Places*

"Written with great clarity and precision. . . . Ellinghaus develops several key insights that will make contributions to historical scholarship on Indians, race, and western American history."

—Margaret Jacobs, Chancellor's Professor of History at the University of Nebraska–Lincoln and author of *A Generation Removed: The Fostering and Adoption of Indigenous Children in the Postwar World*

"A triumph of humanistic scholarship. . . . Many of the topics Ellinghaus covers are of salience to contemporary debates about race and racism."

—Gregory Smithers, author of *Science, Sexuality, and Race in the United States and Australia, 1780–1940*, revised edition

BLOOD WILL TELL

**New Visions in Native American
and Indigenous Studies**

SERIES EDITORS

Margaret D. Jacobs
Robert Miller

Blood Will Tell

Native Americans and
Assimilation Policy

KATHERINE ELLINGHAUS

CO-PUBLISHED BY THE UNIVERSITY OF NEBRASKA PRESS

AND THE AMERICAN PHILOSOPHICAL SOCIETY

Portions of this book were originally published as "The Benefits of Being Indian: Blood Quanta, Intermarriage, and Allotment Policy on the White Earth Reservation, 1889–1920," in *Frontiers: A Journal of Women's Studies* 29, nos. 2–3 (2008): 81–105; "The Pocahontas Exception: Indigenous 'Absorption' and Racial Integrity in the United States, 1880s–1920s," in *Rethinking Colonial Histories II: New and Alternative Approaches*, ed. Penny Edmonds and Sam Furphy (Melbourne: RMIT Publishing, 2006), 123–36.

Library of Congress Cataloging-in-Publication Data
Names: Ellinghaus, Katherine, author.
Title: Blood will tell: Native Americans and assimilation policy / Katherine Ellinghaus.
Description: Lincoln: University of Nebraska Press, 2017. | Series: New visions in Native American and indigenous studies | Includes bibliographical references and index.
Identifiers: LCCN 2016047605
ISBN 9780803225435 (hardback: alk. paper)
ISBN 9781496230379 (paperback)
ISBN 9781496201584 (epub)
ISBN 9781496201591 (mobi)
ISBN 9781496201607 (pdf)
Subjects: LCSH: Indians of North America—Ethnic identity. | Indians of North America—Tribal citizenship. | Indians of North America—Mixed descent. | Indian allotments—United States—History. | United States. General Allotment Act (1887) | United States. Indian Reorganization Act. | Indians of North America—Land tenure. | Indians of North America—Legal status, laws, etc. | Indians of North America—Government relations. | Indians of North America—Cultural assimilation—History. | BISAC: SOCIAL SCIENCE / Ethnic Studies / Native American Studies. | HISTORY / United States / 19th Century. | HISTORY / United States / 20th Century.
Classification: LCC E98.E85 E45 2017 | DDC 970.004/97—dc23
LC record available at https://lccn.loc.gov/2016047605

Set in Charis by John Klopping.
Designed by N. Putens.

For Dahsha and Marlo

CONTENTS

ILLUSTRATIONS

Introduction

The Discourse of Blood in the Assimilation Period

The archives generated by Native American assimilation policies are stained with blood.[1] The terms "full-blood," "half-blood," "mixed-blood" and other fractions making up "blood quantum" pervade these records and the depictions of Native American people therein. The use of such terms was not confined to one statute, one reservation, one agency, or one direction of Indian policy. Blood quantum was an integral means by which white Americans took cognizance of Native American people. It was omnipresent, referred to in almost every document, recorded carefully against names in tribal rolls, used in descriptions of Indian communities and invoked in the complaints of Indigenous resistance from one end of the country to the other. Blood was and is also a term sometimes used by Native Americans in talking and writing of themselves, and in defining tribal membership.

Blood was not, however, specifically mentioned in the General Allotment Act of 1887, the federal legislation that provided the statutory framework for the assimilation period. Nor did the 1887 act define who was or who was not an "Indian."[2] "Oddly enough," Steve Russell has noted, "blood quantum appeared in Indian rolls . . . before it appeared in law books."[3] The section of the Code of Federal Regulations that implemented the General Allotment Act allowed Indian nations themselves to decide who was eligible for allotment according to their own laws and traditions. The regulations stated only that the "possession of Indian blood, not accompanied by tribal affiliation or relationship, does not entitle a person to an allotment."[4] It was not until 1934 that the Indian Reorganization (Wheeler–Howard) Act, which marked the end of the assimilation period, provided a federal definition of Indianness based on blood. Even then, blood remained only one pathway to official Indian status. Section 19 of the Indian Reorganization Act (1934) reads:

> The term "Indian" as used in this Act shall include all persons of Indian descent who are members of any recognized Indian tribe now under Federal jurisdiction, and all persons who are descendants of such members who were, on June 1, 1934, residing within the present boundaries of any Indian reservation, and shall further include all other persons of one-half or more Indian blood.[5]

This book was written by an Australian historian who once sat in the reading room of the National Archives and Records Administration in Washington DC puzzled by the conundrum of the simultaneous presence and absence of blood in Native American assimilation policy. In Australia settler governments regularly passed legislation that contained blood-based definitions of who was an "Aborigine."[6] In the United States, I wondered, if not through legislation, then why and how did blood come to infuse the common understanding of who was an "Indian"? The answer has turned out to be far more complicated than I anticipated.

Blood Tropes

The discourse of blood during the assimilation period carried with it the idea that people of mixed descent and full descent each had distinct personal characteristics. Three tropes concerning Native Americans of mixed descent recurred in the assimilation period. First, drawing on the long-standing European view that racial mixing led to an increase in vigor, white Americans assumed, with easy arrogance, that the addition of white blood made Indians smarter, more business-like, and au fait with Christianity, the English language, and mainstream ways of life. Indians of full descent were assumed to be lower on the evolutionary scale and thus less intelligent and civilized. They were also portrayed as helpless victims deserving of the government's aid. By contrast, people of mixed Indian and white descent were depicted as cunning, exploitative, and undeserving of the benefits and rights that came with Indian ancestry. Native Americans of mixed descent were (and sometimes are still) portrayed as cultural brokers, interpreters, or mediators who got the best out of the allotment process to the detriment of "real" Indians.[7]

A second trope in the discourse of blood helped to barnacle the idea of authenticity to Indian status.[8] Blood was the element that carried a romanticized image of the "noble savage," the Indian of the period before contact and assimilation, portrayed in literature and art. Anthropologists played an important role in cementing the image of the "authentic" Indian by, as Lee D. Baker has shown, "staging, fabricating, authenticating, and editing what was and was not Indian."[9] The presence of any non-Indian blood in a family tree destabilized (to outsiders) their Indianness, contaminating it and casting it into question. As Eva Marie Garroutte expressed it, "full bloods tend to be seen as the 'really real,' the quintessential Indians, while others are viewed as Indians in diminishing degrees."[10] Thus blood operated to divide Indian people into "full-bloods" who were "real Indians" and "mixed-bloods" whose claim to authenticity was on shaky ground.

A third trope embedded in the discourse of blood applied to Native Americans who had, or were perceived to have, African American ancestry. These were treated quite differently to those with white ancestry. African Americans were linked to an image of the "savage" rather than the "noble savage." Indians with African American heritage therefore suffered from the prejudice attached to their African American ancestry.[11] The "one-drop rule" could nullify their Indian status in the eye of the U.S. government as well as some tribal governments. A history of intermarriage with African Americans had a significant effect on how Indian communities were treated.[12]

The belief in blood as a determinant of human characteristics was not new. In 1887, when the assimilation period officially began, blood had long been used by many cultures as a measure and metaphor for pollution and purity.[13] In the sixteenth century Europeans believed that bodily attributes such as skin color were the result of varied climates, not genetics. By the end of the seventeenth century this belief had been replaced by the view that bodily disparities were due not to the external environment, but instead originated within bodies themselves.[14] In this period, blood came to the fore as a way of explaining the differences between the variegated bodies that Europeans were encountering in the early modern world of empire and colonialism.[15] Blood became a racial marker that resided unseen inside the body, a vessel that carried different racial traits and transmitted them to offspring. Of course, Europeans during this period were no longer merely encountering different kinds of bodies but, through cross-cultural relations, were co-creating them. Alongside vague terms such as "half breed," "mulatto," and "métis", blood was used as a means of differentiating people of mixed descent, particularly in Spanish colonial America where the concept of *sangre pura* (pure blood) led to a complex system of racial categorization.[16] In 1705 Virginia legally defined who was a mulatto; several scholars have identified a Virginia statute of 1785 as the first use of blood for such a purpose in a North American law.[17] Jennifer Spear's work is crucial in understanding the entanglement of blood with ideas of race, so that it became both a means of description and itself a racializing force. Using *limpieza de sangre* cases in late eighteenth-century New Orleans, Spear shows that when qualities such as honor, legitimacy, respectability, and reputation were embodied in blood they in turn became racialized.[18] Blood was, and remains, a powerful metaphor. And it is a metaphor, as Patrick Wolfe has noted, well suited to post-frontier settler discourse because it, "being liquid, readily lends itself to quantification" in a way that cultural or political metaphors do not.[19]

This book is concerned with the history of blood in the post-empire age, focusing on its application to the Indigenous peoples of North America in the late nineteenth and early twentieth centuries. A rich literature already exists on how the discourse of blood has impacted and operated within Native American communities at different times and places.[20] There have been, however, few in-depth studies that fully explore the role that blood played in assimilation policy, and explain how blood acquired the meaning most often used in relation to Indigenous North Americans in the twentieth century. As Kimberley Tallbear puts it, blood became a "probalistic social link between an individual and a land-based group."[21] Paul Spruhan has done groundbreaking work on the use of blood in legislation and federal policy from the early colonial period through the present day.[22] One of the first scholars to note the steady introduction of blood quantum through the assimilation period was Jack Forbes.[23] David Chang has analyzed the role of blood in changing the meanings of land and property ownership during the allotment of the Creeks.[24] A number of scholars have examined the role of blood during the assimilation period in their histories of people of mixed Native American and African American descent.[25] Ariela Gross has shown how blood defined race as a kind of "internal essence" in courts of law during the early twentieth century. Angela A. Gonzales has pointed out the centrality of the decennial U.S. census in classifying Native and African American identities in terms of racial science.[26] A number of other scholars have paid attention to Native American people of mixed descent, detailing their border crossings, describing their dual roles and uncertain status, and explaining their significance in the histories of citizenship, racial status, and the fluctuations of the Indian population.[27] But, as Melissa Meyer noted in 1999, notwithstanding the centrality of blood to Indigenous communities, it is curious that "no one has explored in serious scholarly fashion how the enrollment process evolved or how 'blood quantum' . . . came to be one of the most important criteria used first by federal policy makers."[28] There is, Paul Spruhan has argued, a "void" in our understanding of why blood came to permeate federal policy.[29]

In this book I show that while blood was not mentioned in the 1887 General Allotment Act, it nevertheless operated as a set of criteria that could determine whether a person did (or did not) deserve enrollment and allotment. The discourse of blood between 1887 and 1934 is evidence for Ann Laura Stoler's argument asserting the importance of the "unwritten" in colonial ontologies. Blood comprised a set of ideas that could remain largely unwritten because they "could go without saying and everyone knew [them]." It was one of the "pliable coordinates of what constituted colonial common sense."[30] It infiltrated and permeated U.S. government thinking about who was deserving of status as Native

American and operated as a set of ideas about human nature that were powerful and intuitive.

The 1887 General Allotment Act provided that allotments of land were only to be given to members of tribes, but at this time many nations did not have comprehensive written lists of their members. The enormous and complicated task of dividing up reservation land and allotting it to individuals was put in the hands of swiftly increasing numbers of Office of Indian Affairs employees—mostly working as Indian agents and members of commissions (groups of public servants varying in size and complexity sent into the field to make lists of tribal members).[31] As Cathleen Cahill has shown convincingly, it is important for historians to focus not just on legislation but also on the men and women who "actually translated policy into practice."[32] These public servants were given no firm instructions on how to decide who was or was not an Indian. They made decisions nonetheless, and they did so using the language of blood. An individual's blood quantum was often fixed in an arbitrary, haphazard fashion, even though the matter of deciding who was or was not an Indian was crucial to the process of assimilation. Government commissions made crude mathematical estimates according to what they knew of an individual's family—for example, a child of a non-Indian parent and an Indian parent was "half" Indian, and a child with one non-Indian grandparent and three Indian grandparents was "one-quarter."

Other factors came into play as government officials faced Native American people across a table and made their judgments about what indicated a person's ethnic status according to what they saw. As Scott Malcomson has put it: "It had to do with facial features and skin tone; dress, perhaps, language, maybe; family name (surely someone called Whitekiller is an Indian?); and the general tenor of a community."[33] Those making decisions about Indian status often had little information about a person's parentage. They were more often than not low-ranked civil servants who selectively drew upon racial discourses that were available to them, and made assumptions of their own about how an "Indian" should look, sound, and act. Mainstream American ideas about gender roles, as Rose Stremlau has made clear, also filtered into the way allotment was administered.[34] The U.S. government was concerned not merely with assimilation, but with imposing European heteronormative conceptions of family, gender, and relationships, and this also impacted on their decisions.

Despite its scientific-sounding terminology, the discourse of blood as employed in the assimilation period was only indirectly the product of science. Ann McMullen has described blood in this period as a "folk biology," and in the contexts I describe in this book this is perhaps the most meaningful way of understanding it.[35] At the turn of the century scientists as well as the general population conceived of race according to a miscellany of contradictory and competing ideas about blood, civilization, nation, and culture, often using these terms interchangeably.[36] Just as the U.S. government began increasingly to resort to the discourse of blood in deciding who was Native American and who was not, most of the newly minted profession of anthropology was proceeding down a different path. After fiery disagreements on whether different ethnicities were actually different species in the 1850s and 1860s, anthropologists working at the discipline-defining Smithsonian Institution were shying away from physical anthropology (which focused on the relationship between body and culture) because of its political connotations.

From the early 1900s Franz Boas, the "father" of American anthropology, and his followers concentrated primarily on the idea of culture as a means of explaining the diversity of human beings. Boas rejected the idea that ethnic differences could be apprehended by using a fixed and hierarchical model of racial typology and instead investigated how communities defined themselves according to shared social meanings. These views barely made it into government policy—and it is understandable why. The Office of Indian Affairs needed racial certainty and therefore tangible means of categorizing and making sense of a numerous and extraordinarily complex set of communities. Only a marginal group of scientists drew on the discourse of blood to understand race: those who engaged in physical anthropology, those who believed that traits gained during an organism's lifetime could be passed on to its offspring (a theory known as neo-Lamarckism), and a number of amateurs (among them Charles Davenport, Lothrop Stoddard, and the American Eugenics Society) who were interested in eugenics.[37] Occasionally, these nonconformists were asked by the Office of Indian Affairs to assist in particularly troublesome cases where records had proved inadequate to the task of deciding who was Indian and who was not. Some "scientists" do make brief appearances in this book, measuring, photographing, and classifying particular groups of Native American people. But science did little to drive the increasing popularity of the discourse of blood. That was the doing of the Office of Indian Affairs in its efforts to categorize a people according to a universally applicable set of beliefs with the ring of science, but no basis in it.

An Unruly Venture

This book does not tell a neat story, and describes no orderly progression from "something else" to "blood" as means of understanding Indian identity. As C. Joseph Genetin-Pilawa has shown, American settler colonialism had a particular "fluidity and shiftiness."[38] Many times during the writing of this book I have taken comfort from Ann Laura Stoler's remark that although colonial administrations were "prolific producers of social categories," their production was "an unruly and piecemeal venture at best."[39] To describe the role played by the three tropes identified in this introduction in the enormous, lengthy, and complex undertaking of administering the 1887 General Allotment Act, I have focused on specific times and places at which blood rose to the surface of people's racial thinking—and hence entered into the archives. The tendency in some recent Native American historiography has been to focus on one tribal nation, and there is much merit to the method of exploring a complex, local context in intricate detail. My intention, however, has been to create, by the use of multiple and diverse case studies, a nuanced though wide-ranging national picture of the operation of the discourse of blood in government policy.

Blood was transformed from an unofficial, arbitrary marker of Indian status to a component of its official definition in 1934 in three stages. In the first stage, blood was increasingly used, at first haphazardly and informally, during the enrollment of Indian nations. In chapters 1 and 2, I focus on the process of enrollment and allotment on the White Earth Reservation in Minnesota and among the Five Tribes of Indian Territory—the

Choctaws, Chickasaws, Cherokees, Seminoles and Muscogees (Creeks). These two case studies, both of communities made up of many different peoples artificially gathered together at the hands of the U.S. government, show how the discourse of blood began to pervade government decision-making about who was deserving of Indian status and the lands and other benefits that accompanied it before any official blood-based definitions of Indian status existed. In both cases the government followed to some extent the idea that tribal governments and laws should have influence over who was eligible for enrollment and allotment. In both cases the processes became fraught, caught the attention of the nation, and generated much comment, agonized letter-writing and report-making, in part because of the sense that non-Indians were taking advantage of the process to get access to tribal lands and funds. In both cases, tribes and individuals engaged in resistance and negotiation with the policies that were imposed upon them. In this climate the government often acted in the conviction that Indians of mixed descent were undeserving of Indian status, rights, lands, and funds and that "real" Native Americans lived on the reservation and looked and acted in recognizably "Indian ways." At White Earth the process of allotment became fraught because of fraud perpetrated by persons seeking to convince the Anishinaabeg to sell or lease their lands—to an extent that the government could no longer ignore. Government efforts to address that problem by using the racial "science" of the day resulted in labyrinthine legal decisions concluding that the majority of the White Earth population were of mixed descent. In Indian Territory, where the population of Native Americans to be allotted was much larger, administrative chaos was underpinned by the government's conviction that members of the Five Tribes were divided into helpless, deserving, "full-blood" (or "real") Indians on the one hand and scheming, undeserving "mixed-bloods" on the other.

I identify a second stage in the evolution of blood from informal to formal indicator of Indian status in the introduction of the policy of "competency" by the federal government in 1906. The rights of Indians perceived to be of mixed descent had been destabilized by the chaos of enrollment and allotment, but not removed. Competency targeted them and their lands for the first time. Under this policy, introduced with no input from Indigenous people, land held by individual Indians proclaimed to be "competent" could be released from the twenty-five-year trust period to which it was otherwise subject under the General Allotment Act. Competency was unevenly applied in different communities and at different times. Its operation at White Earth and in Indian Territory is considered in the first two chapters. In chapter 3 I show how at the federal level blood was increasingly used to determine who should be declared competent and therefore lose the protection of the trust period. In 1917 the federal government declared all Indians of less than one-half Indian "blood" to be competent, along with Indian students of twenty-one years or older who had completed course work at a government school. Despite diverse and ingenious Indigenous responses to the policy, this had devastating effects on Indian landholdings and cemented the use of blood in federal legislation.

Use of the discourse of blood in the interactions between the U.S. government and Native American nations culminated in a third stage in 1934 with the promulgation, in the Wheeler–Howard Act, of an official definition of "Indian" based on partly on blood quantum for the first time. In chapter 4 I explore the impact of this development. Although the act supposedly ended the assimilation period, it produced little change in the perception that Indians of mixed descent were undeserving of tribal status and government protection. The records created under the 1934 act show that by the 1930s a discernible group of "scattered" mixed-descent Indians stood outside the boundaries of recognized Indian status. I examine the cases of people who tried to seize the opportunity created by the 1934 act to be officially recognized as Indian, even though the potential benefits of such recognition were few. The 1934 definition of Indian status offered two very different paths to official Indian status—tribal recognition and blood quantum. In this we see the essence of a clash that often underlay the administration of allotment policy: the government paid lip service to the principle that Native American nations should define their own tribal membership, yet found the shorthand of blood quantum to be much more convenient to the project of settler colonialism.

The final chapter turns to the state of Virginia, which contained small, federally unrecognized Indian communities as well as a large African American population. I show that in Virginia, far from the "West," ideas about blood were nevertheless similarly utilized to disenfranchise Indigenous people. However, here the concept of "Blackness" was particularly salient. In the 1920s a powerful government official tried to reclassify the Rappahannocks, Chickahominys, Pamunkeys, Monacans and Mattaponis as "colored." The Virginia Indians did not want to be called "colored" and emphasized their Indian blood, insisting that their race be recorded as such on birth and marriage certificates. For the sake of contrast I conclude the chapter by a brief discussion of the Eastern Cherokees, another southeastern nation, as a case of an Indigenous community who used the discourse of blood and its veneration of the "pure, full-blood" to their advantage by promoting their image as pure, authentic Indians.

Blood and Land

Estimates put the amount of land stolen from Native nations during the assimilation period at around ninety million acres. The use of blood quantum to measure Indian status in a context of inevitable and increasing cross-cultural relationships ensured fewer Native people were officially recognized, more land became available for settlers, tribal payments were reduced, and administrative responsibility was diminished for the U.S. government. It is also therefore part of a settler colonial story. As the late, great Patrick Wolfe showed so elegantly, settler colonialism defined Indigenous people in ways that erased them.[40] Blood was part of a broader strategy of elimination, a tool used to efface Native American history, identity, and geography.[41]

One of the great advantages of locating blood and assimilation policy in a settler colonial framework is that it lets us see the global nature of the settler project. As Bruce Granville Miller has shown, many settler states "managed their relations with indigenous peoples . . . simply by failing to acknowledge them or by revoking official recognition and thereby reducing their numbers in various ways."[42] In Australia, where I live (on never-ceded Wurundjeri Willam land), Aborigines of mixed descent were expected to be "bred out" by continued cross-cultural relationships, and it was assumed that Aborigines of full descent would "die out." While the degree of influence of this hypothesis, known in Australia as the idea of "biological absorption," was (and still is) controversial, most historians agree that Australian records show many government officials, public figures, and journalists advocating this sad future for Aboriginal people.[43] By contrast, in the United States, the Office of Indian Affairs and humanitarian reformers almost never explicitly propounded blood quantification as a solution to the "Indian problem," instead advocating the rhetoric, laws and policies of cultural assimilation—allotment, education (child removal), and Christianization.[44]

A number of scholars have argued that the U.S. government nevertheless deliberately engaged in "pencil genocide" by denying people of mixed Indian descent "real" Indian status.[45] Some based this argument on the incorrect assumption, or gave the mistaken impression, that the General Allotment Act set in place a blood quantum requirement for enrollment and allotment.[46] As well as providing a more accurate discussion of the role that blood played in the administration of the General Allotment Act, I hope that this book shows how important it is to differentiate between outcome and intention. It is true that the government's linking of Indian status to a specified quantum of blood opened up the possibility that Indians would eventually be eliminated or absorbed into the general population through interbreeding, and that the connection between blood and right to own land helped to separate Indians from their land.[47] The use of blood in the administration of allotment is, however, often so slippery, surreptitious, or arbitrary that is impossible to regard it as a deliberate government policy. It was not enshrined in legislation, discussed in Congress or in Indian Office publications, or a part of the self-important humanitarianism of the so-called Friends of the Indian. Nor was it a furtive or concealed goal of any of these organs, although it certainly crossed the mind of some individuals.[48] It was sometimes expressed in Indian Office rhetoric, although rarely. In one such case, the commissioner of Indian Affairs, Francis E. Leupp, "styled" the policy of competency "a policy of shrinkage, because every Indian whose name is stricken from the tribal roll by virtue of his emancipation reduces the dimensions of our red race problem by a fraction, very small, it may be, but not negligible."[49] But apart from such isolated examples, a policy of shrinkage was not the U.S. government's stated intention.

The use of blood by the U.S. government during the assimilation period, however, shows how insidious settler colonialism could be. The removal of land from many Indians along with their official status was certainly an outcome of the way in which blood was used in assimilation policy. Even if assimilationists did not mention blood as part of their solution it was an integral part of the worldview of those who enacted and administered Indian policy at this time. The Office of Indian Affairs relied on a belief system—centered on blood—that led government officials to regard Native Americans of mixed descent as less deserving of Indian status than Indians of full descent. This view was unmistakably a component of the government's dealings with Native Americans, and it was also unambiguously of financial benefit to white America—the fewer Indians "on the books," the less administrative time and money would need to be spent on the seemingly unsolvable "Indian problem," and the easier it would become to remove lands from their possession. As Leupp chillingly went on to say in 1905: "If we can thus gradually watch our body of dependent Indians shrink, even by one member at a time, we may congratulate ourselves that the final solution is indeed only a question of a few years."[50]

"Mixed-Bloods"

Indians of mixed descent were a large component of the Indian population during the assimilation period—by 1910 the census reported that 93,423 people, or 37.8 percent of the total Indian population, were of "mixed-blood," and of these 43,937 were recorded as "more than half White" and 4,048 as having "Negro" ancestry.[51] One of the most common stories recorded about people of mixed descent in histories of the assimilation period is that they, along with other people with no Native ancestry at all, took advantage of the chaos of allotment to claim status and land that did not belong to them. In this story the claimants are not "real" Indians but people who took advantage of their education and connections with the white community to better their lives.[52] There is no doubt that many people who had some Indigenous ancestry but little tangible investment in the greater good of Native American people gained tribal status via the complex processes of allotment. There were numerous "grafters," "intruders," "wannabes," and "unscrupulous persons," as they were styled in the records. Tribal governments across the country complained to the U.S. government that people with no genuine claim to a place on their rolls were eroding their sovereignty and lands. To this day people who claim distant Indian ancestors in an attempt to gain access to tribal status or other Indigenous cachet plague Native American nations.

But there is another aspect to this narrative. The discourse of blood created a category of "mixed-bloods" that impacted how claims to enrollment, allotment, and Indian status were decided. It generated the stereotype of the wily, inauthentic, and undeserving person with few tribal ties. This meant that some of those who were classified by the U.S. government as being of "mixed-blood" lost their Indian status during the assimilation period.[53] No doubt some of these people were not recognized by their tribal government as having a solid ties to their nation, and denial of their lack of status was justified. But others would have been members of Native American families, may have lived in Indian communities, and had genuine tribal ties and loyalties. This book does not argue that all those divested of their Native American status during the assimilation period had a legitimate claim. Rather it aims to show that during the assimilation period, in addition to dealing with the claims of fraudsters, Native American nations underwent another attack on their sovereignty: the reduction of the number of federally recognized citizens using the discourse of blood.

How the discourse of blood impacted the legal status and economic standing of many people of mixed descent is an important part of the story of blood and settler colonialism in the United States. In 1917 August Breuninger wrote a letter to President Woodrow Wilson. Breuninger expressed his concern that the category of the "mixed-blood" had undermined, or at least complicated, the citizenship of people of mixed descent. Which nation, he wanted to know, should such people serve in a time of war when they were neither members of Indian tribes (and therefore not wards of the nation) nor American citizens?

Breuninger received a short, dismissive reply from E. B. Meritt, assistant commissioner of Indian Affairs, informing him that such a person was clearly a citizen of the United States under the General Allotment Act of February 8, 1887. Breuninger, a counsellor at law who identified as a Menominee of mixed descent, wrote a second letter pointing out that he had never received an allotment under the 1887 General Allotment Act and so could not have received citizenship in this manner. His father had been born on the old Menominee Indian reservation, and so Breuninger was not a citizen of the United States. Nor was he recognized by the Menominee as a member of their nation. Therefore, his current legal status was "NEITHER white nor Indian." Breuninger went on to report his many attempts to be naturalized. He explained how the officers would "get out their naturalization blanks and everything runs along smoothly, and there is some fond hope that I will receive my full-fledged citizenship paper." But this hope was always dashed. "When they come to the question 'Where were you born?' [and] I answer in this country," he went on, "they drop their pen." In a postscript, Breuninger gave a name to the position he was so strongly protesting against: "I have denominated the people of my status, as the Un-quaw-ians, which means 'clouded.'"[54]

Seventeen years later, an evocative Office of Indian Affairs report on *Indian Land Tenure, Economic Status, and Population Trends* referred to a category of "unenrolled, landless Indians." "An unnatural but important segregation of Indians into two artificial categories has been accomplished through the system of tribal enrollment," the report admitted. "The majority of Indians are enrolled with one particular tribe. . . . Other Indians, though they are biologically of the Indian race, are not officially affiliated with a recognized tribe or band." The report noted a clear correlation between membership of this group and poverty. Indeed, the authors concluded that "it is among the unenrolled and landless Indians that we touch the depths of Indian poverty." They attributed the hardships experienced by this group to their relationship with the Office of Indian Affairs. "The relation of the Federal Government to such Indians is of the most shadowy character," they wrote. "It washes its hands of them and their problems. Local governmental units likewise strive to avoid responsibility for these homeless, non–tax-paying residents."[55] Echoing August Breuninger's 1917 letter, the report described this group as "a people without a country," comprising "the most maladjusted helpless, and poorest [component] of the entire Indian picture, which generally is one of deep poverty."[56] In their characterization of the "mixed-blood" as "clouded" or "scattered and landless," these various descriptions suggest that there were mixed-descent people in the assimilation period who did not fit the stereotype of the shrewd, inauthentic "wannabe."

This book does not attempt the difficult, perhaps impossible, task of estimating how many people of Indian descent were left off the rolls or disenfranchised from their land or tribal membership, nor is it written in support of individual claims of Indian status. But it does argue that the creation of a category of an undeserving mixed-descent Indian is an important, and often unacknowledged, element of the history of the assimilation period. "Identities always serve particular interests," points out Scott Lyons, "and that's probably the most important thing to figure out: just whose interests do they serve?"[57]

When I write about people of mixed descent, I am referring to an extraordinarily complex and fluid category. Individual claims to Indian status are often impossible to assess because government records are simply not equal to the task. Nor do I have the right to engage in such a project. Identity itself is an elusive, private concept. Anne Hyde's work shows how important it is for historians to be aware of how fluid identity can be at a personal level. "Sometimes," she writes, "you can claim an identity, sometimes it is comfortable to wear, but sometimes the culture around you won't let you claim it. And sometimes an identity that once existed disappears."[58] When I cite particular cases in this book, I cannot know the identity of the people contained therein, how they or their communities viewed their status as a Native American, their culture, or their ties to tribal bodies or within the community. In other words, I cannot know whether they were deserving or undeserving of enrollment, allotment, and official status as Native Americans. What the archives do show, however, is the existence of an unmistakable stereotype about people of mixed descent that must have strongly contributed to fewer people being added to tribal rolls, being allotted land, and receiving government support.

Conversations

It would be misleading to suggest that the discourse of blood was no more than a tool of settler colonialism. Kimberley Tallbear warns against seeing the administration of the General Allotment Act simply as a narrative of the federal government "'imposing' dominant 'racial ideologies' and biologically essentialist criteria . . . onto Native American tribes." She advises scholars to pay attention to the "'conversation' between Indian and federal agents throughout the twentieth century."[59] Blood resonated with, and still resonates with, the belief of many Native American people and communities that descent, kinship, family, and relatedness are crucial to Indian identity. Jean Dennison's work on the Osages shows how in the present day the discourse of blood can still be "used as a root system connecting people to the land and the nation."[60] Blood has had, and continues to have, potency within Indigenous communities, often as shorthand for proof of genealogy and tribal connection. As Joanne Barker formulates it, "Blood tales are [also] Indian told."[61]

Recent critiques of settler colonial studies in the United States and Australia have pointed to the potential pitfalls in overriding Indigenous viewpoints and actions.[62] J. Kēhaulani Kauanui's work on blood quantum in the Hawaiian Homes Commission Act frames blood as a discussion between "competing political interests of different nationalisms— those of the Hawaiian sovereignty struggle and the United States."[63] Similarly, in each of my case studies I direct attention to competing sovereignties—bureaucracies supporting a settler colonial government, and tribal nations and individuals seeking to maintain control of their land base and membership. Having regard to the cross-cultural conversations about blood in the assimilation period does not preclude seeing blood as a settler colonial tool of elimination. Native American people grappled with the discourse of blood on many fronts—in their dealings with the government and in their own dynamic communities, constituted by intermarriage and migration. While my major concern has been to interrogate government records, I have tried to view blood not just as an instrument of negotiations between tribes and government, but also as integral to local and personal processes of negotiation and refusal that, at their heart, were assertions of sovereignty.[64]

The U.S. government's use of blood in the assimilation period is a story of a settler colonial power trying to pin down people's identities on paper. This book, therefore, records many instances of ethnographic refusal.[65] In their repudiation of the government's efforts to categorize them in writing, the refusal of Native people to participate in the process of enrollment and allotment can be read as declarations of their sovereign rights. The people in the pages of this book refused to give information, gave the wrong information, organized protest movements, declined to participate in the creation of tribal rolls, resisted being assessed for "competency," sent protest letters to agents and, when they had no effect, to the commissioner of Indian Affairs, the secretary of the Interior, and even to the president. They also painstakingly filled in applications, traveled miles to meet enrollment commissions, endured anthropometric examinations, applied to be designated as "competent," hired attorneys, changed birth certificates, chose the racial status that would serve them best, used multiple surnames, printed their own identification cards, and passed tribal laws in their efforts to define their own citizenship and to gain rights and land. In their many and varied responses to the government policies of the assimilation period, the Indigenous peoples of North America were united in their resistance to being ethnographized in ways that disadvantaged them, their families, and their nations.[66]

The discourse of blood has remained a problematic and contested issue for Native American people to the present day. In the last ten years there have been many controversies relating to claims of Native American identity. There has been the introduction of DNA testing and a growing body of sophisticated analysis of identity issues by Indigenous critical theorists. Native American nations are debating their own tribal membership laws in a variety of contexts: casino royalties, attacks on their sovereignty, decreasing numbers of enrolled members, and increasing applications by Indian "wannabes." Tribal governments have had to fashion membership requirements using practices and ideologies that have long history in a context in which their sovereignty has been constantly under threat.

As a non-Indigenous academic writer I have, as Dian Million phrases it, a "responsibility to more than my own interest."[67] I have tried to write with an awareness of how my words, and the records I have unearthed, might speak to present-day debates and discourses on this subject and have implications for current generations. In the spirit of Audra Simpson's approach to ethnographical refusal ("what am I revealing here and why? Where will this get us? Who benefits from this and why?"),[68] I have suppressed the names, and have chosen not to reproduce images, of people who appear in the archives other than those of leaders, public figures, or participants in already-published cases, and those already named in widely used oral history collections, tribal rolls or who spoke publically about their experiences. I offer this work in the hope that this is the right time—a time when the issue of blood is so fraught—for critique and analysis of the history of this settler colonial phenomenon that continues to resonate.

How that resonance operates or should operate in present-day Indigenous communities are questions for other authors to explore. As Jeff Corntassel puts it so simply, the "question of 'who is [I]ndigenous?' is best answered by Indigenous communities themselves."[69] This book does not purport to answer the question "who is an Indian?" Instead, it asks the question (in Scott Lyons's words): "what *kinds* of Indian identities were in production during a given historical moment"?[70] It concentrates on the "why" of blood (why was it used?), not on the whether (should it be used?) or the who (who uses it?). As Sandy Grande, Timothy San Pedro, and Sweeney Windchief suggest, this opens "spaces of resistance, agency, and possibility, extending the question of 'Who is Indian?' to include the more politicized query of 'Who is asking and for what purpose?'"[71] My aim is contribute to the project of unpacking and disempowering colonial tropes—particularly that of authenticity—that have survived to the present day. My hope is that the book may serve, in some small way, as what Devon Abbott Mihesuah calls a "[tool] of decolonization."[72]

Blood Will Tell tells of matters that are murky, amorphous, and often intangible. It is about a belief system so insidious that government employees applying assimilation policy rarely articulated it in official documents, even as they used it daily to make decisions. It shows how stereotypes mingled with realities to create a tendency rather than a policy—but that tendency had all the impact of a policy. It shows how the discourse of blood acted as a lens for non-Indian Americans in those countless moments when they decided who did nor did not deserve the status of "Indian"—in glances across desks, written marginalia on applications, recommendations and witness testimonies, or when tribal rolls were compiled, court cases decided, and competency hearings conducted. The use of this lens, I want to show, was as important a part of assimilation policy as the clauses of General Allotment Act itself.

BLOOD WILL TELL

CHAPTER ONE

Fraud

The Allotment of the Anishinaabeg

The Anishinaabeg of Minnesota were targeted for allotment in 1889, not long after the General Allotment Act was enacted.[1] Their allotment resulted in such enormous losses of land that, by 1913, it had become a national scandal, the so-called White Earth Tragedy. Allotment also made tribal membership, once regulated by the Anishinaabeg themselves, an unstable and treacherous issue. The various bands of Anishinaabeg that had gathered at White Earth by the beginning of the assimilation period had had a long history of relationships with people from other tribal nations, had participated in the fur trade, and most likely thought of themselves not merely as Anishinaabeg but conceived of their identity in terms of their *nindoodemag*, or kinship networks. The U.S. government attempted to impose criteria determining who was an "Indian" on this complex population. There was, as a result, much confusion about who was, actually, eligible for enrollment and allotment.

William M. Campbell, the first chairman of the Chippewa Commission (the specially formed government body created to allot the Anishinaabeg), directed attention to this confusion early in his term. "There may be many difficulties ahead of me that I do not yet see," he wrote in 1894. "I have submitted a number of questions to the Secretary of the Interior . . . among which [is] . . . '*Who is a Chippewa?*'"[2] Neither the government officials nor the Anishinaabeg themselves knew how to satisfy the Office of

Indian Affairs that someone was entitled to call themselves Anishinaabe. Was it "because my folks knew her Grand parents and God hears what I said to be true [and] [m]y mother always said so," as one man testified in 1897?[3] Or did the receipt of shares in tribal benefits, however small, demonstrate membership? This was what another man argued in 1891, sharing his recollection of his wife's mother with government officials: "She gave mi wife a blanket. She told her in mi presen[ce] there is your share mi daughter."[4] Was it a matter of lifestyle or appearance, as one witness assumed when testifying to the Circuit Court of Appeals in 1917, describing an applicant for tribal membership as wearing "her hair down her back, made moccasins for sale, did bead work . . . [She] was an Indian doctor and midwife; she walked pigeon-toed, as most Indian women do . . . she lived in a tepee."[5] One thing is certain—after the allotment process began, tribal membership was increasingly regulated not by the Anishinaabeg themselves, but by the U.S. government, drawing upon the discourse of blood and related assumptions about Indians of mixed descent. This chapter explores how the Chippewa Commission answered the question of "who is a Chippewa?," and how, despite the resistance of the Anishinaabeg, its response installed blood as a determinant of Anishinaabeg status and made it harder for the White Earth Anishinaabeg to hold onto their lands.

Anishinaabeg means "the original people" or "Indian person." The people who nowadays wish to be known by that name are descended from a number of linguistically and culturally related bands who came from the shores of the Great Lakes. Recent historical work has shown the impact of Anishinaabeg resistance, leadership, and conceptions of nationhood on the politics of the region in the late eighteenth and nineteenth centuries.[6] People indigenous to the Great Lakes region first encountered Europeans when the French entered the area in the first half of the seventeenth century in the hope of finding lucrative trading partners and products. Anishinaabeg history is replete with migrations, amalgamations, intermarriage, and fluid identities. Over the border in Canada, similar conditions had resulted in the creation of autonomous Métis communities, but this did not happen in Minnesota. After 1837 Anishinaabeg treaties sometimes included special provisions for "half breeds," and by the late nineteenth century a number of prominent mixed-descent families lived at White Earth.[7] Historians have demonstrated that intermarriage was fundamental to the Anishinaabeg world long before the Chippewa Commission arrived in Minnesota. Intermarriage and kinship, says Michael Witgen, made Algonquian society "literally like a web."[8] Marriage was a crucial institution to *nindoodemag*, writes Heidi Bohaker, and the kinship networks, or clans, inherited from the fathers dictated obligations, facilitating long-distance travel and access to community resources.[9] Cary Miller has also shown how important relationships through marriage were to Anishinaabe leaders in the late eighteenth and early nineteenth centuries, strengthening ties between villages and allowing leaders to extend the boundaries of their political influence.[10] No wonder William C. Campbell considered that deciding who was a "Chippewa" in conformity with the U.S. government's rigid criteria of Indianness was going to be one of his most challenging duties.

At the beginning of the nineteenth century many diverse interconnected family groups survived by participating in the fur and lumber trade as well as hunting and agriculture. Europeans called them, among other names, "Chippewa," possibly a mutated pronunciation of Ojibwe. The White Earth Reservation, located in northwestern Minnesota, was created by treaty on March 19, 1867. It was the largest of seven "Chippewa" reservations, but the government intended from the beginning to reduce their number and to make White Earth the final home for most of the Indigenous communities in the state. The reservation originally covered 1,300 square miles rich in pine and other natural resources, but was substantially diminished by the events described in this chapter.

The Chippewa Commission

The Chippewa Commission was established by an act of 1889 to negotiate with the Indigenous nations of Minnesota for the relinquishment of all twelve of their northern Minnesota reservations except for White Earth and Red Lake, and the reduction of those reservations in size. The commission, which originally consisted of three Office of Indian Affairs employees, was charged by Congress to compile a census, to direct removals, and to make allotments. This necessitated the definition and determination of who was Anishinaabeg, an undertaking that became ever more complex as time went on. Between 1889 and 1920 a number of ways evolved in which a person could prove their status as a "Chippewa," and myriad ways in which that status could be denied. Mixed-descent Anishinaabeg were never explicitly excluded. Once blood was introduced as a determinant of membership of the White Earth community, a complicated mix of criteria for qualification or disqualification (such as tribal involvement or place of residence) was applied if the person in question was judged to be of "mixed-blood." Allotment was followed by an extraordinary volume of fraud and confusion, leading the government to experiment with novel ways of turning folk biology into a science. By the end of this process, the discourse of blood had resulted in a tragic loss of land for the White Earth community.

During the course of allotment the government adopted numerous policies that ostensibly sought to impose logic on the process of claiming Anishinaabe status, but in practice they resulted in fewer and fewer people being eligible for enrollment. Each time new rules were formulated, more and more Anishinaabeg were denied their share of the lands that once stretched from the edge of Iroquois territory in the Northeast to the Great Plains. The Anishinaabeg negotiated the application of these rules with persistence and often success.

From the very beginning of the Chippewa Commission's work, as it traveled around Minnesota in 1889 holding tribal councils with the various bands, many Anishinaabeg expressed concerns about tribally disconnected Anishinaabeg and intermarried whites. According to Anton Treuer, such concerns had been voiced in Anishinaabe country at least since the White Earth removal treaty of 1867.[11] In many cases, the persons in question were the speaker's relatives, but more generalized anxieties arising from changes in the White Earth population and the effect of allotment on the sharing of resources were also at play. At the sixth tribal council held at White Earth on July 21, 1889, one member of a prominent mixed descent family, expressed his concern that "quite a number of Indians who belong to no reservation" might "come up here and decide to take land. . . . If all the Indians in the state should eventually decide to come here, there would be hardly enough land."[12] He was not alone. Another man raised the same issue at the seventh council four days later. "There will not be land enough for the whole; that is what I know positively," he told the commission.[13] He also worried that "those I call my sons-in-law" (intermarried whites) would select the best pieces of land at the expense of the "Indians, the original owners." "Those who are intermarried among us take advantage of the Indian," he told the commission, "and in time, if there is no strong protection thrown around the Indian . . . the others are just selfish enough to put the Indian at one side and say the claims are theirs." "Those who talk the best," he opined, "who are so solicitous of their own interests and . . . who have more foresight than we" would get the best allotments, just as they had gotten the "seed-grain first" and "anything issued."[14] He anticipated that men would "marry into our tribe just for the purpose of picking out choice pieces of land. . . . Those who are here, and who have made it their home with us before this arrangement was perfected, we wish to retain, but now there will be no end to emigration [sic] into this country by claiming relationship with us."[15] The Anishinaabeg were also well aware that many people who firmly belonged to their community were not of full descent, and the tribal councils revealed the complicated relationship between "mixed" and "full." Thus a third man wondered whether a woman married to a white man would lose her right to remain on the reservation. "There is a thing I cannot comply with," he said. "My heart still beats for my children. I can not deprive them of any right to which they are entitled . . . they have married for love."[16]

The commission frequently reassured the Anishinaabeg that enrolled members would have a say in deciding who could join them on the rolls. "The mixed bloods . . . acknowledged as belonging to your tribe will be treated the same as yourselves. . . . If there are any others who apply to be admitted . . . and you object, the matter will be referred to Washington," Commissioner Rice told the Mille Lacs.[17] "You are the judges in the matter of the census which will be taken; you know who ought to be on the rolls and who not," he said on another occasion.[18] He repeated the assurance at the ninth meeting of the tribal council at White Earth: "No one will be permitted to settle here to whom you object . . . no one shall receive an allotment without your consent. We shall not open the door to such people nor will we assist others to do so."[19] The commissioner of Indian Affairs, Thomas J. Morgan, similarly instructed the chairman of the Chippewa Commission, D. S. Hall, that on the subject of tribal membership "great consideration" should be given to the views of Anishinaabe chiefs.[20]

These assurances were not honored. In just over six years, the Chippewa Commission shifted from their 1888 position of allowing the Anishinaabeg to identify their own members to a strict definition based on blood and geography. From 1895 a "Chippewa Indian" was anyone who was a resident of Minnesota when the 1889 act was passed, and was of "Chippewa Indian blood" (no degree being specified), had "a recognized connection with one of the bands of Chippewa Indians in the State of Minnesota," and lived on one of the Chippewa reservations "with the bona fide intention of making it his permanent home."[21] Although chiefs were sometimes consulted in individual cases, after the initial consultation process they had little input into how Anishinaabe status was defined. The government was motivated by mistrust of Anishinaabeg testimony, suspicion that people were claiming Anishinaabe status to gain resources unfairly, and adherence to the notion that blood was a provable index of status. It deeply misunderstood how the Anishinaabeg thought about their nation and its boundaries. Melissa Meyer notes that the "bands" recorded by the government in the end "bore little relation to those that functioned in reality."[22]

The shift from tribal control to a blood-based definition was gradual but inexorable. After the commission compiled a census in 1889 it spent a significant part of the next decade adding and subtracting names. It did not take long for the census to become contentious. Meyer noted the existence of a "considerable folklore" among the Anishinaabeg surrounding the politics of enrollment, including stories in which liquor played a role and "band leaders . . . placed their friends on the rolls or people for whom they 'felt sorry.'"[23] In December 1890 the commission chairman told the commissioner of Indian Affairs that he believed the process of identifying the Anishinaabeg had become complicated because of the linking of that status with rights to land and annuities. The commission was concerned that people were claiming Anishinaabe status in order to acquire land. "A large number of persons who have never lived with the Indians, or upon any Reservation within this state, are now claiming the right to do so," he wrote. "Some of them undoubtedly have rights, and some who were born in Canada have none, and some elsewhere who have no Anishinaabe blood in their veins, as well as some so faded that other evidence than their looks will be required to establish the right they claim."[24] The process was further complicated by the fact that some Anishinaabeg did not look as "Indian" as non-Indian Americans expected.

In December 1891, in response to a number of applicants who had hired attorneys, the assistant attorney general ruled that the census could be amended to allow people who had unjustifiably missed out on enrollment to be included, and undeserving applicants to be excluded, and that the commission had a duty to "hear as carefully and thoroughly as possible each case," after which the commission's decision would be final. With this ruling the federal government acknowledged that some who had legitimate rights had been left off the lists of tribal members, but also that it suspected there were many who were undeservingly on them. The commissioner of Indian Affairs warned the commission that "great pressure will probably be brought to bear by claimants who have no bona fide rights to enrollment among these Indians" and by "a great many unscrupulous and dishonest people of full or part Indian blood."[25] Meanwhile, Anishinaabe people negotiated the process of enrollment by hiring attorneys and, as Jill Doerfler reports, even writing directly to the secretary of the Interior and the commissioner of Indian Affairs to argue their case.[26]

At the same time the government decided that Anishinaabeg who did not reside in Minnesota should be ineligible. This decision was made in response to the commission's report of 1889, which acknowledged that there were more people entitled to be on the census than the 8,304 originally enumerated, that many of them were of mixed descent, and that many lived off the reservations. "In Michigan, Wisconsin and elsewhere we know there are persons of Chippewa blood that will claim, and no doubt many are entitled to, benefits under the recent negotiations," the report admitted. While the commissioners felt that the "safe rule to be observed will be to consult the chiefs and head-men as to the justice of their claims," the assistant attorney general read the original statute to mean that "Congress legislated in this act only for the Chippewa Indians actually resident in the State of Minnesota and that none other should be enrolled."[27]

Enrollment hearings were tedious, confusing, and time-consuming, and the commission gave few applicants, or witnesses, the benefit of the doubt. The single volume of testimony that survives in the archives (relating to eleven enrollment cases heard in the period 1897 to 1899) shows that the official concern of the commission was to ascertain whether mixed-descent claimants were recognized as Anishinaabeg by other Anishinaabeg. Ironically, its distrust of Anishinaabe witnesses undermined this approach.[28]

Most of the questions asked of witnesses at enrollment hearings aimed to find out how long they had known the claimant, whether they knew details of the claimant's family, particularly whether a parent had maintained tribal ties, and whether they believed the claimant was of Anishinaabe descent. Although all claimants brought along several Anishinaabeg willing to swear to their status, the commission did not always find such testimony convincing. In other words, it assumed that applicants were likely to lie in order to exploit the system and to gain land. In cases in which the chairman's reasoning was recorded, it mostly consisted of weighing the various witnesses' testimony against each other. Thus, in the case of a claim by two sisters, Chairman Hall disregarded Anishinaabe notions of kinship in holding that Chief May-zhuck-ke-ge-shig's claim of a "relationship for his mother in law to their grandmother . . . is about as vague and indiffinate [sic] as it well could be." In his view a contemporary of the sisters' parents who explained that the sisters failed to come to White Earth to enroll in 1889 because their father, "being an old soldier, was trying get a pension," was "a better witness for the petitioners" than the chief. But Hall eventually rejected the claim because the sisters had not come forward until ten years after the beginning of the commission's work, even though the "petitioners and their parents were almost neighbours to Chairman Rice, all residing in St Paul." Another woman's claim was rejected by Hall because "she does not seem to be very well identified by her witnesses, none of them having seen her for thirty or forty years." Yet another application was refused simply because the evidence was not "sufficiently clear," even though a previous chairman had placed her sister on the rolls. Thus, although the commission certainly asked questions about tribal recognition, in this sample of cases its decisions overrode the evidence of Anishinaabe witnesses because of suspicion that both the applicants and the witnesses were lying.

The commission soon tired of relying on the opinion of chiefs and headmen, whom they perceived as being unduly influenced by internal politics. As early as November 1891 Chairman Hall wrote to the commissioner of Indian Affairs to ask his advice on forty names on the census that were marked "objected to by the chiefs." The commission called a meeting and asked the chiefs to state the nature of their objections, but this they failed to do to the commission's satisfaction.[29] Hall noted on another occasion that "there is a great deal of politics upon an Indian reservation. The chiefs in some instances have brought us names and asked us to place them upon the rolls of the Chippewas of Minnesota, and after inquiring into the matter, and questioning them closely, we have found in a number of instances that the parties were from Canada, or from out of the state, who were very evidently not entitled to be enrolled or to receive the benefits of the Act."[30] The possibility that these were people with a legitimate claim was not entertained. After 1891 the commission no longer accepted chiefs and headmen as the final arbiters of Anishinaabe status and used pre-prepared, blank "Affidavits for Enrollment" that it felt would bypass any "favoritism."[31] The attitude that these men were untrustworthy sources of information about their community strengthened as time went on. In 1894 Chairman William M. Campbell expressed the government's growing mistrust of Anishinaabe headmen emphatically: "They are old and simple men who are ready to make affidavit when asked, and . . . no importance should be attached to their recollections unless the same can be corroborated."[32] Thus the commission's original promise to the Anishinaabeg that their chiefs would be heard on who could be enrolled was broken.

The Office of Indian Affairs now stipulated that the commission, instead of relying on chiefs' opinions, should apply the criterion of residence on the reservation in deciding enrollment cases. Campbell's 1893 correspondence with the commissioner of Indian Affairs cited the example of an "intelligent mixed-blood" who married a white man, moved off the reservation, and raised a daughter who in turn married an Episcopal clergyman and raised three daughters of her own in Chicago. As these three "young ladies of education and wealth . . . [were] travelling in Europe" the commissioner of Indian Affairs, the secretary of the Interior, and the Chippewa Commission debated whether they, and their mother and grandmother, should be granted allotments of land, as they had all emphatically refused to move back to the reservation. According to the commissioner of Indian Affairs, this last aspect of the case resulted in their disqualification from allotment.[33] Tropes of gendered dependency no doubt also worked against them: as wives of white men, and mothers of children with mixed ancestry, they could be treated as undeserving of Indian status because they were being financially supported by their husbands and were in no need of White Earth resources.

Reservation land was not for those who, from the government's point of view, had already been assimilated. Allotment was thus a privilege for Indians still bunched in a recognizable group on the reservations, not for those living elsewhere. By dint of their acculturation they had forfeited the benefits that came with Native American ancestry.[34] The requirement that people live on the reservation was, however, not intended to encourage more Anishinaabeg to stay. Rather, it was a means of demonstrating an individual's ties to the community, and therefore his or her tribal status. Official insistence on a so-called bona fide intention to live with the Anishinaabeg on White Earth was unshakeable, even for those who had proved their Anishinaabe status. The commissioner of Indian Affairs made it clear that even if applicants were Anishinaabeg they needed to take up residence on the White Earth Reservation before they were entitled to allotment.[35]

By 1893 it was no longer sufficient for applicants to produce evidence that the community recognized a person as having Anishinaabe ancestry. Applicants also had to show that they had lived with the Anishinaabeg prior to 1889 and drawn treaty annuity payments, as well as to demonstrate an intention to live permanently on the reservation.[36] By 1894 the commission had formed the belief that all Anishinaabeg of mixed descent were taking advantage of the system of allotment, and were using their business acumen to secure pine-rich lands for themselves. Some Anishinaabeg also worried, as one chief put it, that many "Indians, half-breeds, and whites" were interested in their tribal ties "only on account of the land, with their ears open to listen to any-thing that will give them a chance to get an allotment made in pine."[37] Chairman Campbell complained to the commissioner of Indian Affairs that "almost every mixed-blood or white man who is married to an Indian woman makes strenuous efforts to get on the pay-roll [of the Indian service] without any regard, whatever, to their ability to discharge the duties of the position they seek."[38]

In May 1895 the assistant attorney general introduced, for the first time, a blood-based definition of a "Chippewa Indian," making "Chippewa Indian blood," tribal recognition, and residence on the reservation essential to tribal membership.[39] Although at this point there were still Anishinaabeg designated by the government as being of mixed descent living on the White Earth Reservation in possession of their lands, this loss of control of the rolls, together with the incorporation of blood in the official definition of tribal membership, was to have devastating effects in the early years of the new century on those defined as "mixed-bloods."

The Anishinaabeg's own understanding of who was a "Chippewa" had little to do with biology or blood and much to do with culture and lifestyle. Jill Doerfler has meticulously traced the Anishinaabe use of the terms "mixed-bloods" or "half-breeds" back to the treaty period. She argues that while it is still not completely clear how the Anishinaabeg understood these terms during the allotment period, oral testimony shows that White Earth Anishinaabeg did not "use blood as a metaphor for ancestral/racial ancestry," and the terms "'full-blood' and 'mixed-blood'. . . were flexible terms generally tied to a variety of lifestyle choices, such as clothing and religious affiliation, as well as economic conditions."[40] In court cases held to decide Anishinaabe status, Indigenous witnesses clearly indicated that their conception of racial status stemmed from culture and kinship as much as from descent. Doerfler writes: "During questioning, some refused to use these categories and repeatedly asserted that this was not the way that they understood identity, language and translation of the terms 'full-blood' and 'mixed-blood.'"[41] For example, one man testified that "mixed-bloods" were self-identified, but were also those who "looked it. They could be distinguished what they were." He also told the court that, on the other hand, "full-bloods" might have a "small amount of white blood" but culturally "[lived] as an Indian."[42] Doerfler reports that some witnesses refused to grapple with the definitions of Indianness offered to them by government representatives and "purposefully refused to recall or describe the skin color of the individual in question as a calculated strategy to assert that it was not important."[43] Issues of translation further confused the issue. Thus it may be that the term "white blood" was completely nonsensical to Anishinaabe witnesses because "the root of the Anishinaabe word for blood, *miskwi*, is *miskw*. *Miskw* is the color red, and probably references the literal color of blood."[44] There were historically rooted differentiations in the Anishinaabe nation, but they were not those identified by the Chippewa Commission. The Chippewa Commission believed that blood and culture were intimately related, that blood in fact equaled culture, and that all Indians of mixed descent were acculturated cultural brokers with the skills to take advantage of less capable "full-bloods."

Competency

Although the Chippewa Commission had moved swiftly to a definition of Anishinaabe status that disadvantaged those designated as mixed descent, many such Anishinaabeg remained on the rolls who had been included in the original census, or been lucky in their enrollment hearings, or who had inherited land and enrollment status from their parents. By the turn of the century, however, they found their status challenged by proponents of the view that they ought to lose the special protections and rights that came with Anishinaabe ancestry. In the main, this was prompted by the desire of white Americans to acquire the pine-rich lands available on the White Earth Reservation. In 1906 and 1907 Congress added amendments or "riders" to the Indian Appropriation Acts that removed restrictions on the sale, encumbrance, or taxation of allotments held by adult "mixed-bloods" of the White Earth Reservation. The sponsor of the "Clapp riders," Senator Moses Clapp of Minnesota, though motivated by the goal of opening up lands for white purchase, purported to have the best interests of the Anishinaabeg at heart. The Clapp riders took advantage of the Burke Act, passed earlier in 1906 by Congress. The Burke Act, which applied to all Native Americans, allowed the commissioner of Indian Affairs to award, on application, a "fee patent" to Indians who were perceived as capable of managing their own affairs that gave them control over their lands before the expiry of the twenty-five-year trust period dictated by the Dawes Act. The Clapp amendments also removed the commissioner's power under the Burke Act to decide who was or who was not competent at White Earth. Instead they simply declared that all adult "mixed-bloods" were competent.

Fraud perpetrated by unscrupulous whites quickly followed on the heels of the Clapp riders. Once they were passed, all Anishinaabeg of mixed descent were free to sell or lease their allotments without restriction or protection. Melissa Meyer has described how land and lumber companies, anticipating the amendments' passage, hired prominent mixed-descent men to gain access to the best farmed and timbered land by securing mortgages from allottees who claimed to be mixed-bloods (Meyer uses the terms "mixed-blood" and "full-blood" in a symbolic rather than genetic sense). "For many Indians whose thoughts fastened on their next meal instead of advantageous real estate transactions," Meyer writes, "the promise of immediate cash was seductive."[45] The Indian Rights Association duly found that the removal of restrictions upon the sale, encumbrance, or taxation of lands allotted to mixed-descent Anishinaabeg had led to "increased suffering among the Indians," and expressed the fear that "as funds received from the sale of their allotted lands are exhausted and the cold increases in the rigorous winters of that northern region . . . there may be need of urgent appeals for aid."[46]

In 1909 the Office of Indian Affairs embarked on a series of investigations into fraud and a revision of the rolls. Numerous court cases ensued, contesting the legality of land sales, and continued over the next decade. In early 1909 Warren K. Moorehead, an archaeologist, amateur anthropologist, and recently appointed member of the Board of Indian Commissioners who worked at the Smithsonian Institution, investigated the conditions at White Earth and began to publicize them. The situation soon evolved into a national scandal and became known as the "White Earth Tragedy." In July the commissioner of Indian Affairs, R. G. Valentine, sent Moorehead back to White Earth to conduct further investigations. Inspector E. B. Linnen of the Department of the Interior accompanied Moorehead.[47] Their report, delivered a few months later, told a horrific story. In less than three years after the passing of the 1906 Clapp rider, 90 percent of the land allotted to Anishinaabeg of full descent had been mortgaged or sold, and 80 percent of all reservation land had passed into private ownership.[48] The Office of Indian Affairs responded instantly, and in the summer of 1910, Marsden C. Burch, a special representative of the U.S. Attorney General, began to file complaints in the U.S. District Court at Fergus Falls, Minnesota, contesting the ownership of 142,000 acres of land.

In the fall of 1910 Burch, with the help of John Hinton, a special Indian agent, began putting together a roll which recorded the blood status of each White Earth Anishinaabeg.[49] Hinton sent out a form letter telling White Earth residents that the "government wishes to know the status as to Indian blood of every allottee on the White Earth Indian Reservation, Minnesota, and of every Indian entitled to an allotment thereon." The letter asked recipients to state "how much Indian blood you have; that is, whether you are a full blood, 4/4, or less, say, 3/4, 1/2, 1/4, 1/8, 1/16, 1/32, or any other fractional part as the case may be."[50] Some Anishinaabeg unsurprisingly found this request confusing. In a letter to one man, Hinton felt obliged to give an elementary lesson in fractions. "You say that your father was a person of 1/2 Indian blood and that your mother is a full-blood (4/4)," Hinton wrote, "and that you therefore think you are of "1/4 Indian blood. You doubtless mean that you are of 1/4 white blood and 3/4 Indian. . . . Add the fractions 4/4 (the Indian blood of your mother) and 1/2 (the Indian blood of your father) and divide the sum by 2."[51]

While much outrage and effort was expended on behalf of the "full-bloods and minors" who had lost their lands, Anishinaabeg of mixed descent were portrayed, if not as the enemies and exploiters of the former group, then at least as not deserving of the government's sympathy. The first trials for fraud did not begin until November 1911 and some commentators were openly critical of the fact that the Department of Justice proceeded first against defendants of mixed-descent status, rather than against whites, with the consequence that many of the latter were able to escape prosecution because a three-year statute of limitations applied.[52] No one questioned the premise behind the Clapp riders: that Indians of mixed descent did not deserve government protection for their lands.

The Anishinaabeg did their best to navigate the laws in ways that would benefit them. The government's failure to recognize that they understood the situation very well make the government-produced records of this period a rich source of frustratingly half-told stories of negotiations between the parties. Sometimes the logic of Anishinaabe actions and the motivation behind their communications with government officials can only be guessed at, but their intent to maneuver around the complicated legal definitions of Indianness is clear. Now that the law had made the issue of blood so crucial, some Anishinaabeg began proactively to claim the status that most advantaged them. If they claimed to be of mixed descent, then they could have control of their land and had the right to sell it. If they had been cheated of their lands, and could prove they were of full descent, then they had a chance of retrieving them. In 1910 a group of prominent Anishinaabeg of mixed descent voiced their desire for an authoritative roll that fixed their blood status and put them fully in control of their property and rights. The attorney general acknowledged "a feeling of uncertainty and unrest" both among Indians and potential purchasers of allotments, caused by the investigations of the Office of Indian Affairs, and a "clamor for some solution of their difficulties and adjustment of the same." The attorney general expressed sympathy for mixed-descent Anishinaabeg, and suggested making a list of the "60 to 75 per cent . . . who are undeniably of the mixed blood" so as to "settle the status of a considerable majority of Indians beyond dispute, and, therefore, settle a like percentage of the difficulties and annoyances incident to the allotments and status of both Indians who have alienated and the purchasers."[53] The government felt that these mixed-descent Indians, no longer in need of its protection, should be allowed to alienate their lands without encumbrance.

Mixed descent equaled competency, which in turn gave Anishinaabeg of such status the freedom to do what they wanted with their land. It was thus in some respects a desirable status. John Hinton, employed to rewrite the White Earth rolls, had little doubt that Indians were prepared to manipulate their own status, and the status of others, to their advantage. He reported to the commissioner of Indian Affairs that as soon as he began the work of investigating applications for fee-simple patents, some Indians who had previously claimed full-descent status were tempted to undergo a "change of heart." One man, for example, had come to him to express a doubt that his wife was of "full-blood." Hinton believed the reason for this doubt was the rich timber on his wife's lands that could be sold if she were designated as of mixed descent.[54]

Not all Anishinaabeg who took advantage of the 1906 and 1907 Clapp amendments' removal of restrictions on the sale, encumbrance, or taxation of allotments held by mixed-descent adults of the White Earth Reservation were victims of fraud or deceit. Thus one mother, after the passing of that legislation, sold her allotment to her son for $500.00 cash. Her son, who was in charge of family affairs, supported his aging mother out of this money and built her a house, so she no longer had to support herself by fishing. This satisfying arrangement was predicated on the premise that the mother had at least one white or African American ancestor, however distant, and was thus able to sell her land. When the government began investigations, the case came under scrutiny. One witness testified that the mother "was always known as a full-blood Indian" by her community and her family, and that she "always lived as an Indian, in a wigwam . . . up to the time that these lands were being sold, then she lived in a hut, a little house, that [her son] built for her; but before that she always lived as an Indian woman . . . [by] fishing." Unlike many White Earth allottees who were taken advantage of by white "grafters," selling their lands for far less than they were worth for the convenience of a cash settlement, this mother and son seem to have utilized the government's laws to take control of their own finances and lives. This family were perhaps not at the mercy of "grafters," but rather claimed the status that suited their needs the best.[55]

On the other hand, claiming to be of full descent was in the interest of Anishinaabeg who felt they had been unfairly done by in their business dealings—if judged to be with a "full-blood" such dealings were illegal. This is shown by the 1915 case *United States of America v. John C. Cabanne*, which centered on the purchase of land by Cabanne from a woman who claimed (successfully) to be of full descent, thus making the transaction illegal. Many Anishinaabe witnesses in the trial were interrogated about the physical characteristics of her ancestors, and their answers show their awareness not only of the artificiality of the government's notion of Indianness, but also their conviction that it could be defined both biologically and culturally. One witness who was asked "would you be a full blood if you had not sold your land?" told the court that he "would have been an Indian if I had not sold my land. I tried to be, but—if it had not been given to me that I was a half-breed, why, I could not have sold my land." He clearly felt that being of full descent was something that someone could "try to be," in other words, it was a status awarded by the government, not something integrally linked to a personal identity that he probably understood in a completely different way.[56]

The rolls compiled by Linnen and Moorehead, and then Hinton, attracted much criticism and continued to be sources of contention. In 1913 the government decided to try to achieve a fairer enumeration of tribal members and a roll commission was established, once again, to enroll all members of the White Earth Reservation by sex, age, and blood status. The government considered that a legal definition of the term "mixed-blood" was now required. Three test cases were brought to prompt the courts to decide how much white ancestry made an Indian of mixed descent. In June 1914 the U.S. Supreme Court affirmed in *United States v. First National Bank* that "the term mixed blood includes all who have an identifiable mixture of white blood."[57]

What exactly an "identifiable mixture of white blood" was, and how to discern it, was now the problem. Witness testimony and paper records were no longer sufficient. After a year, the government called on anthropologists, specifically those who worked in the field of physical anthropology, to play a proactive role in the fraud cases.[58] This was not a common practice, and shows the desperation of the Office of Indian Affairs to find a "scientific" solution to an increasingly complex political situation. The office consulted Dr. Aleš Hrdlička, since 1903 the first curator of physical anthropology at the U.S. National Museum (later the Smithsonian), on the physical characteristics of "pure-blooded" Indians. According to Matthew Bokovoy, Hrdlička was at the margins of a group of scientists who were promoting eugenics and other conservative racial theories and policies aimed at maintaining racial hygiene.[59] As was the common practice of the time, Hrdlička was a collector of bones who proudly, by way of example, described having excavated fifty-seven Lenape skeletons, studied them, and then donated them to the Museum of the American Indian in New York.[60] Hrdlička was also an enthusiastic measurer of living specimens. He examined about seven hundred people at White Earth to test the "purity" of their blood, and later published his findings on the characteristics of fifty-nine of those he designated as "full-blood."[61] Professor Albert E. Jenks, an anthropologist from the University of Minnesota, who was also called to testify in fraud cases involving Anishinaabe people, utilized racial science as a tool to determine who had an "identifiable mixture of white blood" and who did not. Court decisions began to rest upon physical anthropology, the practice of measuring and inspecting human bodies to discern mixed ancestry. In 1914 Jenks traveled to Minnesota, and went around the reservations measuring Anishinaabeg "as to head breadth and length, face breadth and length, nasal breadth and length, color of eye, skin and hair, texture and quantity of hair, and nature of incisors." He also later published the findings of this study.[62]

Whereas once Anishinaabe informants were put on the stand and questioned about community ties, they were now quizzed on ancestry and physical characteristics. In 1914 Jenks was subjected to questioning by Ranson J. Powell, an attorney acting for persons accused of buying allotment land from Anishinaabeg of full descent who were not allowed to sell it. Over many days and under direct and cross-examination, Jenks argued that there were certain common physical characteristics by which Anishinaabeg of mixed descent could be recognized and identified. He testified that:

> the tendency of coarse, black, lank hair is to become finer and lighter;
> ... for the complexion to lighten, for the nose to narrow, for the hair

on the body and the face to become more profuse, and, depending upon the gametic composition of the white parents for the eyes also to become lighter; the whole face tends to assume a more upright position.[63]

Jenks's judgments were not made strictly on a phenotypical basis. He admitted under cross-examination that even when the physical signs were ambiguous, his opinions were swayed in at least one case by the "known fact of the long period of amalgamation in that particular region between the Whites and the Indians." It seems fair to say that Jenks's opinions were influenced by his assumption that all Anishinaabeg were of mixed descent. "Personally," he told the court, "I question very seriously whether there are any pure-bloods up there."[64]

Jenks's assumption that most of the Anishinaabeg were of mixed descent dovetailed with the government's interest in having as many Anishinaabeg as possible declared "mixed-blood." It was beneficial for grafters who were defending their lease or purchase of Anishinaabe property to prove that the sellers were of mixed descent, and it was also much less trouble for the government if fraud cases were resolved by finding that the seller was of mixed descent. The upshot of Jenks and Hrdlička's work was that many Anishinaabeg were declared to be of "mixed-blood" according to racial "science." The events at White Earth reveal the government's selective use of racial "science" at this time—both Jenks and Hrdlička had opinions about racial mixture that were far more complex than appeared from their work in Minnesota. Hrdlička, for example, was positive about the potential of people of mixed ancestry to make the United States a better nation and was at odds with eugenicists such as Charles Davenport who were promoting conservative racial theories at this time.[65] Gregory Smithers has argued that Hrdlička believed in a single origin for mankind and (cautiously) in the potential of intermarriage to wipe out racial distinctions, making him the author of "an antiracist discourse that was itself tinged with the racial biases of its age."[66]

By 1915 the government had contrived a solution to the situation at White Earth that was based on compromise. All land transferred from those who were unquestionably of full descent should be restored to them. Claims of fraud involving the transfer of land from those of mixed descent who had been judged competent to take control of their lands were to be dismissed. Defendants in the remaining cases were to pay the difference between what they actually paid and the fair market value, plus 6 percent interest, and anyone not satisfied with this could pursue their claim in court. Significantly, no means were provided to recover lands that had been fraudulently acquired from Anishinaabeg declared to be of mixed descent.[67] Their lands were gone. This compromise meant that legal claims to recover land could concentrate on identifying Anishinaabeg of full descent, vastly cutting down the number and complexity of cases. As the status of "mixed-blood" was defined as including all who had any white ancestry at all, the discovery of an Anishinaabeg who could convince a court that he or she was "full-blood" was bound to be a rare event.

In July 1911 a House committee began a full investigation of what had occurred at White Earth, sitting first in Washington, and then, from January 1912, in Minnesota and Detroit. The report of the committee, which was tabled in January 1913, perceived the exploitation of the Anishinaabeg to have been the natural consequence of contact between inferior and superior civilizations: "Considering their unsophisticated character, the operations of great and greedy lumber concerns and anxious speculators in farming lands, the march of settlement, and the great influence such interests could wield with the Government, particularly in the legislative and executive branches, it is but natural that results as we found were likely to follow sooner or later. In this instance it was sooner."[68] While the report expressed regret and outrage in equal measure, this shoulder-shrugging view of the events at White Earth shows that in essence the committee regarded the government as powerless to do more than to point the finger at those responsible. "We would respectfully urge a careful perusal of . . . the record, which we submit in the hope that it may help bring about better conditions," was the committee's vague recommendation.[69] Perhaps understandably, the committee did not wish to accuse Congress, or individual government officials, of anything more serious than "a dreadful blunder."[70] Indeed, a few members of the committee even hesitated to put their names to criticisms leveled at former commissioner of Indian Affairs Leupp and Indian Inspector James McLaughlin.[71] The committee saw the Clapp riders not as an attempt to loosen the legal ties binding Indian-held land, but merely as a kind of scientific gaffe, acknowledging that the "theory on which the [Clapp riders seem] to rest, namely, that a slight admixture of white blood would by some magical process bring discretion and business capacity, was thus demonstrated to be without foundation, and proved to be a cruel blunder."[72]

The number of Anishinaabeg who were eligible to be allotted land had diminished considerably over the decades since the establishment of the Chippewa Commission in 1889. In 1920 the U.S. District Court approved a "Blood Roll" that classified the 5,173 allottees of the White Earth Reservation as either of mixed or of full descent. A total of 408 people were included on the roll as "full-bloods."[73] The larger picture is that the process of allotment, the decisions of the government officials sent to Minnesota, and the specific legislation directed at White Earth had allowed the Chippewa Commission to conclude that the majority of Anishinaabeg were of mixed descent and undeserving of Indian status and lands.

The allotment period was one of overwhelming loss for the Anishinaabeg, a time when the discourse of blood, and the implicit assumption that Anishinaabeg of mixed descent did not deserve government protection or tribal assets, set in motion policies and practices that were devastatingly unjust. It was not that the U.S. government explicitly excluded people of mixed descent from the nation or from their share of its resources. But the assumption that such people were not entitled to tribal membership pervaded the many policy decisions of the period and gradually shaped a tendency to deny them recognized Anishinaabeg status. The lands allotted to people of mixed descent were less protected— that is, more open to competitive acquisition—and the government was hesitant to award them any tribal resources.

The people living at White Earth during the allotment period found themselves in the nonsensical position of having rigid categories of Indianness imposed on a community with a complex and fluid sense of identity. By utilizing the categories imposed upon them by the U.S. government to their own ends, or by rejecting them entirely, the Anishinaabeg of White Earth negotiated this intractable situation in different and powerful ways. The actions of the White Earth community during this period, particularly their testimonies in legal cases and enrollment hearings and their negotiation with the policy of competency, are best understood as examples of survivance or refusal.[74] In the end, the Anishinaabeg outlasted the so-called White Earth Tragedy and maintained a cohesive community. In 2012 the White Earth Nation ratified a constitution that removed the requirement of "Chippewa blood" from the nation's membership requirements and made family descent the crucial requirement for citizenship, just as the tribal councils had suggested in 1889.[75]

CHAPTER TWO

Chaos

The Dawes Commission and the Five Tribes

Joseph W. Howell was an attorney sent by the Department of Interior to investigate the contested enrollment of the Five Tribes of Indian Territory between 1898 and 1907. In his 1909 report, he revealed the existence of "what we termed the 'equitable box'" in which were placed unsuccessful applications for enrollment and for which he and his team hoped that "Congress might possibly give remedial legislation of some character." We can only speculate how many such applications were kept in the "equitable box." One such case was the daughter of a Cherokee mother and a non-Cherokee father. She had been taken to California at the age of three after her parents' separation, "during which time she was kept in ignorance of her Cherokee blood and Indian rights." Even though her mother was on the 1880 Cherokee roll, the woman's application was rejected as too late. On December 14, 1904, the assistant attorney general ruled that although her "natural right, by reason of her birth, was perfect, and . . . she had not . . . voluntar[ily] . . . forfeited her citizenship during her absence . . . the Commission to the Five Civilized Tribes was . . . without jurisdiction to receive or consider her application, and . . . her minor children should also be denied enrollment."[1] Although we do not know what the Cherokee nation felt about the merits of this case, it was just one of many instances where administrative attempts to address the mammoth task of enrolling and allotting the Five Tribes—like the act of May 31, 1900, that set a deadline for applications—made people of mixed descent vulnerable to losing tribal membership.

This chapter shows how the messy, chaotic undertaking of enrolling and allotting the Five Tribes was, from the beginning, permeated by the discourse of blood and the stereotypes about Indians of mixed and full descent that it entailed. In part because the Dawes Commission (the body entrusted with the task of allotting the Five Tribes) believed Five Tribes governments were run by scheming "mixed-bloods," the U.S. government gradually reduced the power of the Five Tribes to regulate their own membership, despite policies to the contrary and in the face of increasing activism by the Five Tribes themselves. People of mixed descent were not overtly disqualified from being enrolled and allotted, but the assumption that many members of the Five Tribes were of mixed heritage and thus did not deserve tribal lands and resources was underpinned by the overwhelming, confusing, and messy nature of the administrative task itself.

The Five Tribes—the Choctaw, Chickasaw, Cherokee, Seminole and Muscogee (Creek) nations—had been forced by Andrew Jackson to leave their homelands in the 1830s and settle in Indian Territory, which became the state of Oklahoma in 1907. Indian Territory was inhabited by other Native American nations, some whose lands lay in the area—the Caddos, Wichitas, Quapaws, and Apaches—and others who had been relocated there, including the Kickapoos, Miamis, Delawares, Cheyennes, Pawnees, Kiowas, Comanches, and Osages. Indian Territory lands were rich and desirable, and white immigrants, or "intruders," swamped the region during the Reconstruction period, weakening the authority of the tribes and placing much pressure on Congress to release "wasted" Indian land to European hands. Would-be settlers, known as Boomers, gathered on the borders and repeatedly ventured into Indian Territory to seize land. The Five Tribes at first avoided allotment, having been exempted from the 1887 General Allotment Act. Their period of grace ended in 1893, when settler pressure to open up even more Indian Territory lands prompted the government to create the Dawes Commission and charge it with the task of convincing the Five Tribes to submit to the allotment process. Three commissioners, including the eponymous Henry L. Dawes of Massachusetts, whose name was attached both to the commission and the General Allotment Act, were given the task of traveling to Indian Territory and negotiating with the Five Tribes. But in 1898 the Curtis Act ended the possibility of any real negotiation by imposing allotment on the Five Tribes without the consent of the tribal governments. The Dawes Commission went through a number of personnel changes during its existence and was ultimately absorbed by the Office of Indian Affairs agency based in Oklahoma in 1914.

The work of the Dawes Commission resulted in an overwhelming loss of land for all members of the Five Tribes. In 1912 the Dawes Commission summarized its work in Indian Territory between 1894 and 1912 as follows: "Applications were made for the enrollment of over 200,000 persons, of which number 101,221 were enrolled and found entitled to allotments."[2] The commission also conceded that as of June 30, 1910, when allotment was completed, unallotted land totaled 1,815,189.22 acres.[3] Once allotment of Five Tribes lands began, surplus land began to be officially opened to white settlement. The famous images of land rushes—with white settlers literally running to claim previously Indian-owned lands—originated in this time and place.

As Gregory Smithers has shown, during the post–Civil War period, a "kaleidoscope of people—Northern and Southern whites, freedpeople, and wartime refugees of every race, religion, and ethnic background" entered the lands of the Five Tribes. "By 1885, 25,000 white people called the Cherokee Nation 'home,'" Smithers writes. "Five years later, that number had increased to 140,000."[4] Historians have graphically described how non-Indians who flooded Indian Territory and managed to get themselves onto tribal rolls dispossessed Five Tribes people of their lands.[5] There is plenty of evidence that the Dawes Commission was complicit in the process of placing ineligible people on Five Tribes rolls and allotting them. Kent Carter and William G. McLaughlin have detailed how, in the years leading up to and during allotment, the U.S. government attempted by various means to force Five Tribes governments to open membership up to freedpeople and intruders: it ignored their complaints, made lists of people who they considered had been unfairly excluded, created and used censuses and rolls that nations did not consider a fair representation of their citizenship, forbade officers of tribal governments from removing intruders, and generally meddled with the Five Tribes' right to determine their own citizenship. Each of the Five Tribes was vocal in its resistance to these attempts.[6] As the activist Wilson Jones, aka Chitto Harjo, put it in a petition to Congress in 1904: "The United States . . . encouraged the influx of both white and colored people by permitting them to enter and settle in the Indian Territory, and by its many approvals of illegal adoptions to citizenship . . . of both white, colored, and mixed."[7] However, the settler colonial strategy of removing Indigenous lands and placing them in the hands of non-Indians is not the focus of this chapter. Rather, it draws attention to another way the Dawes commission undermined the Five Tribes' sovereignty: its use of the discourse of blood to promote a view of mixed-descent people as undeserving, so that at the same time as people ineligible for citizenship were being enrolled, people perceived to be of mixed descent—who were not intruders, and who were eligible for allotment under tribal laws and practices—were susceptible to being dispossessed.

Until 1908 (when a blood-based policy of competency was introduced) no law or policy specifically disadvantaged Five Tribes citizens of mixed descent in the allotment process. The 1898 Curtis Act did not give a definition of Indianness according to blood, nor did it prescribe a particular blood quantum for inclusion on the Five Nation's rolls.[8] Nonetheless, the discourse of blood, the idea of authenticity, and the trope of the "real" Indian pervaded the allotment process. The Dawes Commission relied on blood unquestioningly to decide who was or was not deserving of Indian status. The Five Tribes had a long history of cross-cultural relationships, and a large proportion of their population were of mixed descent. In 1910 Oklahoma had by far the greatest number of Indians reported for any state—74,825, or more than one-quarter of all the Indians in the United States.[9] Of this population, 62.6 percent, or nearly two-thirds, were reported in the 1910 census as being of mixed descent, making Oklahoma stand out in this respect from the other states with large Indian populations.[10] The mixedness of Five Tribes Indians was a constant refrain in the reports of government officials and other experts who visited Indian Territory. In 1884, after such a visit, the well-known reformer and Indian educator S. C. Armstrong expressed his concern that as Five Tribes communities became more "Anglo-Saxon than Indian" by the "admixture" of blood, "we shall ultimately have in this Territory an Indian problem without Indians."[11] In 1890 the authors of an extra census bulletin focusing on the Five Tribes wrote that, in the towns of Indian Territory, so-called pure Indians were few and far between. "One constantly hears the remark from travelers in the Indian territory," they reported, "Why, where are the Indians?"[12]

The Dawes Commission

From the beginning, the Dawes Commission operated on the assumption that there were three kinds of Indians in the Five Tribes: people of full descent, who were helpless and deserving victims in need of the government's help; Indians of mixed white and Native American descent, who were believed to have inherited a love of capitalism from their white ancestors; and Indians with African American ancestors who were seen as hardly Indian at all, the salience of their Black blood far outweighing the red. The commission regarded people of mixed Indian/white descent as cunning, exploitative, and undeserving of any of the special benefits or rights that came with Indian ancestry. Its reports are saturated with the sentiment that mixed white/Indian descent people were taking advantage of allotment at the expense of people of full descent, who were portrayed as primitive and uneducated victims. In its 1912 report, the commission distinguished between the "highly educated part Indian business and professional man, who is Indian only in name, and over whom any sort of governmental supervision is not only unnecessary but absurd" with the "real full-blood of the Five Tribes."[13] Superintendent Dana Kelsey contrasted the "competent ne'er-do-well, the part-blood business or professional man—Indians only in name—and the simple-minded, trusting-natured, easily influenced full-blood."[14]

In this context white ancestry was a factor that removed the special privileges of indigeneity. By classifying someone white, or nearly white, those in charge of parceling out Indian Territory could justify the removal of the legal protections that had been put in place to protect Indian land. Mixed-descent people were portrayed as shrewd, manipulative, or corrupt (euphemisms, perhaps, for some level of acculturation) and undeserving of special status given to those with more visible Native American attributes. Their very requests for help (or demands for action) by the government undermined their "real" Indian status. "My most severe criticism of the field work," wrote one administrator in 1913, "would be that the time of our men is too much given over to complaints and work for the broad-shouldered, reasonably competent, shiftless class who, when getting into trouble, was the first to ask help of the government. We ought to speedily put these people on their own resources entirely, and exert all our efforts toward helping the wholly uneducated real full blood to live more comfortably."[15]

The Dawes Commission regarded Five Tribes Indians with African American ancestry as undeserving for different reasons. In treaties signed by the government after the Civil War, the Cherokees, Seminoles, and Muscogees (Creeks) agreed to give their former slaves tribal citizenship (the Choctaws and Chickasaws refused, although the Choctaws eventually adopted their freedpeople in 1883). These people and their descendants were supposed to be enrolled in the category "freedmen" and were entitled to be allotted land. Despite their legal entitlement, the Five Tribes were hesitant to include people of mixed African American and Indian descent as full citizens. Like their white/Indian counterparts, they were generally not regarded (by the Dawes Commission or sometimes the Five Tribes) as "real" Indians, and were additionally subject to the same racial segregation that existed elsewhere in the United States. They were also casualties of the categories of enrollment. The division between "Indian" and "freedmen" failed to take into account the extensive intermarriage between these groups. People of mixed Indian and African American descent were often enrolled as freedpeople, erasing any official recognition of their Indian ancestry. Historian Tiya Miles has made an in-depth investigation of the plight of people of mixed Cherokee and African American descent in her study of the Shoeboots family, who, she argues, fell victim to what has been called the "pencil genocide" of the allotment era. According to Miles the "vast majority" of such people were not placed on the "Cherokee by Blood" rolls even if they had proof of Cherokee ancestry. "Because they appeared 'black' to Dawes Commissioners and because they were usually identified as former slaves," Miles says, "Afro-Cherokees were listed on the 'Freedmen' roll, which didn't record a degree of Cherokee 'blood.'" The decision to keep Five Tribes people with mixed African American descent off the "blood rolls" has serious implications for families in the present day, who have no way of proving their Indian descent.[16] Many have to rely on what Kevin Mulroy has termed "behind-the-rolls information" to work out their ancestry.[17]

An Exceedingly Onerous Task

In 1887, the year in which the General Allotment Act was passed, Woodrow Wilson, then an academic who would later be president, wrote an article on public administration that advocated morality in government via the reform of the civil service.[18] The records of the Dawes Commission demonstrate that Wilson was right about the need for reform. The commission was beset by confusion, bad record keeping, and a workforce unable to cope with the size and complexity of its task. The General Allotment Act was enacted at a time when new technologies infiltrated government offices—the telephone, typewriter, monotype and linotype machines, and vertical filing cabinets. The Dawes Commission, working far from urban centers, was unable to take advantage of this new equipment. It was also rife with corruption (agents could profit from their positions). Merely receiving applications for enrollment "occupied a space of nearly nine years," the 1905 report explained. The commission had to travel all over Indian Territory, carrying all its camping gear and paper records that encompassed more than one hundred thousand citizenship claims and the accompanying testimony, evidence, and correspondence.[19] At field camps, the commission pitched two tents, one for Indians and one for African Americans, and applicants for enrollment were directed, often with only a passing glance, by an agency official or tribal member employed for the purpose, into one or the other, thereby fixing their racial status forever. After questioning heads of families, field agents looked for applicants' names on one of the tribal rolls in their possession.

If they found them, the family was enrolled on a "Straight" card. If not, they were recorded on a "Doubtful" or "D card."[20]

Its reliance on the discourse of blood and authenticity and its segmented view of the Five Tribes made the Dawes Commission's enormous task of enrolling and allotting the Indian Territory even more difficult. In its 1899 annual report the commission portrayed itself as working hard to correct the "general impression [that] exists among those unacquainted with conditions in Indian Territory that the work of making rolls of 'Indians' is a comparatively simple matter." The commission blamed the large numbers of Five Tribes members of mixed descent for the complexity of the situation. "Were Indian Territory merely a reservation peopled only by full-blood Indians, that impression would have foundation in fact," the commission went on. But the completed rolls would, the commission predicted (correctly), "contain the names of full-blood Indians, Negroes, and white men, with every intervening degree of blood."[21]

The commission itself admitted that many people failed to gain Five Tribes citizenship because of the complexity of the enrollment process and the scale of the work. According to the commission, the volume of disputed cases had, by 1896, "exceeded all expectations."[22] When the date for closing the rolls began to approach in 1907, the work of ensuring that "no person entitled to enrollment might be omitted" became "exceedingly onerous." It required the engagement of additional employees, and even then "the entire workforce worked day and night in order that all the work might be completed."[23] By the commission's own admission, these factors led to shoddy record keeping. "Under such conditions," together with confusion caused by the Five Tribes' naming practices, the commission's 1905 report stated, "it is not to be expected that absolute accuracy could be attained, and it is hoped that such errors as creep into the rolls will not be regarded by the Department as indicating carelessness on the part of the Commission or its employees engaged in the preparation of the citizenship rolls."[24]

In his study of the Dawes Commission, Kent Carter included countless examples of the convoluted administrative tasks that faced the commission. "Congress," he says, "never appreciated the complexity of the policy it was asking the Dawes Commission to implement, and there was almost no precedent for what it was attempting to do." The commission had to rely on tribal rolls that were incomplete, withheld, missing, and unindexed. Before 1899, when the commission completed an index to the Chickasaw rolls, "clerks had to search hundreds of pages for the names of applicants." In the meantime, "rolls became out of date even before the ink on them could dry because people listed on them died and others were born." Congress also demanded that the commission begin allotting land before the enormous task of enrollment had been complete, and thus the commission was obliged to divide up almost twenty million acres of land concurrently with receiving and assessing claims and issuing certificates to thousands of people.[25]

The commission's method of enrollment was imperfect or even, as Joseph Howell argued in his 1909 report on its work, fundamentally flawed. The biggest injustice, Howell contended, was the burden had been placed upon the applicants by requiring them to meet personally with the commission.[26] Children, the ill, the elderly, and the disabled were immediately handicapped. As only the Muskogee office was open continuously, Indians living in rural areas were at a disadvantage. "I was strongly impressed," Howell reported, "with the fact that, as a general rule, persons hav[ing] the most meritorious cases were the least able to take the necessary steps to secure their enrollment." Howell described how "such persons were frequently unable to undergo the expense of travelling by rail, even a few miles, in order to have their cases investigated . . . when it came to leaving their homes and incurring hotel expense, even for a short time, the impossibility of their doing anything for themselves was still more certain." "Distance though short," he concluded, "was an impossible barrier between them and their rights."[27] "It often proved," moreover, "that applicants . . . were totally ignorant of what was expected of them and . . . had but little knowledge of what would constitute legal evidence of their rights."[28]

One year after the passing of the 1898 Curtis Bill that began the actual allotment process, the commission prescribed six criteria by which an Indian could become eligible for enrollment. The first and clearest path to enrollment was "inheritance of Indian blood." Blood was not, however, on its own a path to citizenship, but became so only when "coupled with continuous affiliation and residence with one of the Five Tribes" as well as previous recognition and enrollment. The other five legal paths to enrollment had nothing at all to do with racial background. Pursuant to earlier treaty stipulations, citizenship might be attained through tribal adoption; through intermarriage; by being an ex-slave or their descendant (except the Chickasaws); and finally by appeal to a U.S. court in Indian Territory, or any other legally constituted court, committee, or commission designated by one of the Five Tribes. The Dawes Commission created separate rolls for "Indians by blood," for intermarried white citizens, and for ex-slaves or freedpeople.[29] Thus, blood was an important pathway to enrollment, but only when it was coupled with a tribal affiliation of some kind, usually demonstrated by inclusion on a prior tribal roll. In fact, the commission privileged tribal rolls (which were sometimes incomplete, withheld, or difficult to read) over everything else. Kent Carter, an archivist who worked through the 1980s and 1990s on the extensive records of the Dawes Commission held in the National Archives, describes the commission's basic postulate thus: "all the real Indians are already upon the tribal rolls and that those seeking admission thereto are not Indians but white people, some possibly having a trace of Indian blood in their veins." The Dawes Commission, Carter argues, had "decided that its task was not to find everyone who had Indian blood; it was to enrol only those people who met the exact requirements of the law as they defined it."[30]

There were no laws or policies applied by the Dawes Commission that specifically prevented Five Tribes people of mixed descent from being enrolled. Nevertheless, there were four aspects of the commission's practices that disadvantaged them: it conferred on mixed-descent children the status of the mother; it enrolled mixed-descent Indians of African American ancestry as freedpeople, not as Native Americans; it imposed residence requirements; and it made administrative errors when it recorded individuals' supposed blood quanta.

The decision to give children with parents of different tribal origins the same enrollment status as their mother was based on tribal practice. The adoption by the commission of this gendered policy was also, as Rose

Stremlau has convincingly shown in the case of the Cherokees, part of its assimilationist strategy of imposing heteronormative, Western ideas about family, gender, and relationships onto the Five Tribes.[31] This policy disadvantaged people of mixed descent because children of parents with different statuses (who were likely to be of mixed descent) had a 50 percent chance of missing out. For instance, Grant, Lydia, and Dolly Feather, who were the children of an enrolled "full-blood" Cherokee man and an unenrolled white woman, were denied a place on the rolls because "there was no legal marriage, and the children, being illegitimate, must take the status of the mother and cannot be enrolled as citizens of the Cherokee Nation, notwithstanding the enrollment of the father."[32] Children of mixed descent with mothers who were not enrolled were thus likely to be denied status, even if their father had a strong claim to citizenship in one of the Five Tribes. In some places women had been omitted from the rolls because of a tendency, notwithstanding that it was not federal policy, of allotting heads of households. Thus the Chickasaw Annuity Roll of 1878 was not only unbound, un-indexed, and incomplete, but "it showed only the names of the heads of families, omitting the names of women, when not heads of families, and minors."[33]

People of mixed African American and Five Tribes descent were more likely to be enrolled as freedpeople than as Indians, redefining their racial status as more African American than Native American. In 1906, in the course of an ongoing legal claim by Joe and Dillard Perry to be enrolled as Chickasaws of blood and not as freedpeople, lawyer Albert J. Lee stated to Congress that "any person going before Commissioner McKennon's tent and making application for enrolment as citizen by blood . . . who appeared to have any negro blood, was ordered to proceed to Commissioner Needle's tent, and any protest of statement made by them to the effect that he was not a freedman, but entitled to enrolment as a citizen by blood, was not recorded."[34] Joe and Dillard Perry were the children of an African American mother and an enrolled Chickasaw father. Joe and Dillard's names had been placed on the roll of Chickasaw freedpeople, but their mother applied for their names to be transferred to the roll of citizens by blood, and the ensuing legal case hinged upon whether they had applied before a certain date.[35] In his 1909 investigation of the inequities of the Dawes Commission's work, Howell reported that "freedmen . . . were accorded but little, if any, protection by the law," and argued that the children of Choctaw freedpeople (of whom he thought five thousand had been unfairly left off the rolls) and Creek freedpeople had received especially unjust treatment.[36]

A residence requirement, dictated by the Curtis Act, provided that no one could be enrolled who had not moved to and settled in the nation in which they claimed citizenship before June 28, 1898. This reflected Cherokee tribal laws that, beginning in 1841, extended citizenship to Cherokees from North Carolina and elsewhere who had not removed to Indian Territory if they emigrated there.[37] The residency requirement turned the assumption that "real" Indians lived in Indian Territory into policy. For five years the commission denied enrollment on this basis. People of mixed descent were less likely to live in Indian Territory, and therefore were sometimes not allowed to enroll at all. The assistant attorney general reversed the policy in 1903, but according to Howell only some cases were readjudicated.[38] James P. Sneed is a case in point. He moved to Indian Territory from Murphy, North Carolina, to fulfill the residency requirement, but to no avail. He told an interviewer:

> I run a livery stable in Cherokee Co., N.C., Murphy was the town. Mr. Campbell Taylor came out there and talked us into coming out the Cherokee Nation. I did not want to come, but Mr. Taylor told me I could get my allotment if I would come, but when I got here I was too late—I did not get any land, and I am one-fourth Cherokee.[39]

As Smithers has shown, the Cherokee were a particularly diasporic nation. Moving from one place to another could make claiming citizenship difficult. One woman, for example, who claimed to be from a Cherokee family recognized as such in North Carolina, emigrated to Cherokee lands (she said at the invitation of the Cherokee Nation via delegates appointed by Chief Bushyhead) in 1880. In 1897 she moved to Muscogee in the Creek Nation. She had applied for citizenship in 1881 but said she was denied a hearing "because she had no attorney and no money to employ one." In 1897 she asked again for a hearing, this time from the Dawes Commission. She was unsuccessful.[40]

Blood quantum—the amount and its source—was sometimes recorded incorrectly, even arbitrarily, on the rolls. Mary Grayson recalled that:

> My mother, who was Creek, was called white and my father, who was Cherokee, was called Creek by the Government during the Creek allotment. I just figured that the Dawes Commission couldn't get everything right.[41]

Jobe McIntosh, a Creek man, told an interviewer: "Well, when they was filing for my land, why I should have been three-quarter Indian and one-quarter white. But they reversed that, they make me three-quarter white and one-quarter Indian. So, anybody had as much as half-half-breed have, to pay tax. So, I had to pay for every foot of Land I had. . . . I sold all but forty. I held it till tax just ate it up. Took it away from me."[42] People who had ancestry from more than one nation sometimes only had their mother's ancestry recognized, or had to choose one or the other at enrollment. Hattie Pierce Nelson told an interviewer that her family was told by "Old Indians" that "we are more Chickasaw than Choctaw, but we are enrolled as one-sixteenth Choctaw. One could not enroll as of mixed-blood. Had to be Choctaw or Chickasaw or what have you."[43] Such mistakes could have serious consequences later when people were granted the legal right to sell or lease their land according to their blood quantum.

The Cherokee and the Choctaw and Chickasaw governments noted that people whom they regarded as legitimate citizens were being passed over. The Choctaws and Chickasaws explained that "there are some few scattering Choctaws and Chickasaws who were left off the tribal rolls by mistake as a result of their own ignorance in failing to apply, and possibly some few others whose names were stricken from the rolls by mistake." These people had "no connection whatever with the class of fraudulent applicants and imposters that is being represented by attorneys and lobbyists at Washington."[44] In 1891 the principal chief of the Cherokee Nation wrote to the National Council to remind them of the necessity of correcting the census rolls because "there is no doubt but many names of bona fide citizens were left off."[45] Long after enrollment had concluded, some individuals remembered the issue. Cook McCracken recalled that "many an Indian and a Freedman was butted off of the rolls that I know personally should have been on there."[46] "I wish to say that some Indians received lands who should not and some who should have received lands never did," Mary J. Barker, who was enrolled as "full-blood" Cherokee, advised an interviewer in 1938.[47]

Five Tribes Resistance

Each of the Five Tribes had existing, and fluctuating, ways of defining their membership according to clan, kinship, and tribal law when the Dawes Commission began its work, and the commission, at least at the beginning, had a stated policy of following tribal practices. As with the Anishinaabeg (and as Stremlau has argued in the case of the Cherokees), it is more than likely that the Five Tribes regarded blood as an indication of cultural orientation and upbringing rather than of ancestry.[48] Also like the Anishinaabeg, the Five Tribes were concerned before the Dawes Commission began its work that people with no tribal connection were gaining rights—particularly through intermarriage. The Muscogee (Creek) had not created any statute law on the subject of citizenship prior to the allotment period but, as Pleasant Porter wrote to the commissioner of Indian Affairs in 1899, there were "time immemorial well established rules and customs by which citizenship was determined."[49] The Affidavit of Witness form used by the Creek Citizenship Committee shows how important recognition by members of the tribe was to gaining the right to enroll. The form asked the affiants to state how many years they had known the applicant, and that the applicant "is and has been recognized and treated by . . . neighbors, acquaintances, and the public generally, as a person having . . . Indian blood, and that the complexion, physical appearance, language and manners, of the said . . . indicate that the said . . . is of Indian blood."[50] The Choctaws had a law of 1883 specifying that intermarriage with "freedmen of African descent" did not confer rights of citizenship.[51] The Chickasaw legislature passed a similar law discouraging intermarriage that was approved in 1876.[52] A Choctaw law of 1840 allowed white husbands to become eligible for citizenship if their marriage lasted for two years. The Chickasaw constitution of 1856 also made it possible for white people to be adopted into the nation through intermarriage or by an act of the legislature. The Muscogees and Seminoles similarly allowed for intermarried whites to be adopted, but intermarriage was not an automatic path to membership.[53] The Cherokees, too, had laws governing the conferment of Cherokee citizenship on intermarried whites, and from 1869 onward used their supreme court as a body to which people could apply for citizenship.[54] However, in 1871 the court reversed the practice of allowing freedmen to gain citizenship through marriage to Cherokee women.[55]

The Cherokees lobbied tirelessly for their right to oppose the enrollment of intermarried whites. In 1876 Cherokee chief Oochalata wrote to President Ulysses S. Grant, arguing that if his nation was not allowed to "define its own identity it can not determine its own destiny."[56] Lobbying and legal challenges continued throughout the allotment period. In 1899 Commissioner Tams Bixby wrote to Henry Dawes to tell him that the Committee on Indian Affairs had lost patience with the Cherokees' activism. "The expression 'let them hold the hot end of the poker,'" he wrote, "is not infrequent among them."[57] Despite blows dealt to their opposition to the Curtis Act and allotment by judicial decisions in *Stephens v. Cherokee Nation* (1899) and *Cherokee Nation v. Hitchcock* (1902), the Cherokees were able to negotiate the terms on which the Curtis Act was applied to them (via what is known as the Cherokee Agreement of 1902), and won a battle in 1906 when the U.S. Supreme Court upheld their right to deny citizenship to people who had married into the nation after November 1, 1877.[58] On a smaller scale, individuals such as Robin Stann, a deputy sheriff and interpreter, helped individual Cherokees to navigate enrollment and allotment and "saw that allotments were made to his people of the lands on which they lived and did not care to leave."[59]

According to Kent Carter, the Muscogees (Creeks) made several attempts to preempt the commission's enrollment work by taking their own census both in 1896 and 1899.[60] Gary Zellar also describes the Muscogee Nation's attempts to control which names ended up on Creek rolls, but concludes that, once the Curtis Act was passed, the nation could no longer "dodge the punch" of allotment.[61] The Choctaws and Chickasaws similarly protested against the government's interference in writing. They complained against the reopening of the tribal rolls, arguing that "a great mistake" had been made when the government assumed jurisdiction over tribal membership. Had the tribes been allowed to judge who was entitled to the right of citizenship, the "great horde of fraudulent claimants that besieged the courts and the Commission would have been unheard of." The 1896 act that authorized the commission to decide citizenship cases had, the Choctaws and Chickasaws complained, lifted the "flood-gates." The act was "taken by the numerous applicants to be an invitation . . . to 'all persons' to apply for citizenship in one or the other of the nations; at least, a great many persons applied to the Dawes Commission for citizenship in the tribes now had never before claimed or thought they were Indians." The Choctaws and Chickasaws expressed a special resentment of certain attorneys who, they said, were representing "Creoles, Negroes, Mexicans" and other "persons of dark complexions" and claiming they should have membership in the tribe.[62] Jesse T. Schreier asserts that the Choctaw tribal government went so far as to station representatives outside the commission's tents to direct the flow of people with a special focus on freedpeople and people of mixed Choctaw and African descent.[63] Katherine Osburn argues that the lawyers representing the Choctaw Nation used a political and legal definition of Choctaw status, as opposed to the discourse of blood relied on by the Dawes Commission, to maintain the right of the Choctaw Nation to decide their own membership criteria.[64]

Resistance to allotment also operated outside tribal government structures and legal systems. The Muscogee Crazy Snake movement, led by Chitto Harjo, and the Cherokee Keetowah Society and Nighthawk movement, led by Red Bird Smith, refused to participate in the process of allotment, believing, as Stremlau puts it, that "any acknowledgment of or involvement in the allotment process legitimized it."[65] The protestors went into hiding whenever the commission arrived to take names, sent back certificates (some annotated in both English and Cherokee with the statement "I don't want this. If I want it I will come and get it"), created alliances with protesters from other nations (for example, the Four Mothers Society), made speeches, and sent delegations to Washington and memorials and petitions to Congress.[66] In 1902 several Nighthawk men were arrested, shorn of their hair, and put in jail.[67] Protest could also take the form of simple silence, as Stremlau shows in the case of Nighthawk Jenny Oakball, who refused to speak to a Dawes Commission employee.[68] In response, the commission made arbitrary allotments to the protestors and their children, used a special railroad car to distribute certificates that protestors refused to collect, and portrayed them as "full-bloods" who were being manipulated by cunning people of mixed descent.[69]

The tribal governments were themselves victims of the division of the Five Tribes into "full/deserving" and "mixed/undeserving" Indians in the minds of government officials. The Dawes Commission believed that the tribal governments of the Five Tribes were mostly run by mixed-descent people and were thus corrupt and inauthentic, and useless to the "real" Indians. The commission had been informed by the secretary of the Interior at the outset that "success in your negotiations will mean the total abolition of the tribal autonomy of the Five Civilized Tribes and the wiping out of the quasi-independent governments within our territorial limits."[70] The corruption of tribal governments was a common theme in the Dawes Commission's writings and speeches, and it was the reason why the dissolution of tribal governments was presented as the fairest solution for the Five Tribes.[71] The commission did not hesitate to state "the effacement of the tribal governments" as one of its objectives. This was a democratic goal, the commission asserted, because of the "incapacity of the tribe for self-government."[72] The 1898 Curtis Act also inflicted several severe blows on tribal sovereignty. As Circe Sturm has shown, it closed down tribal courts and instead gave federal courts jurisdiction over Indian Territory.[73]

The commission blamed tribal governments for its lack of success in convincing Five Tribes Indians to agree to allotment, describing them as having fallen under the control of "mixed bloods and adopted citizens . . . while the real full blood has been left destitute and crowded out upon the mountains and unproductive land, to take care of himself as best he can."[74] Thus the commission's argument was that it need not pay attention to the opinions of the tribal governments because they were corrupt and, perhaps even more significantly, inauthentic and not really "Indian" at all. Although an act passed in 1906 permitted the tribal governments to continue to exist, by 1913, as the commission itself reported, "the tribal officials had been divested of practically all governmental functions," and all "tribal records, papers, documents, etc., [had] turned over to the custody of this office." No tribal elections were held after 1906, and the president assumed the power to remove any tribal official and reappoint someone in his or her place.[75]

Competency

In 1908 people designated as "mixed-bloods" were confronted with a significant challenge to retention of their land: competency. In 1904 Congress had passed legislation that released lands belonging to "Indians who are not of Indian blood"—those designated on the rolls as whites and freedpeople—from the twenty-five-year trust period that prevented those lands from being sold or leased. In 1906 Congress had extended this trust period for "full-bloods." But, in 1908, "an act for the removal of restrictions from part of the lands of allottees of the Five Civilized Tribes, and for other purposes" was passed, applying to all whites, freedpeople, and people "of less than one-half Indian blood." Indians designated as having more than one-half and less than three-quarters Indian ancestry were henceforth free to sell their surplus land, although their homesteads remained subject to restrictions. Those designated as having more than three-quarters Indian blood also remained restricted.[76]

Those declared competent lost most of the special benefits and protections attached to Indian ancestry. This was the most concrete legislative expression of the presumption that Five Tribes Indians of mixed ancestry did not deserve land or Indian citizenship. It meant that people of mixed descent were more likely to sell, mortgage, or lose their land, as was Lillie Gordon Franks's experience:

> My mother, father, four brothers, three sisters, and myself each received an allotment of a hundred and sixty acres. My allotment was near Bixby. Since we were not full bloods we had to pay taxes. I sold my land when I was about ten. Mother held hers until her death about ten years ago, after which it was sold.[77]

Many mixed-descent people were the targets of "grafters," who, as Gertrude Bonnin, Charles H. Fabens, and Matthew K. Sniffen documented in 1924, had a variety of creative schemes to unlawfully gain their land. They reported that:

> These grafters often keep a "birthday book" so they will know when the minors with estates become of age (which means the restrictions on the lands of mixed-bloods are automatically removed). They have been known to go to the Government Indian schools to call on these minors, and promise them presents of gold watches, or invite them to share their homes after they leave school, or become of age.[78]

The government quickly realized that assuming a certain amount of non-Indian blood was a measure of the capacity to resist "grafters" was a mistake.[79] Thanks to the chaotic practices of the Dawes Commission, many allotted Five Tribes Indians did not even know how much land they had been allotted or where it was.[80] "Viewing the situation at this time," the superintendent of Indian Affairs in Oklahoma reported in 1916, "it is apparent that the basis of quantum of blood was an unfortunate one. Time and developments have demonstrated that quantum of blood does not indicate business capacity or lack of it." In the superintendent's view the "startling probability" existed "that approximately 90 per cent of the members of the Five Civilized Tribes, who have had their restrictions against alienation of their lands removed by congressional acts, have parted title thereto." In less than ten years, he marveled, "a race of landlords . . . have been transformed into a race of tenants."[81] In 1913 Warren K. Moorehead, a member of the Board of Commissioners for the Office of Indian Affairs and one of the investigators of the "White Earth Tragedy" detailed in the previous chapter, described the rarity of mixed-descent people who had held onto their land. "There are some few Indians, mixed bloods and freedmen, living upon their original allotments," he wrote, "but they are so few that . . . white citizens in the community are sure to point out to the traveller that such and such a man held on to his property, and the grafters were unable to take it away from him." Nevertheless, Moorehead, like so many other government officials, thought mixed-descent Indians were likely to be swindlers. "Many of these men are estimable citizens," he admitted, "but others are quite as harmful to the best interests of the more ignorant full bloods as the white grafters themselves. Being able to speak both languages, and possessing a knowledge of the white man's ways, they act as interpreters for the grafters, and engage in swindling their own people."[82]

In 1907 Congress closed the rolls of the Five Tribes and withdrew the chance of people like Ben Hartness, a Cherokee, to be entered on the rolls. Hartness remembered that his family "proved up the blood," but the rolls had closed before they were placed upon them. He agreed with his interviewer that people like his family were called the "too lates." His family's case was still pending when he was interviewed in the late 1960s.[83] Closing the rolls also instantly deprived the next generation of Five Tribes Indians from citizenship in the Five Tribes. After the rolls were closed the Dawes Commission did not recognize the children of the Five Tribes born after March 4, 1906, regardless of their ancestry, "as members of the tribes, or [as having] any rights to lands or moneys, except as they may inherit." Whether this was the result of a notion that allotment had done the job of assimilation in only one generation, or simply an administrative washing of hands, is not clear. Dana Kelsey, the superintendent of the Union Agency, the government body given the task in the new state of Oklahoma of supervising the Five Tribes, was a strong advocate of the distinction between "deserving full" and "undeserving mixed" Indians. But even he was astounded at the finality of this legislation. "It is very seldom considered," Superintendent Kelsey wrote in the 1912 annual report, "that there is a rapidly growing class of real Indians that are not so recognized."[84] The following year Kelsey painted an even more dramatic picture of the problem, portraying it as the next important challenge facing the state of Oklahoma. "We fail to appreciate," he pointed out, "that the hills contain thousands of children not officially recognized as members of tribes, but who are really Indians in every sense." This "unallotted generation," largely residing in the "remote districts . . . [were] unable to speak English, scantily and slovenly clothed, presenting a hopeless subject from which we expect a self-supporting American citizen in but a few years."[85] With the next generation completely wiped from the rolls, and only able to rely on inheritance to maintain their hold on what was left of their lands, the Dawes Commission could claim to have taken an enormous step toward appeasing settler pressure to open up Indian-held lands. The Dawes Commission's work may have been complex and chaotic, but in an extraordinarily short time it managed to significantly reduce the numbers of Five Tribes Indians who were officially recognized by the federal government.

The Dawes Commission did not deliberately exclude people of mixed descent from enrollment and allotment. Rather, they were made vulnerable to omission from the rolls of the Five Tribes through a variety of administrative processes—residence requirements, enrolling mixed-descent children according to their mother's status, enrolling people with African American ancestry as freedpeople, incomplete rolls, time limits, and incorrect record keeping. The government assumed that mixed-descent people were better able to negotiate the complex process of allotment—gaining access to the right tent, having the right documents, possessing money for an attorney, living in the right place, or manipulating tribal government to their own ends—and that they used their skills to advantage themselves and disadvantage people of full descent. The trope of the undeserving mixed-descent Indian had no place for deserving, mixed-descent victims. Today, a significant part of one set of records in the National Archives is made up of letters from the Office of Indian Affairs informing people of Indian descent that they were too late to enroll.[86] Some, though of course not all, may have deserved a place in Joseph Howell's "equitable box" mentioned at the start of this chapter. "The fact that a person . . . has Indian blood in his veins of any degree would not entitle him to any right to participate in the distribution of lands or funds belonging to any of the tribes in the Indian Territory," stated the Office of Indian Affairs' reply to one such letter. "There are a great many people," it continued candidly, "who possess various degrees of Indian blood, but who are in nowise citizens of the Five Civilized Tribes. . . . notwithstanding the popular and widespread opinion to the contrary."[87]

After the 1887 General Allotment Act was passed, the process of allotment proceeded across the country with notable haste, as pressure from white settlers to release Indian lands mounted. Just as in Minnesota and Indian Territory, discussed in this and the last chapter, Native American nations across the United States had their populations enumerated and allotted by commissions of various kinds. And, just as in Minnesota and Indian Territory, tribal rolls often became the sources of intricate legal cases and government bureaucracy. The Anishinaabeg, Choctaws, Chickasaws, Cherokees, Seminoles, and Muscogees were nations with diasporic populations, competing sovereignties, and significant numbers of mixed-descent people in their populations. Their devastating experiences of enrollment and allotment demonstrate the pervasiveness of blood-based myths about people of mixed descent. In Minnesota the myth of the undeserving cultural broker of indeterminate racial status predominated. In Indian Territory the related idea that Indian communities were divided into deserving, helpless "full-blood" or "real" Indians and cunning, undeserving "mixed-bloods" prevailed, butting against the Five Tribes' efforts to maintain the right to decide their own citizenry.[88] In both Minnesota and Indian Territory the connection between blood and Indian status was solidified in competency laws. Meanwhile, the assumption that Indians of mixed descent were not worthy of enrollment, allotment, or official recognition of their Indian status began to infiltrate the government's policies, making a lie of their protestations that they followed tribal custom when enumerating Indian populations. In 1920 Congress included a section in the appropriations act giving funding to the Office of Indian Affairs that authorized the "final enrolment of tribes." The secretary of the Interior was authorized to make final rolls of the membership of any Indian tribe, which should contain "ages and quantum of Indian blood." These rolls were to constitute the legal membership of the respective tribes.[89] The discourse of blood, now cemented in the enrollment process, made it difficult for people to prove their status and therefore lessened the number of people on the rolls who deserved land and benefits. The following chapter continues the story of Native American land loss by examining the policy of competency in the national arena.

CHAPTER THREE

Practically White

The Federal Policy of Competency

In his classic work on assimilation policy, Frederick Hoxie described a ceremony at an unnamed reservation at which competency was granted to a group of Native American people. Candidates "were dressed in traditional costume and armed with a bow and arrow." After ordering a candidate to shoot his arrow into the distance, the presiding officer, usually the agent, would announce, "You have shot your last arrow." The arrowless archer would then return to the tipi and reemerge a few minutes later in "civilized" dress. He would be placed before a plow: "'Take the handle of this plow,' the government's man would say, 'this act means you have chosen to live the life of the white man—and the white man lives by work.'" The ceremony would close with the newly competent landowner receiving a purse (at which point the presiding officer would announce "this purse will always say to you that the money you gain from your labor must be wisely kept"), and an American flag.[1] This ritual represented competency as a reward for—and inspiration toward—acculturation. In reality, however, the administration of the policy of competency was driven by the notion that some Native Americans were undeserving of government protection of their lands.

In 1906 the Office of Indian Affairs began the practice of distributing "fee patents," also known as certificates of competency, to individual Indians. These documents allowed them to sell, lease, or mortgage their land without interference from the Office of Indian Affairs. The concept of a competent Indian person was adopted to overcome a stipulation in the 1887 General Allotment Act that the government held the title to each allotment in trust for twenty-five years. In 1906 the government decided that a modification of this regime was desirable, and the legal status of competency was created by an act (the Burke Act) that released the holder's allotment from the trust period. Indians could be declared competent and awarded a fee-simple patent (a fee patent), or later a certificate of competency, after an application process that supposedly measured their level of acculturation and business acumen. Competent Indians exempt from the special laws and protections that accompanied Native American status were allowed to sell, mortgage, and lease their lands and were no longer exempt from taxes. They were also likely to sell their land or have it taken from them because of unpaid taxes, defaulted mortgages, or exploitation. Simple financial need thus contributed to their long-term financial hardship and the overall reduction of Native American landholdings. This benign-sounding policy was the catalyst for an enormous transferral of Native American lands to non-Indians and was the vehicle by which measuring Indianness according to blood quantum became firmly embedded in federal policy.

We have already encountered the concept of competency. In chapters 1 and 2 I dealt with legislation that declared mixed-descent members of individual nations (the Anishinaabeg in 1906 and 1907 and those comprising the Five Tribes in 1908) ipso facto competent. Such specific legislation proved a clumsy mechanism, and was only sparingly used by the federal government. The Burke Act provided a broad alternative avenue for the award of certificates of competency across the country to individual Native Americans who could apply for assessment by the Office of Indian Affairs and for a certificate of competency from the secretary of the Interior.

Although the Burke Act required an assessment of each individual applicant, a method ostensibly very different from the collective award of competency to certain members of a specified nation considered in chapters 1 and 2, a close examination of the process by which individual awards of competency were made under the Burke Act shows that federal policy was driven by the same assumptions and purposes that lay behind legislation that declared mixed-descent Indians of specified nations competent without any assessment. Competency was the first policy of the assimilation period that directly used the language of blood. Competency policies were imposed from the top down—the legislation was passed with no tribal consultation or even limited effort to follow tribal policies or practices as there had been during the processes of enrollment and allotment.

In this chapter, I examine the background of the Burke Act, and the practices and policies pursued in its implementation by the Office of Indian Affairs until 1917, when the office abandoned the process of individual assessment in favor of an automatic award of competency to all Indians of a specified blood quantum, and the effects and aftermath of these strategies. I then provide a case study, examining the decisions made by the Cheyenne/Arapaho competency board during 1917, showing to what extent the rhetoric of federal officials translated into local practice. Finally, I examine how Native American people themselves viewed and negotiated competency.

Rhetoric and Reality

Competency implied equality—it gave individuals a form of citizenship allowing them to be treated as white persons under the law and giving them the right to sell, lease, or mortgage their land. For those in charge of dictating Indian policy and solving the "Indian problem," competency was an application of the principles of assimilation that underlay the Dawes Act. Commissioner of Indian Affairs Francis E. Leupp wrote of "releasing Indians from federal control" and enabling the Office of Indian Affairs to "manage the affairs of the helpless class with undisputed authority [while] on the other hand, [removing] from the roll of dependents the ever-increasing number of Indians who no longer need Government supervision."[2] The Indian Rights Association urged the government to expand the reach of competency, arguing that it was "little short of a crime to the Indians to continue their servile and dependent condition, so lacking in experience and individuality for assuming the duties of citizens."[3] While this gospel of equality sounded good in the cool marble halls of Congress,

Certificate of Competency of a Kansas or Kaw Indian

ALLOTTEE No. ____77.____

WHEREAS, _____,

a member of the Kansas or Kaw tribe of Indians, has made application for withdrawal from said tribe and for

the issuance of a CERTIFICATE OF COMPETENCY as contemplated by Section 10 of the Kansas or Kaw

Agreement, which was accepted, ratified, and confirmed by the Act of Congress approved July 1, 1902 (32

Stats. L., p. 636); and,

WHEREAS, Upon consideration and examination of the request, I have found said _____

_____ to be fully competent and capable of

managing and caring for ____his____ individual affairs:

NOW, THEREFORE, I, _____Assistant_____,

Secretary of the Interior, by virtue of the power and authority vested in me by Section 10 of said Act of

Congress of July 1, 1902, hereby issue to said _____

this CERTIFICATE OF COMPETENCY and do hereby invest ____him____ with the power and authority

to sell and convey any or all lands deeded ____him____ by reason of said Agreement, and do hereby declare

____him____ to be fully competent and capable of managing and caring for ____his____ individual affairs.

Done at the city of Washington this ____29th____ day of ____May____, 19_8

_____
Assistant Secretary of the Interior.

it masked the reality of the reservations where land-hungry white people found it all too easy to use the policy to exploit Native American land-holders. Competency hastened the removal of special status from Indian lands and allowed them to pass into the mainstream market, open to the tactics (and crimes) of capitalism without restriction.

Once a Native American person was declared competent, he or she was open to manipulation, deceit, scams, and bad advice. Activists soon brought the frauds perpetrated as a result of the policy of competency to the public's attention. Three members of the Indian Rights Association, Gertrude Bonnin, Charles H. Fabens, and Matthew K. Sniffen, published a pamphlet in 1924 calling the allotment of the Five Tribes "legalized robbery." In it, they included some colorful stories of the creative methods by which white people managed to cheat Indians out of their land.[4] The government was well aware of the rapidity with which competent Indian people sold, leased, or forfeited their land. But public awareness of the situation made no difference. In 1934 Commissioner of Indian Affairs John Collier reported to the Senate and House Committees on Indian Affairs the shocking statistic that allotment policy had reduced Indian landholdings from 138 million acres in 1887 to 48 million acres.[5] Janet McDonnell, whose 1991 study of assimilation policy is perhaps the most comprehensive source of information about competency, estimates that 23 million acres of the transferred land had been fee patented.[6]

There was, though, another side to the policy. Being awarded competency allowed people to sell unwanted land and make their own financial decisions. Where day-to-day survival was frequently a struggle, the opportunity of an immediate, large payment of money was inevitably welcome. Many allotments were unsuitable for farming, and many

Fig. 1. Certificate of Competency of a Kansas or Kaw Indian, 1918. File 22558–18–127, CCF 1907–39, RG 75, NARA–Washington DC. The image shows a rake, hoe, bales of hay, and other farming implements, all presided over by the American eagle. Although competent Native American people were often imagined by the U.S. government as self-sufficient farmers, in reality competency meant lands could be sold, leased, mortgaged, or taken through fraud or non-payment of taxes or loans. Conversely, competency sometimes also entailed a form of economic freedom that may not have included working the land.

people were not interested in farming or ranching or did not have enough capital to succeed. Money from the sale of lands might help to start a business, build a house, or buy more valuable land elsewhere. Philip Deloria points out that the idea that Indians "squandered" or "lost" their money or their lands (a common refrain in agent's reports) smacks of paternalism: "It proved easier to think of sold allotments as squandered than as swindled, for that placed responsibility on Indian people rather than those who cheated them."[7]

Competency was a second stage in the dispossession of Indians during the assimilation period implemented by the discourse of blood. Chapters one and two show how blood infiltrated the hasty processes of tribal enrollment and allotment that followed the Dawes Act of 1887. In this chapter I show how the use of the discourse of blood in the policy of competency operated to jeopardize the landholdings of Native Americans, especially those perceived to be of mixed descent, who had survived enrollment and allotment with their status and landholdings intact.

Soon after the process of enrollment and allotment under the Dawes Act had begun it became clear that some allottees and some pieces of allotted land were not suited to farming. Four years after the Dawes Act was passed, a further act of Congress authorized the secretary of the Interior to permit leases of allotments, when "by reason of age or other disability" an allottee could not make personal use of them. Many years later, a 1935 government report into Indian land tenure, economic status, and population noted that, although the legislation authorizing the leasing of land was to have the most "profound effect" on the implementation of the policy of allotment, "its passage attracted comparatively little interest." The right to lease their land was ostensibly granted to Indians who could not work their land, but the report noted that it was "entirely favorable to the western land-seekers and business interests, who did not fail to apply pressure to the Office of Indian Affairs."[8] Individual Native Americans also requested, or had agents who requested on their behalf (not always with the purest of motives), that their trust period be lifted and the fee patents to their land be handed over to them. In each case, Congress was required to enact special legislation, or tag an extra clause onto existing Indian-related legislation, to grant a fee patent.

In 1905 the Supreme Court ruled that, under the Dawes Act, an Indian granted an allotment immediately became a citizen of the United States and was thenceforth eligible to buy alcohol (the sale of alcohol to Indians had been banned since an amendment to the Indian Appropriations Act in 1897). This prompted Charles Burke, the representative from South Dakota, to sponsor an amendment to the General Allotment Act. The Burke Act provided that an allottee could become a citizen only at the end of the twenty-five-year trust period. However, because some Native Americans were competent to manage their lands, and the government had acknowledged and encouraged this phenomenon, the secretary of the Interior was given the right to abbreviate the probationary period for Indians judged competent to manage their affairs.

The Burke Act allowed the secretary of the Interior to issue fee patents, after an application process that began when an individual approached a local superintendent, who completed the application, posted it on the reservation for thirty days, and then forwarded it to the commissioner of Indian Affairs. If the commissioner approved it, it was forwarded to the secretary of the Interior for his signature. Later the same year in Minnesota, as described in chapter 1, the first Clapp Rider was passed conferring competency collectively on "mixed-blood" Anishinaabeg.

After the passing of the Burke Act, the Office of Indian Affairs began actively to look for applicants for competency. As early as May 1907 the acting commissioner sent a letter to agents and superintendents requesting the names of Indians "who are sufficiently capable, and who wish to manage or lease their lands," in order to enable the Office of Indian Affairs to "make the experiment of giving to progressive Indian allottees greater freedom in the management of their allotments."[9] And again in November 1907, Circular 172 requested agents and superintendents to "forward complete lists of Indians in their charge who were competent to handle—realizing the nature and consequences of their acts—the money belonging to them as individuals."[10]

At first competency was awarded relatively cautiously because government officials were aware that fee patents often led to Indians selling their land or being defrauded by avaricious white real estate agents, mortgage brokers, lawyers, and scammers. Laurence Schmeckebier's history of the Office of Indian Affairs reports that between 1909 and 1912 about 3,400 applications were approved and 200 denied.[11] During this time, commissioners of Indian Affairs displayed different levels of enthusiasm about competency, which was a divisive subject. "No phase of Indian administration is more controversial than this question of freeing the Indian from government control," wrote Schmeckebier in 1927, who argued that on the one hand the Office of Indian Affairs was represented as "a great bureaucracy which stifles the initiative and advancement of the Indians," and on the other "it is claimed that if the individual Indian were given full control of his property he would soon be cheated out of or dissipate it and become a pauper."[12]

Although the Office of Indian Affairs was supposed to be hesitant to award fee patents without applications, this was not always the case. In 1910 the Indian Office sent blank agreements of sale to Wyandottes who owned land in Oregon but did not live on the reservation.[13] In 1912 Commissioner of Indian Affairs Robert G. Valentine told the superintendent of the Yakima School that a Native American "amply able to look out for himself . . . should, from a true social point of view, be a full-fledged member of his local community" and should be pressured to apply for competency. Such people were "no longer morally justified in not applying." The matter should be "brought clearly to [their] attention," and if that did not work then "the Department should avail itself of its power under the law to issue a patent in fee without request on the part of the patentee." The superintendent was requested to submit the names of "not more than six Indians on your reservation whom you believe clearly should share the burdens as well as the privileges of their local communities."[14] Reports from agents and superintendents on the reservations received by the Office of Indian Affairs contained both positive and negative reports about the practice of pressuring people to apply—in some cases describing shocking cases of land theft resulting from it, in others applauding it as an effort to make Indigenous peoples independent and self-supporting.

Federal Competency and Blood

The concept of competency was an old one, stemming from John Locke's theory of liberal democracy, but it found particular expression in the United States during the nineteenth century.[15] In the legal arena, as Felix Cohen pointed out in 1945, the term incompetency was used to refer to people—such as children, the mentally ill, or the elderly—who were unable to enter into a contract, give evidence in a court of law, or serve on a jury.[16] In the hands and minds of the Office of Indian Affairs, however, the term "competent" took on racial implications. The office assumed that Native Americans were, racially, mostly childlike and in need of protection, and government agents were empowered to decide whether the removal of restrictions was in the "best interests" of the person in question.[17] Competency was for Native Americans who were intelligent, educated, had "business sense," and required no guardianship. It dovetailed perfectly with the racial stereotype of the "mixed-blood" undeserving of protections offered to "real" Indians. No wonder it quickly became linked with the discourse of blood.

Washington officials at first unofficially and then later officially took the view that competency was particularly appropriate for people of mixed white and Indian descent, in the belief that their non-Indian ancestry and their presumptive connections to the white community made them candidates for acculturation. In draft legislation never passed, Congress addressed the "Rights of Mixed Blood Indians" as early as 1896, proposing that "mixed-blood Indians who are possessed of land in severalty shall at once receive patents in fee for their lands." A Senate committee noted that "a mixed-blood Indian having one-quarter or less Indian blood in his veins is quite as competent to perform the duties of citizenship intelligently as many white men, and that the percentage of incompetency among the Indian tribes of one-quarter Indian blood or less is not greater than that to be found among a like number of white persons."[18] In 1910 Leupp, the commissioner of Indian Affairs, elaborated this idea in a publication on how to solve the "Indian problem." Leupp described the Indian of mixed descent as having a particular aptitude for assimilation, having inherited from "his Indian blood . . . keenness of observation, stoicism under suffering, love of freedom, a contempt for the petty things which lay so heavy a burden on our convention-bound civilization." To these qualities the mixed-descent person (whom Leupp assumed was a man even though the policy was not gendered) could add, thanks to "his white blood," the competitive instinct, individual initiative, resourcefulness in the face of novel obstacles, and a constitution hardened to the artificialities of modern life.[19]

Leupp was not alone in thinking that Native Americans of mixed white/Indian descent were especially fitted for release from government supervision. In 1913 Cato Sells took up the position of commissioner of Indian Affairs, determined to declare Indians competent whether they wanted it or not. Sells, whose term as commissioner featured the strongest emphasis on competency as a means of solving the "Indian problem," ordered superintendents to submit the names of all people under their control who had less than one-half Indian blood, along with their age, sex, blood quantum, and descriptions of their land.[20]

In many cases the assumption that white blood equaled greater acculturation led to unflattering views of the morality of mixed-descent Native Americans. Alexandra Harmon has argued that Indians accused of monopolizing land at the expense of their countrymen in Oklahoma were nearly always accused of being of mixed descent by both whites and Indians.[21] Many government officials believed that some competent Indians deliberately refused fee patents because they were taking advantage of their special status in order to avoid tax. In 1917 the Competency Commission who had worked on the Pottawatomi Reservation in Kansas reported finding "several very competent Indian allottees . . . who have refused to sign applications for patents in fee on the sole ground that they will have to become tax payers" and expressed the hope that "some way can be found whereby patents can be issued to them." Such people (who might be retrospectively read as financially astute and/or activist in the sense described by Audra Simpson as refusal), the chief clerk at the Office of Indian Affairs felt, "are the very ones that we desire patents in fee issued to." Even though the law did not require it, he said, the office preferred to have such individuals sign an application form, thereby indicating their desire to be declared competent. However, he reminded the superintendent of the push to give fee patents to those of mixed descent and encouraged him to recommend "all Indians, whether of full or mixed blood, who are fully qualified to care for their own affairs" to be awarded competency.[22]

When government officials recommended awarding competency to Native Americans of mixed descent, the non-Indian blood component they envisaged was most often white. It was mixed white ancestry that was most salient when the government spoke of acculturation. Black ancestry carried with it quite different connotations. It was not associated with acculturation, intelligence, or business sense. It did, however, destabilize the authenticity of those who possessed it, rendering them as undeserving of the special protections accorded to "real" Indians as those of white/Indian descent. When laws like those that targeted the Five Tribes and the Anishinaabeg living at White Earth (see chapters 1 and 2) stated that Indians of less than one-half blood were ipso facto competent, Indians of mixed African American descent were included with those of white descent.

Because of the general view that Native Americans of mixed descent should be on their own to sink or swim, applications for competency were often approved even when the government was presented with clear evidence that this could lead to a financial situation in which applicants would have to sell their land. Thus, a financially successful couple from the Quapaw Agency in Oklahoma, who owned land valued at approximately $160,000, were awarded competency. The superintendent of the agency in his report described the husband as "educated, strong, healthy . . . without any occupation, except riding over the country in a big Pathfinder Auto and pestering his lessees for money to spend in luxurious living." This was in part because they were graduates of Carlisle and Haskell, and thus came within the Office of Indian Affairs' policy of awarding competency to educated Indians. But there was another reason—their success made them unworthy of protection. The superintendent predicted that they would not "have a dollar . . . within less than five years." But, he said, "it is very doubtful whether it will make better citizens of them by endeavouring to hold them in leash any longer. If they are given full control of their land they no doubt will live a riotous and luxurious life for a short time, then be compelled by want to earn their living by the 'sweat of their brows.'"[23]

The policy required government agents to assess individuals according to whether they were "civilized" and had enough "business sense" to take on the responsibility of controlling their own property. In this process gendered norms played an important role. "Civilization was performed and evident in one's behavior," writes Rose Stremlau, and Native American women were judged by standards of behavior that were "informed by the gendered expectations of Anglo-American society."[24] Women were seen as needing greater protection, and their "business sense" was often adjudicated by whether they were attached to the right kind of man. One confidential report about an Osage woman who was married to a non-Indian man urged consideration of the fact that "this young woman is married and would be subject to her husband's will in matters of estate, expenditures, routine matters, etc., perhaps an investigation of his abilities might be a deciding factor in cases like this."[25] The Indian Rights Association was worried that the pendulum of equality "might swing too far," particularly for Native American women who "may have no conception whatever [of] the nature of a deed of conveyance of land, and might easily be deluded and induced to execute a legal transfer of title to her allotment."[26]

Although the Office of Indian Affairs was cautious about removing restrictions from lands that were rich in oil or gas, the view that Native Americans of mixed descent were undeserving of protection sometimes prevailed even in such cases. In 1908 the agent at Muskogee wrote a long report to the commissioner of Indian Affairs about oil-bearing tracts of land in the Cherokee Nation whose owners had submitted applications for fee patents. He justified the removal of restrictions by inviting "attention to the fact that the great majority of these cases are of less than half blood."[27]

Where Indians of mixed descent had been defrauded of their lands, the Indian Office showed little inclination to help them. One Quapaw woman from Oklahoma was defrauded of her land by a Mr. Scott, who threatened her with prison if she did not sign a deed of sale. In 1937 the woman hired a lawyer and took Scott to court. She received no help from the Indian Office when she wrote to ask for advice on whether she should accept his settlement offer. The local agent voiced the Indian Office's attitude in writing that "since she is practically a white woman, I do not believe the Government has any moral duty to protect [her] any further."[28]

Blood-Based Competency

In 1917 Commissioner Cato Sells issued a "Declaration of Policy" that explicitly avowed the connection between competency and blood and, with immediate effect, declared competent all Indians with less than one-half Indian blood; all Indians with one-half or more Indian blood who after careful examination were found to be competent; and Indian students twenty-one years or older who had completed course work at a government school, received a diploma, and demonstrated competency. "This is a new and far-reaching declaration of policy," wrote Sells. "It means the dawn of a new era in Indian administration. It means that the competent Indian will no longer be treated as half ward and half citizen. It means reduced appropriations by the Government and more self-respect and independence for the Indian."[29] During the three years that followed, 10,956 fee-simple patents were issued, compared with 9,894 in the ten years from 1906 to 1916.[30] In 1921, after a devastating amount of land had shifted from Native American to white ownership, the new commissioner of Indian Affairs, Charles H. Burke, reversed the policy of awarding competency according to blood.[31] Then, in 1927 and 1931 Congress passed a general law authorizing the cancellation of fee-simple patents issued to Indians without their consent before the expiration of restrictions in their original patents.[32] While the policy was in operation, however, untold numbers of enrolled and allotted people of mixed descent were declared competent and their lands subjected to the open market and the efforts of fraudsters.

The 1917 Declaration of Policy was not a sudden change in strategy, but rather the expression of a view that had been formed over decades. "While ethnologically a preponderance of white blood has not heretofore been a criterion of competency," wrote Sells, "it is almost an axiom that an Indian who has a larger proportion of white blood than Indian partakes more of the characteristics of the former than of the latter." For Sells, the mixed-descent Indian in "thought and action, so far as the business world is concerned . . . approximates more closely to the white blood ancestry."[33] In an article published in the *American Review of Reviews*, Sells promoted his policy as permitting the Office of Indian Affairs to "release from governmental control the 'White Indians.' . . . It is the beginning of the end of the Indian problem."[34]

By 1918 and 1919 the Office of Indian Affairs was enthusiastically awarding patents to Native American people whose names had appeared on lists of persons of one-half or less Indian blood or who had graduated from large off-reservation boarding schools such as Chilocco.[35] The Office of Indian Affairs sent out circulars requesting lists of all allotted Indians of "one-half or less Indian blood" from agents, superintendents and farmers-in-charge.[36] In July 1919 the office issued an order precluding children who were not under federal supervision from enrolling in any government non-reservation boarding or day school. The Indian Rights Association quoted Sells as saying that "for several years attempts have been made to eliminate from Indian schools pupils whose parents are citizens, particularly those possessing only a small degree of Indian blood." The association noted that this particularly affected the children of Indians declared competent in 1917.[37] In 1920 a subcommittee of the House Committee on Indian Affairs, after traveling to reservations in the Southwest and Northwest, bemoaned the fact that competency commissions did not have the right to declare Native Americans competent unless they desired it, "since [only] a very small percentage of the Indians desire to become citizens," and recommended that the law be changed. The committee's view was that there were "many thousands of Indians who are thoroughly competent to be citizens who are still within the supervision of the Indian Bureau and who should at the earliest possible moment be thrown on their own reserves."[38] A year later an ultimately unsuccessful bill was placed before the House that provided for competency for any Native Americans of any blood quantum who had reached the seventh grade and turned twenty-one, and also removed several steps from the application process.

In justification, the committee quoted from the annual report of the secretary of the Interior for 1914, which conceded that there were many thousand "entirely self-supporting, capable, thrifty, farsighted, sensible" Indians who are "so farsighted that they do not wish to enjoy full independence because their property would then become subject to taxation."[39]

The Declaration of Policy caused a drastic rise in the numbers of people declared competent between 1919 and 1922 and a corresponding amount of land with no special protection. A 1935 government report blamed the granting of fee patents for the "loss" of about 23,000,000 acres, noting that "Indians who retained their land after coming into full control over it were rare exceptions." The report concluded that the granting of fee patents was "practically synonymous with outright alienation."[40]

The Cheyenne and Arapaho Competency Commission

Decisions about whether or not individual Indians were competent were entrusted to diverse administrative bodies during the many decades when competency policies were implemented, and in many cases their decisions were not consistent with national policy or with each other. Indeed, the administrative process was so massive that whether an Indian was declared competent often depended on when and where they applied and who received their application, or on what particular set of assumptions a specific competency commission or government official was operating under. It is important, therefore, to pay attention to local decision-making processes as well as federal policies and rhetoric. At the local level mixed ancestry was often an influential factor, sometimes under a specific law that pertained to a particular nation and sometimes because of the assumptions held by government officials about whether Indians of mixed descent deserved Indian status or not. As described in chapters 1 and 2, specific laws declaring mixed-descent people automatically competent were passed applying to the Five Tribes in Oklahoma and the Anishinaabeg in Minnesota. The Osage were similarly targeted in 1921 by an act that removed "all restrictions against alienation . . . of all adult Osage Indians of less than one-half Indian blood."[41] It is telling that the U.S. government passed specific competency legislation for nations with assets such as desirable lands, oil, and timber, like those owned by Osage, the Five Tribes, and the White Earth Anishinaabeg.[42]

In other places a law was not required for almost the same effect. The decisions of a board sent to Oklahoma to examine the Cheyennes and Arapahos for competency in January and February of 1917 provide just one illustration. This board operated just before the April 1917 "Declaration of Policy" made all Indians of half or more white descent competent. No law or policy as yet directed them to award competency invariably to mixed-descent Indians, but they did so nevertheless, acting on the view that Cheyenne and Arapaho people of mixed descent did not deserve government protection.

The Cheyennes and Arapahos were two distinct peoples, both of the Algonquian language family, who formed a coalition in the nineteenth century. They held lands in present-day Colorado, Kansas, Nebraska, Wyoming, New Mexico, Oklahoma, and South Dakota. After much violent conflict, they signed a treaty with the U.S. government in 1867 and eventually agreed to a combined reservation in western Indian Territory. They were allotted under the Dawes Act in the early 1890s, and excess land was almost immediately opened to white settlement. The Cheyennes and Arapahos were well aware by 1917 that the cost of being declared competent would be theft of their land and "valuable possessions."[43] As long as a decade earlier, the Office of Indian Affairs had begun to ask agents and superintendents in Cheyenne and Arapaho country to submit lists of names of people they considered "capable of handling their own and their children's allotments." Commissioner Leupp received some enthusiastic replies, which he forwarded to the secretary of the Interior with recommendations that fee patents be issued, and at least fifty-three were.[44] In March 1909 the superintendent of the Cheyenne and Arapaho Agency wrote to the commissioner of Indian Affairs to report that the new process of awarding fee patents was destined to cause "much trouble ahead." "Indians to whom this privilege has been granted," he wrote, "have in many cases exceeded the privileges granted them." The superintendent claimed that Indians declared competent had made "leases for a longer term than those provided by the regulations; accept[ed] full payment for the entire term in advance, taking goods and chattels as part payment, etc." The superintendent was reluctant to help individuals who had consequently found themselves in trouble, for example a man whose lessee refused to vacate his land when the lease had expired. "I have expressed the opinion that if these Indians are capable of leasing their own lands," the agent wrote, "they are capable of forcing the lessee to vacate the land." Therefore, he stated, "it is not the duty of the Agent or Super-intendent to take up the quarrels between the lessor and the lessee."[45] A few months later the same agent reported that in "many cases these Indians have collected three to five years of rent in advance, have spent the money, not always wisely," and were now reduced to jointly farming their "friends' allotment[s]." The agent reiterated his belief that the Cheyennes and Arapahos ought to sink or swim on their own. "The Cheyennes and Arapahos have been spoiled in years past by over-indulgence," he wrote. "It is hard to eradicate from their minds the belief that the simple fact that they are Indians places the Government under obligation to them." "They are gradually learning better," he added ominously.[46] Notwithstanding a further negative report about the effects of competency from this agent in October 1909, in 1913 the superintendent of the Cheyenne and Arapaho school was asked to submit more names because "it is evident that there are not as many Indians availing themselves of this privilege as there should be."[47]

Given this history, it is no wonder that as a competency board was on the way to interview the community in 1917, a Cheyenne-Arapaho dele-gation was traveling in the opposite direction to ask the commissioner of Indian Affairs to call the board's visit off. Showing they were well aware that their community was at risk of having its lands stolen by fraudulent whites, one member of the delegation told Assistant Commissioner E. B. Meritt: "We realize that if we were given . . . the right of conducting our own business affairs and our land turned over to us, that then all of our property and money would fall into the hands of grafters." The delegation informed Meritt categorically that they were "not ready to prepare ourselves to compete with civilized people in a business way."[48] In January 1917 the president received a petition from the Cheyennes and Arapahos asking him to extend their trust periods for an additional twenty-five years. "We realize that we are not sufficiently advanced educationally to take over the full burdens of citizenship," they wrote.[49] Their request was ignored.

The Cheyenne and Arapaho board was constituted of only three members: O. M. McPherson, a special Indian agent and Department of Interior representative, Captain Trowbridge of the secretary of the Interior's office, and W. W. Scott, the superintendent of the Cheyenne and Arapaho school.[50] We do not know much about the board's experiences in Oklahoma. We know that the weather was cold, a "howling wilderness of wind" as McPherson described it.[51] We know also that the board covered an impressive distance during the month they were at work, interviewing between twenty and seventy people a day in six different towns between January 19 and February 23. On February 6 at Cantonment, they interviewed eighty-four people in one day. For all interviewees the board recorded a variety of information: their age, their ancestry, the amount of land they held (for most the standard 160 acres allowed by the Dawes Act), whether they spoke English, what kind of schooling they had, and their state of health. With time the board got more efficient at working out exactly what information it needed, and its entries in the minute books that provide the main evidence of its work became shorter and more pointed. Thus, an entry about a non-competent Cheyenne or Arapaho read as follows:

[Name], 45, Cheyenne, Full blood (wife [Name]). Owns 160a, [. . . .] 70a under cultv, does not farm any rent all his land, cash $185 per year has leasing privileges, all fenced and two room house 2 horses 1 set harness, 1 farm wagon. Has farmed until the last year. Has cultivator [. . .] Value $4500. Never went to school. Does not understand or speak English. Non-competent. Does not want patent. Has 1 boy 16 years old.[52]

An entry about a competent Cheyenne or Arapaho read:

[Name], ½, 35, married, wife [Name], now [Name], 160 acres, 90 a under cultv. Rents 40 + another 50 corn. Good 4 room farm house; barn 28x14, hay barn [. . .] few fruit trees, well and windmill, [. . .]

6 work horses, 3 colts, 40 hogs, 2 goat, 1 farm wagon, 3 sets harness [. . .] 1 sulky plow [. . .] small tools, [. . .] Indian Mission School [. . .] 6 years, Cheyenne School 2 years, finished 5th grade, speaks Cheyenne. Competent. Does not want patent.[53]

The information thus recorded by the board reflected Office of Indian Affairs' policy on competency. The board attempted to distinguish between Indians who had demonstrated an ability to organize their own financial affairs and exhibited signs of "intelligence, industry and thrift," and those who lived in the "depths of helplessness, ignorance and vice," as Commissioner of Indian Affairs Leupp put it in 1909.[54] They collected information about farms and schooling but also relied on assumptions of what "civilization," "assimilation," "business sense," and (of course) "blood" looked like when personified by the people standing before them.

Historian Donald Berthrong has also investigated the Cheyenne-Arapaho board's decision-making process, although he does not focus on the issue of blood. He argues that the Cheyenne-Arapaho board's "criteria of business competency were unclear." Berthrong shows that many fee patents were in fact issued to Indians who showed no sign of "industry"—who "pursued no vocation and lived on lease money"—and that "little consideration was given to the allottee's previous record of handling his or her money and property." But while the Cheyenne-Arapaho competency board clearly did not regard "industry" as an overriding criterion, it did not award competency randomly. In its minute books, the board described many interviewees to be "old and ignorant," or "old, ignorant and blind," "old and deaf," "old, crippled, ignorant," or "old and feeble"—and none of the people thus described were awarded competency. Berthrong confirms that age was an important factor. "Of the 167 whose restrictions on the land were removed," he writes, "76.5 percent were between the ages of twenty-one and thirty-nine."[55] The ability to speak English was also important: 105 of 128 people (82.03 percent) who were declared competent could speak English or had some knowledge of English. Every single person declared competent had had some schooling, whether at one of the large, well-known off-reservation boarding schools such as Carlisle, Haskell, or Chilocco, or at local schools, where they had at best received a rudimentary education (some of those who attended the latter could still not read or write English).

The Cheyenne and Arapaho board was conservative when it came to the number of Indians they awarded competency. In a letter to the president summing up its work, Secretary of the Interior Franklin K. Lane reported that of the 3,331 Cheyenne and Arapaho Indians allotted under the Dawes Act whose patents were due to expire in May 1917, only 168 ought to be declared competent. The rest, the board had recommended, should have their patents extended and remain incompetent.[56] This low number might lead one to think that the government had the best interests of the Cheyennes and Arapahos at heart, but two telling practices contradict this assumption. First, the Cheyenne and Arapaho board's decision-making process was, to some extent, "inherently coercive," a phrase Janet McDonnell has applied to the competency commission sent to the Omaha reservation in Nebraska in 1910. There, she says, the "government issued fee patents on the basis of the commission's recommendation without any application or consent from the individual involved and sometimes over his protests."[57] And indeed, the Cheyenne and Arapaho competency board's records show that only 11.2 percent of the people it interviewed indicated that they wanted a fee patent. The great majority, 87.4 percent, stated firmly that they did not want a fee patent. Notwithstanding, just over 10 percent of the latter group were awarded one anyway.

Second, Indians perceived to be of mixed descent were more likely to be declared competent. The Cheyennes and Arapahos who were interviewed in 1917 were mostly categorized as being of full Indian descent—only 5.72 percent were recorded as being of mixed white ancestry. But a quarter of those declared competent were of mixed descent. The proportion of interviewees of mixed descent who were declared competent was larger than the proportion of the total group of mixed descent. Thus, being of mixed descent was not an automatic path to competency, but certainly helped to sway the board in that direction. A close analysis of the decisions made by the Cheyenne–Arapaho board in 1917 shows that in addition to youth, rudimentary signs of acculturation and white ancestry were regarded as reason enough to declare individuals competent.

The board manifestly operated on the assumption that people of mixed descent were more likely to have the "intelligence, industry, and thrift" that indicated competency.

Native American Responses to Competency

Competency put many Native Americans of both mixed and full descent in a difficult position. On the one hand, being awarded competency left them open to exploitation and fraud and the consequent theft of their land. On the other hand, competency gave them control over their own property and removed government supervision from their financial affairs. Hence responses to competency varied. Some Indians wanted and applied for competency on their own initiative. The Quapaw Competency Commission that worked in Oklahoma through the 1910s recorded applicants' reasons for applying for competency on the application form. Most responded with reasons of the utmost practicality. "I desire a Certificate of Competency so that I may be enabled to dispose of this land described in my application so that I can purchase a team and farming implements which will enable my husband to farm a portion of my lands where we now live," wrote a woman.[58] "I wish to sell this tract which is of no use to me and use the proceeds to buy a small place at Commerce, Oklahoma, where my husband is employed and where my parents live," wrote another.[59] A third applicant's reasons were geographical and financial: "I am now living at Joplin, Missouri, and cannot look after the renting of my land conveniently. I can loan my money out here in Joplin for eight and ten per cent. And have less trouble than renting my land and get more out of it."[60] David Chang reports that many Creeks were eager to sell or mortgage their land in order to obtain money or goods. These short-term benefits, he points out, were often meant to assist individuals in longer-term goals of sustaining communities and remaining a part of them.[61]

A Quapaw woman from Ottawa County, Oklahoma, wrote an angry letter to the commissioner of Indian Affairs on finding out in 1919 that her name had been put on a list of incompetent Indians. The applicant wrote that she was doing very well for herself—she was a beneficiary of a mine, which operated on her allotment, and whose lease she had negotiated herself and felt she hardly deserved the designation. "How would [you] like to have this done to you?" she asked Sells, "you and every other white man has the right to do what you want with your things; why can't I have it?" Other letters in her file reveal that the superintendent of the Quapaw agency declared her incompetent after the mine was closed down and she defaulted on a loan to buy a new Cadillac.[62] The mention of the Cadillac resonates with Philip Deloria's argument that mainstream Americans were reluctant to see Indian people interacting with modernity. The incongruity of a Native American (particularly a woman) "squandering" her money on a Cadillac may well have been a factor in the Quapaw agency's treatment of her.[63]

Others were similarly offended by the implications of being declared incompetent. C. L. Ellis, a member of the Quapaw Competency Commission, recognized this in 1910 while at work in Oklahoma. "Some [potential applicants] so far refuse to reply to our inquiries for information," he reported to his supervisor, "mostly, we suppose, in the spirit of resentment at inquiry into their affairs as they have always considered themselves competent."[64] Hazel and Quinton Harper, an Osage couple, were interviewed in 1968. Quinton said that being incompetent "means they're calling us ignorant." Hazel disagreed, "No, it [sic] not, again now this word incompetent is that you're not able to do what you're supposed to do with your own thinking. . . . Competent is you're capable of handling your own affairs, your own business. . . . I don't like it myself, cause it doesn't give you a fair shake." The Osages had the concept too, she said, "but we don't call it competency, I mean dumb, not able or something." Hazel was well aware of the legal implications:

> Once when you get those papers, competency papers, or certificate, why then your land goes on the tax roll, which it already is, but soon as they get that they start paying taxes. Start living like a white man, being a white man, they call it, have to be that way. The agency can't help you if you get in trouble over [a] lease or roadway or something like that. You have to go to county court, you can't go to the agency. The agency turn you loose, you're free. You're not really free, you're just turned loose.[65]

Some high-profile Native Americans fully supported the legal equality implied by the policy. Yankton Dakota woman Zitkála Šá (Gertrude Bonnin) wrote to President Wilson on behalf of the Society of American Indians, a political organization run by high-profile Indian activists of various backgrounds, to congratulate him on Sells's "Declaration of Policy." It was, she said, "an advance step in response to the urgency of this Society, as expressed in its platforms in recent years. It contemplates not the vanishing of the Indian but the disappearance of the race as a special problem and the releasing of restrictions and federal control."[66]

On the other hand, other Indians recognized the value of the special legal status their lands enjoyed in the eyes of the federal government and thought it worth retaining. As early as 1878, delegates from the Cherokee, Choctaw, Seminole, and Creek Nations showed remarkable foresight when they memorialized Congress on this subject. "The history of Indian legislation from the first settlement of the country shows that the restrictions upon alienation were meant for the benefit of the Indian," they wrote, "having their origin in the desire to guard against danger from the designs of evil-disposed white men." The delegates argued that "every member of Congress who carefully examines the subject could not help but appreciate the wisdom of retaining those restrictions."[67]

Some Native Americans have recorded memories of relatives who did their best to manipulate the policy to their own ends. A Delaware, Joseph Rogers, remembered his aunt explaining that some "full-blood" Delawares claimed to be "mixed-bloods" in order to sell their land, or even just to hasten the tedious process of enrollment:

> Some of 'em done so they could sell their land. Some of 'em married white men that wanted to sell their land. . . . And I don't know how else to say it. Some of 'em get over there because they couldn't afford to stay up any longer. Half-breed line was getting shorter and the quarter-breed line. And the full-blood line. Which ever it was. Some of 'em just change over to one to get in there. Now that's what Aunt Julia said.[68]

Clarence King, an Ottawa, also remembered people claiming a lower blood quantum when applying for competency, and clamering [*sic*], to get a roll, to lower their Indian degree of blood. To make . . . the Competency Roll in order that they could sell their land. In order to make a Competency roll they had to have someone to vouch that they were less Indian than they were. If they get down, low enough degree that was considered competent and they would make that competency roll. . . . And lots of them was worse off than before they ever made the allotment. The elder members that was full-bloods and those that had allotments they were held as wards and were never released they couldn't sell their land. So that's the reason most of the full-bloods up until their deaths had their allotments.[69]

Ross Swimmer, a former chief of the Cherokee Nation of Oklahoma, has also described how "a lot of ingenious Cherokees who were full blood, registered as a quarter, eighth or sixteenth blood so they could sell their property. And a lot of those who really were a quarter or an eighth or a sixteenth and who didn't want to pay taxes registered as a full blood so that they could have their land restricted and nontaxable."[70] These accounts seem to some extent to be conflating the processes of enrollment and competency, and are most likely referring to the requirement that applicants for competency provide a statement of their blood quantum as part of the application process. Indigenous peoples' responses to competency were complex, varied, based on personal circumstances and different understandings of what the policy meant, and its implications for their lives and property.

Did the U.S. government deliberately use a blood-based policy of granting competency to hasten its acquisition of land? The government received constant reports of reduced land holdings resulting from competency, and yet continued to grant it. It is impossible to view this "loss" of land as an unexpected, unwanted consequence. Commissioner Leupp wrote in 1909 that once the Office of Indian Affairs was freed of its task of administering lands held in trust, "there will be no more reservations; white settlers will have all the surplus lands, their farms will join those of the Indians, and the latter, by the removal of restrictions will pass rapidly from the trusteeship of the Government into the care of their owners." Leupp looked forward to the time, "in about a generation, [when]

'Indian lands' and the 'Indian problem' will simultaneously disappear in the vortex of a general American citizenship."[71]

In 1924, when the Indian citizenship bill was discussed in Congress, the idea that competency was solving the "Indian problem" by ridding the government of responsibility for all but the most vulnerable Native Americans was alive and well. One member painted the Office of Indian Affairs as an over-bloated authority in charge of less than 200,000 Indians. The rest, thanks to competency and various other legal processes, were freed from government control.[72] Another idea still current was the trope of the undeserving person of mixed descent. Carl Hayden, member of the House of Representatives for Arizona's at-large district, asserted that on every Indian reservation there were Native Americans who were "discontented . . . this is particularly true with the mixed breeds; Indians who have in their veins white blood, and who are shrewder, perhaps, on that account. It is often they who seek to rob their full-blood brother out of his property."[73] It was in this climate that Congress, in a one-sentence act, declared all "non-citizen Indians born within the territorial limits of the United States" to be citizens.[74]

Citizenship did little to protect Native American lands. While politicians waxed lyrical about bestowing it, government agents lamented the reports of people cheated out of their land. The government was not of one mind, and its numerous agents clearly interpreted the legislation in a variety of ways and felt very differently about the reduction of Indian-held lands. But many were clearly influenced by the attitudes about Indians of mixed descent that prevailed in the Office of Indian Affairs. The convenience of the outcome to a colonizing government, whatever expressions of regret it might make, is hard to ignore. It was competency that intertwined the special protection of Native American land with blood quantum and thus represents Patrick Wolfe's "logic of elimination" in its purest form. Ultimately, the policy of competency provides a clear instance of a settler nation using citizenship as a means of dispossession, and the discourse of blood was an integral part of the process.[75]

CHAPTER FOUR

The Same Old Deal

The 1934 Indian Reorganization Act

In 1939 a woman from St Louis, Missouri, wrote the Office of Indian Affairs to tell the commissioner, John Collier, that she had been "Cherokee-conscious" for many years. She wanted the opportunity, she said, to "establish [her] Cherokee identity" and to be recognized by the federal government as an Indian. Her letter was prompted by the passage of the 1934 Indian Reorganization (Wheeler–Howard) Act, in which she "saw a ray of hope . . . If I am not mistaken, the provisions of the Act gives [sic] me an opportunity to establish my Cherokee identity and have my claim adjusted." She thus wrote to the Office of Indian Affairs to find out how to make her claim.[1] Did she have ties to the Cherokee Nation that would be recognized today? Was she enacting the ubiquitous myth of the Cherokee grandmother? Was she hoping that recognition as a Cherokee would result in financial gain, perhaps relieving her of economic suffering caused by the Great Depression? Did she have a more fluid understanding of Cherokee identity than that enshrined within strict government categories? The records do not disclose, nor reveal whether her application was successful or not. In truth, the "ray of hope" she perceived was a weak one at best. The 1934 act recognized that there were Native Americans of mixed descent that were not tribally enrolled, but the opportunities it offered them to be officially recognized as Indian were few. Although the act was part of an "Indian New Deal" that was constituted as a radical departure from the previous policy of assimilation, established ideas about blood, people of mixed descent, and authentic Indian culture survived intact into the new era.

The New Deal incorporated the first official inclusion of blood in the federal government's definition of who was an "Indian." Blood was not, however, the only determinant of Indian status. Section 19 of the 1934 Indian Reorganization Act defined an Indian as belonging to one of three groups. First, "all persons of Indian descent who are members of any recognized Indian tribe now under Federal jurisdiction." Second, all "descendants of such members who were, on June 1, 1934, residing within the present boundaries of any Indian reservation." Finally, and most controversially, the definition included "all other persons of one-half or more Indian blood."[2] Blood as an official measure of Indian status was thus immaterial to persons who were enrolled in one of the nations recognized by the federal government, or to descendants of such persons residing on a reservation. Their Indian status was assured. But for those Native Americans who had, for one reason or another, failed to be officially enrolled, the possession of Indian blood became a tenuous path to government recognition as an Indian.[3] As Patrick Wolfe has pointed out, in 1934 "blood quantum discourse was now aimed primarily at people living *off* the reservations, the 'all other persons' who were not 'of one-half or more Indian blood.'"[4]

The 1934 act provided a chance for people who had missed out on enrollment and allotment, or who were descendants of enrollees not resident on a reservation, to be officially declared Indian. The advantages of such a declaration, however, were minimal. Successful registrants could apply for loans for tuition and might be given preference in employment by the Indian Service. Some funds were made available for land purchases and for other loans. Many applications were received, which left the Office of Indian Affairs with a problem: how to decide the merit of an application. Because the majority of applicants were not present on tribal rolls, the lack of paper evidence led the Office of Indian Affairs to rely on anthropometry and cultural factors to indicate race, as well as on administrative brush-offs. The government's disposition that mixed-descent applicants were undeserving of Indian status ensured that few were successful in taking advantage of this opportunity.

The Indian Reorganization Act was the product of a philosophical reaction against, and a legislative reversal of, previous policies of land allotment and assimilation. According to Senator Burton K. Wheeler (Montana), one of the cosponsors of the bill, its purposes were to stop the alienation of Indian lands, enable the acquisition of land by landless Indians, stabilize and empower Indian nations, encourage the formation of Indian business corporations, open up a line of credit for Indians, help Indians to enter mainstream schools and colleges, and encourage the employment of Indians by the federal Indian Service.[5] In other words, the new policy was predicated on the tardy realization that the General Allotment Act had been unsuccessful in solving the "Indian problem." As a pamphlet published in 1938 describing the new policy acknowledged, the "attempt to 'Americanize' the Indians by making them individual property owners [had] failed. . . . The new policy encourages tribal life and community control of lands and resources."[6]

The new policy largely represented the vision of one man, John Collier, the newly appointed commissioner of Indian Affairs. Collier's philosophy was rooted in the Progressive reaction to immigration and urban life. According to Kenneth Philp, after a visit to Taos Pueblo in 1920, Collier became convinced that the Pueblo peoples lived in a golden age, possessed lost human qualities of communal living, and "offered a model for the redemption of white society because it concerned itself very little with the material aspects of life."[7] Most scholars agree that Collier's promotion of Indian culture originated in a deep romanticism. Underlying the 1934 act was the desire to resurrect and retain Native American culture, promote tribal government, and halt the effort to assimilate Indians into the white mainstream. Collier told a House of Representatives committee in 1935 that "only sheer fanaticism would decide the further destruction of Indian languages, crafts, poetry, music, ritual, philosophy, and religion."[8] He summarized the radical departure he wanted Indian policy to take by starkly contrasting it with "historic policy: That Indian property must pass to whites; that Indian organization must be repressed and prevented; that Indian family life must be dismembered; that Indian cultures must be killed; and that Indians as a race must die." The new policy was to ensure that "Indian property must not pass to whites; that Indian organization must be encouraged and assisted; that Indian family life must be respected and reinforced; that Indian culture must be appreciated, used, and brought into the stream of American culture as a whole; and that the Indian as a race must not die, but must grow and live."[9]

Historians are divided on whether John Collier and his policies were of benefit to Indians or merely another means of colonial oppression, forced assimilation, and indirect colonial rule. Most scholars agree that Collier failed to understand the diversity of Indian nations and treated them all as if they were the Pueblo peoples he knew most about.[10] While there were some positive results, the lasting legacy of the New Deal was not self-government but the imposition of European structures of political organization.

The new attitude toward Indian culture meant little change for Native Americans of mixed descent, who were assumed to be more acculturated, less authentic, and less Indian, and had little place in Collier's idealistic vision for Indians. In an editorial published in 1936, Collier suggested teaching Native Americans of mixed descent to be more Indian while teaching "the tribal Indian" to be more technological. "Mixed-blood Indians," he said, "have much to gain through being put into contact with Indian tradition."[11] This view of Collier's was particularly misguided considering that the Pueblo, from whom he drew his romantic view of Indian culture, had a long history of intermarriage with other peoples. Vine Deloria Jr. and Clifford J. Lytle describe an "ugly exchange" between Collier and Joseph Bruner, a Creek (Muscogee) man from Sapulpa, Oklahoma, and president of the National Indian Confederacy. Bruner's opposition to Collier and his policies provoked a vitriolic response from Collier, revealing that he subscribed to the same ideas about people of mixed descent that had been held by his assimilationist precursors. Collier called Bruner "one who gains attention at all only through being an Indian, and yet who gains the attention through presenting the anomaly of an Indian ferociously trying not to be one. But when an Indian is subconsciously driven not to be an Indian, almost unavoidably he falls into imitation of the less attractive traits of the white man." "You are," he wrote to Bruner, "unfortunately, made less interesting through your choice of the white-man qualities you will imitate."[12] Harry J. Brown writes that the new policies were based on the assumption that people of mixed descent were "lingering somewhere between the primitivist utopia of the reservation and the wasteland of modern civilization." Thus, he states, "the politics of the New Deal only offered more of the same old deal."[13]

Notwithstanding his subscription to the discourse of blood and authenticity, Collier's original vision of Indian status was somewhat more inclusive than the final piece of legislation. The original bill included those enrolled as members of federally recognized nations and their descendants who were living on the reservation, as well as "all other persons of one-fourth or more Indian blood."[14] The object of this definition, Collier told the Senate and House Committees on Indian Affairs, was to "include all Indian persons who, by reason of residence, are definitely members of Indian groups, as well as persons who are Indians by reason of degree of blood."[15] According to Lawrence C. Kelly, the bill was debated extensively throughout the spring of 1934, and was drastically altered in the process. The quantum of blood required for Indian eligibility under Section 19 was changed from Collier's original one-fourth to one-half.[16] Section 19 was amended by the Senate committee.[17] Responding to Collier's proposal that Indians be defined as having "at least one-fourth Indian blood," Senator Wheeler argued strongly for a "one-half blood" quantum: "If you pass it to where they are quarter-blood Indians you are going to have all kinds of people coming in and claiming they are quarter-blood Indians and want to be put upon the Government rolls," Wheeler claimed. "What we are trying to do is get rid of the Indian problem rather than add to it."[18] During the debates on the bill in the House, the member from Oklahoma (who was an enrolled Cherokee) also expressed his concerns about the "doubtful language" used in the bill's definition of Indianness, which "may enable claimants from Maine to California to assert rights."[19] Another member of the House expressed concern that the one-fourth definition would "take existing power and authority away from the tribes and its operation would be to include many people who do not now share in tribal property, lands, moneys, or governments."[20]

In the remainder of this chapter I examine in detail the operation of the 1934 Indian Reorganization Act in relation to unrecognized Native Americans of mixed descent. I investigate how people who claimed Indian descent but were neither listed on tribal rolls nor lived on reservations, as well as some federally unrecognized nations, fared under the New Deal. It was no surprise to find that the Indian Reorganization Act, which had at its core the idea of upholding and preserving traditional Indian culture, grudgingly gave only a marginal place to those of mixed descent. In their effort to encourage and retain Native American culture, Collier and his staff conceived of Indian status as static, as something that had to be immunized against white or Black infiltration, whether geographical, economic, political, or genetic.

"Scattered" Indians

In general the Office of Indian Affairs was uninterested in what it called the "scattered" people of Native American descent who no longer had ties to a tribal nation. "While it is true that the Act has placed an obligation upon the Government to assist one-half blood Indians," wrote the assistant commissioner to one such person, "there are thousands of such Indians who must be considered, and of these the one-half bloods who are grouped together more or less in communities will be first considered. As for the scattered individual half-bloods there actually is not a great deal which can be done for them as provided for in the Act."[21] Another person, who had applied to be recognized as Cree, was told by letter: "There are many persons having some degree of Indian blood in different parts of this country, but who never belonged to such a tribe. Such persons usually have no claim to tribal benefits which can be substantiated. If you have this status, as seems to be the case, it is regretted that no assistance can be rendered [to] you or your son in this matter."[22] At a meeting of an enrollment committee concerned with the plight of an unrecognized group of Indians from Montana (also known alternately as Chippewa-Cree, Cree, and Rocky Boy's band), the committee members explored at length whether it was "the intent of Congress in writing Section 19 of the Indian Reorganization Act to extend recognition and assistance to scattered, unaffiliated individual Indians on the basis of their Indian blood, regardless of whether or not they resided in an Indian community?" The committee concluded that the answer was no. Their priority was to recognize "members of Indian groups, rather than . . . individuals who long ago severed their affiliation with Indian tribes and have lived as white people in white communities."[23] Although the 1934 act had introduced blood as a determinant of Indian status, this did not mean that the government was interested in identifying all those of one-half or more Indian blood and declaring them to be Indians.

The registration process used by the Office of Indian Affairs to decide whether applicants were deserving of Indian status reflected its suspicion that inauthentic Indians were trying to access tribal or government assets and its reluctance to recognize any "new" Indians. O. H. Lipps, a long-time employee of the office, did not bother to hide these sentiments in his final report on the enrollment of the Chippewa-Cree of North Dakota. "One may doubt their claim," he wrote of the Chippewa-Cree who tried to register under the 1934 act, but "they are generally able to meet all the requirements as to affidavits of persons who knew their parents and grandparents and thus prove the correctness of the claim."[24] Officials were disconcerted by the eagerness with which many people attempted to become registered, notwithstanding that the potential concrete benefits of registration were minimal. The Office of Indian Affairs created a form letter to answer what must have been a significant number of inquiries about registration under the act. It consisted of five paragraphs, against which one or more checks would be made in dealing with a particular application. It was signed by John Collier and told applicants that residence and ties to a nation were more important that Indian blood:

> Membership in a tribe is not an hereditary right. That is to say, although your parents may have been enrolled with a tribe, if you were born away from the reservation and never took up residence among the Indians of your parents' tribe, you probably were never enrolled and

you have no claim to enrollment, except as the tribe in question might, in its discretion, adopt you into membership.[25]

The letter explained that nations which had been enrolled "under specific authority of Congress" had undergone a "final closing of the tribe's membership books. . . . [which] cannot be reopened to admit the names of persons who . . . through over-sight or error were not included."[26] In other words, it made clear to applicants that they should not view the 1934 act as providing a chance to rectify their omission from tribal rolls.

The letter went on to state that non-enrolled persons who wished to be registered as Indians needed to prove they were of one-half or more Indian blood. Documentary evidence of their "degree of Indian blood . . . such as registration at an Indian Agency" was required. Alternatively, "the applicant should at least support his statement with [an] affidavit executed by reliable witnesses who have known him and members of his family over a long period of years." Applicants were warned that the "authority to decide whether or not proof of Indian blood is adequate rests with the Commissioner of Indian Affairs."[27]

The final paragraph of the letter spelled out the few benefits to which a person registered as an Indian under the 1934 act was entitled. The Office of Indian Affairs sought particularly to discourage any hope that applicants might have of accessing funds available under the act for the acquisition of land: "These funds . . . are very limited and at the present time no land has been purchased for individuals, nor is it likely that such purchases will be made in the future."[28] "In replying to inquiries," resolved one enrolling committee, "care should be exercised not to encourage the idea that the benefits are extensive or that they may be enjoyed by everyone."[29]

The application process was elaborate and required applicants to give information about both blood and culture. A four-page application form asked for details of any ancestors "ever enrolled for land, annuities, or other benefits by the United States or any State"—parents, grandparents, and even beyond—and of the degree of blood for each enrollee, as well as for the names of "tribal officers, members, or organizations which believed you to be a person of Indian blood." A series of questions aimed to ascertain the degree of acculturation: "Have you abandoned tribal life and adopted the habits and customs of the white community? Have you voted in State, county, or city elections? What Indian languages, if any, do you speak? How well?" In addition, there were questions about education and occupation, amount of property owned, and annual income, as well as a space for attaching photographs that "should be head study, front and profile views."[30]

Even applicants with strong tribal ties backed by documentary evidence would have found this process difficult, and for those who had lost track of one or both parents, who were in the dark about some details of their family history, or who were confused by what the government meant by "degree of blood" it must have been formidable. Unlike the rolls, lists, and forms filled out during enrollment and allotment, or generated by the policy of competency, these applications were to be filled out without the "assistance" of government officials. In a note signed "Bruce (Land Division)" written on the margin of a list of pending cases, one government official noted:

In several instances, there is nothing in the file to corroborate the applicant's claim. I refer to those who do not appear on any census roll. A considerable number of these applicants do not know the degree of blood of either one or both of their parents. Some of the inconsistencies pointed out hereinabove would indicate that some of the applicants who allege they know the degree of blood of their parents do not, in fact, know what such degree of blood actually is.[31]

Illiteracy and lack of education were a further barrier. One applicant was firmly rejected because his application gave "no information at all," even though a white attorney of his acquaintance wrote a letter of support

Fig. 2. The application form asked for detailed answers to questions about blood quantum, family, tribal ties, and acculturation. Page 1 of blank application for Registration as an Indian, February 26, 1938, box 1, E616, Applications and Other Records Relating to Registrations Under the Indian Reorganization Act of 1934, 1935–42, RG 75, NARA–Washington DC.

Application No. ....

Action taken ....
(N. B.—Applicant will not write in the above spaces)

Name of wife or husband ....

Application No. ....

APPLICATION FOR REGISTRATION AS AN INDIAN

(Separate applications must be made by husband and wife.
Adult children may also make separate applications)

Town ....

County ....

State ....

The SECRETARY OF THE INTERIOR,

Washington, D. C. Date ....

SIR:

I, hereby make application for the registration of myself (and ....
minor children) as an Indian (or Indians) of one-half or more degree of Indian blood, in accordance with the provisions
of the Act of Congress of June 18, 1934 (Indian Reorganization Act; 48 Stat. L. 984–988).

1. NAME { English ....

Indian ....

(If a married woman give maiden name) ....

(a) Date of birth .... Place of birth ....
(Month)   (Day)   (Year)

(b) Sex .... Marital status ....
(Single, married, divorced, widow, or widower)

(c) Degree of Indian blood claimed ....

(d) Name of tribe, band, pueblo, or group to which you belong or from which you claim descent ....

(e) If your parents or any of your ancestors were ever enrolled for land, annuities, or other benefits by the United
States or any State, give the following information:

Name of such enrollee(s):

(1)... Relation to you ....

(2)... Relation to you ....

(3)... Relation to you ....

(Add others, if known.)

(f) If degree of Indian blood was specified in such enrollment, state degree for each enrollee: (1) ....

(2) .... (3) ....

(g) If land was allotted to any of these enrollees, give allotment numbers: (1) .... (2) ....

(3) ....

(h) If enrollment was for other purposes than land allotment, give roll numbers or application numbers ....

6—9166

1

("simply as an act of kindness for which I expect no compensation") telling the Office of Indian Affairs that the applicant had "filled out [the application] to the best of his ability, but in consequence of lack of education, he is apprehensive that he may have failed to comprehend the import of some or perhaps many of the questions, and that consequently he may have failed to convey the information desired."[32]

Another applicant did not give a numerical estimate of her blood quantum, but wrote that she was part Cherokee, part Choctaw and part Creek. She had no enrolled relatives and was unable to give the details of her relatives demanded by the application, although she did her best to give as much information as possible, resorting in many sections to writing simply, "I do not no [sic]." She spoke no tribal languages and had never applied for enrollment herself, but had lived on a reservation in Oklahoma and had been recognized there as an Indian person. She said she had not abandoned tribal life or adopted a white lifestyle. Her application was rejected because of its "inadequate information. In place of her father's name, she has given the name of her husband. The father was evidently part Irish and part Creek, and spoke no Indian language. The mother is said to be part Choctaw and part Cherokee and evidently spoke no Indian language."[33] Did this woman have ties to a nation that would be recognized today? We cannot know. Without a paper trail, she had little chance of success under the 1934 act.

Even when people had information such as roll numbers, this did not always guarantee success. One man enclosed a letter from a man who he said was his father, which stated his Cherokee roll number and continued "if there is anything else you want to no [sic] tell me just exactly what you want to no [sic] and I'll try to find out just what you want to no [sic]. I'm enrolled as full blood. Let me hear from you soon. Your dad." The Office of Indian Affairs rejected the application, informing the applicant that they could not find any record on the Cherokee rolls of the children of his alleged father, adding, "The letter from [your alleged father] . . . does not establish beyond reasonable doubt the matter of your relationship to him . . . Any statement . . . on this matter ought to be in the form of an affidavit sworn to before a notary and should be corroborated by competent witnesses." The alleged father does, in fact, appear on the Cherokee enrollment cards under the roll number that he gave in his letter, designated as a "full-blood." Was he writing a letter for the applicant claiming to be his father in order to help him claim a spurious Indian status? Or were they in fact related? Records do not show, but what is more certain is that the Indian Office greeted incomplete applications with little sympathy.[34]

Families that had intermarried with the mainstream population were also viewed with suspicion. Thus, although the Office of Indian Affairs had "no objection to the approval" of one applicant, they hesitated to register his children: "I do not know whether [the applicant's] present wife is mother of the children or not. She appears to be a white woman. I have met one of his sons who also has a white wife. These facts raise some question in my mind as to the wisdom of registering this type of Indian as Indian," wrote the superintendent of Rocky Boy's Agency in Montana.[35] Another revealing letter from Fred H. Daiker, the assistant to the commissioner of Indian Affairs, to the superintendent of the Hoopa Valley Agency in California warned against approving "individuals intermarried with white people." If the California Indians had formally adopted such people, he said, "you should withhold land assignments from them." He explained that:

> The land purchase funds authorized by the Indian Reorganization Act are intended primarily to benefit Indians, as defined in the Act. A person, one half or more Indian, married to a white man or woman might receive individual benefits, such as educational loans or Civil Service preference, but since funds are limited, I do not see how we could justify the granting of a land assignment when a white person is involved. Too many Indians have yet to be provided for.[36]

At the Turtle Mountain Agency in North Dakota, Supervisor of Education Henry Roe Cloud transmitted a list of 105 Chippewa-Cree people for enrollment under the 1934 act. He stated he was following gendered reservation policy by rejecting women who had married white men, even if they had proved they possessed "½ degree Indian blood," while accepting Indian men who had married white women. Tribal policy was that an enrolled husband imparted his status to his wife and children—but only after some administrative consternation it was decided that women who had married white men would be able to apply to register as "Indian" under the 1934 act. Seemingly, however, they lost their membership in the Turtle Mountain nation.[37]

Age was an important factor in the Office of Indian Affairs' responses. The office advised a person applying on behalf of an acquaintance not to bother continuing with the application process because "the person in question, who you state is 84 years old, could not take practical advantage of" the benefits provided by the 1934 act, "since these benefits are limited to education loans, employment preference in the Indian Service, land purchase for subsistence use, and credit for productive purposes."[38] Another letter on behalf of a brother and sister who claimed "their father was three-fourths Chickasaw and their mother a full blood Choctaw" also received a reply asserting that it was pointless for elderly people to claim Indian status.[39] Thus, even when applicants seemed to have a legitimate claim to one-half Indian blood, the Indian Office did not hesitate to reject their applications. The uncertain and difficult process by which "scattered" Native Americans were required to prove their Indianness ensured that the act was administered inconsistently.

Physical Anthropometry and Unrecognized Nations

As conclusive documentary evidence of a person's ancestry was so difficult to obtain, the Office of Indian Affairs had before long to address the slippery issue of otherwise determining whether an unenrolled Indian was of one-half Indian blood. Although by the 1930s anthropometry or physical anthropology had been relegated to the margins of the anthropological profession, inside the Office of Indian Affairs an Anthropological Unit was newly established to consider the possibility of resorting to anthropometric measurements. The office was not prepared to embrace physical anthropology fully as a "magic formula," but a committee meeting in July 1936 to consider the procedure of enrolling Indians of one-half or more degree noted that "when we consider what little else we have to go by we ought at least to give that data a chance to prove itself." The science could not, the committee stressed, relieve the office of the "responsibility of judging cases for itself, but at least it will supply some of the factors on which to base judgment."[40] Further discussions over subsequent months led officials to agree upon a mixture of tribal connection, Indian culture, and anthropometric criteria. A memorandum dated September 22, 1936, outlined the policy the Office of Indian Affairs had adopted in determining an applicant's degree of Indian blood. "Determination of the degree of Indian blood is entirely dependent on circumstantial evidence; there is no known sure or scientific proof," the memo began. "Nor has any legal standard of universal applicability been set up by statute for the determination of who is, and who is not, an Indian." In these circumstances, the office prescribed the following procedure. In cases that were "marked by some measure of reasonable doubt," five possible forms of evidence were to be used in making a decision. They were, first, documentary evidence on tribal rolls; second, "testimony of the applicant, supported by family records, official records other than tribal rolls showing blood degree, and similar documents"; third, "affidavits from persons who know the applicant"; fourth, "findings of a qualified physical anthropologist based on examination of the applicant"; and finally, "testimony of the applicant and supporting witnesses, tending to show that the applicant has retained a considerable measure of Indian culture and habits of living."[41]

In the absence of conclusive documentary or scientific evidence, the commissioner of Indian Affairs was given "administrative discretion" to give greater "comparative weight" to cultural factors than biological factors—a policy in keeping with the New Deal's reverence for traditional Indian culture. "Where genealogical or biological data still leave doubt as to the applicant's claim," the memo stated, "the Commissioner may consider whether or not the attitude of the applicant and his manner of living tend to show the inheritance of Indian characteristics." Thus, Native Americans could in effect be "punished" for acculturating. The policy did allow for exceptions in the case of people of mixed ancestry who could demonstrate a connection to and practice of Indian culture. But the biases of the officials made the recognition of such cases unlikely. If a person of mixed descent had outwardly done what he or she had been encouraged to do by the government in the last four decades—assimilate—then this would hardly have resulted in the continuation of a traditional lifestyle to an extent that would satisfy the New Dealers.

The 1934 act acknowledged that there were many Native Americans who were members of nations who had not received federal government recognition. The legislation distinguished between "recognized" and "unrecognized" Indian nations, but provided no criteria to help officials to identify which was which.[42] The Office of Indian Affairs therefore had carte blanche to make these decisions. It did so, unsurprisingly, on the basis of New Deal ideas of the characteristics possessed by "traditional" Indian groups, influenced by Collier's long admiration for the Pueblo peoples of New Mexico. Paul Spruhan has shown that the Office of Indian Affairs classified some nations as ineligible because they were not Indian enough, and their members were only eligible to register as Indians if they were of more than one-half Indian blood. These included the Mississippi Choctaws, the St. Croix Chippewas, the Nahmas and Beavers of Michigan, and the Lumbees of North Carolina.[43] Collier eliminated all Eastern Indian nations from consideration altogether, calling them "folk groups."[44]

The office did allocate some time and funds to certain groups who for one reason or another they regarded as deserving special attention from anthropologists (and in one case, an individual).[45] The work of Carl C. Seltzer of the Peabody Museum at Harvard provides the most striking example of the use of anthropology in teasing out the complexities of Indian status as defined by the 1934 act. Seltzer was a marginal figure in the world of anthropology, best known for his questionable research into the health benefits of cigarette smoking. During 1937 Seltzer examined more than two hundred individuals in Robeson County, North Carolina, at the request of Collier. These peoples, now known as the Lumbee Indians (although some call themselves Tuscarora) whose ancestors were mainly Cheraw and Siouan-speaking peoples, had been classified as "Free Persons of Color" between 1835 and 1865, had no legal designation between 1865 and 1885, but were legally recognized as Indians by the state of North Carolina in 1885 and by the federal government in 1956. Nevertheless, they are not yet a federally recognized nation.[46] According to Malinda Maynor Lowery, in 1936 the Lumbee Indians, who of course had their own notion of identity grounded in kinship and connection to their homeland, had already spent three years lobbying to get a bill passed that recognized the Indians of Robeson County as "Siouan Indians of Robeson County" rather than as "Cherokee Indians of Robeson County," the name approved by the state of North Carolina in 1911. Collier suggested to them that racial science might help their cause, and they agreed to submit to anthropological testing.[47]

Seltzer physically examined, photographed, and measured Lumbees who applied for registration under the 1934 act, and took samples of their blood. Seltzer's "racial diagnoses" were made "*solely* on the manifestations of physical characteristics of known racial significance as interpreted by the science of physical and racial anthropology." He used a scale of measurement based on Aleš Hrdlička's 1920 work on anthropometry. In other words, the applicants' own statements about their ethnicity were ignored, and "no distinctions and designations were made as to the tribal affiliations of the subjects."[48] Because he only factored anthropometric information into his decisions, Seltzer gave different racial designations to the members of the same family, in some cases assigning different statuses to full brothers and sisters. Rather than causing him, or the Office of Indian Affairs, to doubt his methods, these inconsistencies were explained by Seltzer as due to marital infidelity, incest, and hidden illegitimacy.

Seltzer claimed that illegitimacy was "of special significance" among the "so-called 'Indians' of Robeson County" because of its "marked prevalence all through the community."[49] Seltzer often had no evidence of illegitimacy apart from his own anthropometric findings, but he did not hesitate to give his opinion that there were cases of illegitimacy in some families "which have not been disclosed either through the medium of the blood groupings or of direct testimony."[50] On this basis, Seltzer felt confident enough to label individuals illegitimate on his family charts.

Seltzer's logic might have been stunningly off, but his methods were certainly thorough. He used an array of instruments, including an "anthropometer, spreading calliper, sliding calliper, and steel tape." For skin color, the Von Luschan color scale was utilized (Von Luschan was a pioneer of pre-Nazi racial "science" in Europe). Photographs were taken by means of a "Leica camera . . . with f1:4–9cm lens."[51] For example, a fifty-two-year-old farmer had his skin color examined on various parts of his body, his face and body intimately and accurately measured, and his hair, eyes, nostrils, eyebrows, ears, and ear lobes rated on a detailed chart.

The farmer claimed to be more than "½ Indian blood," but Seltzer concluded that he was "almost a border line case" of "about equal parts of White and Indian plus a recognizable strain of Negroid," and rejected his application. He listed his "non-Indian features" as "the presence of vascularity of the skin as evidenced by the scratch test, the possession of the low wave variety of hair form with distinct curliness in the front of the head . . . . the moderate to pronounced nasion depression, the deep set of the eyes. . . . the well-marked prominence of the chin, ears which are reminiscent of the usual Negroidal form, [and] Negroidal limb proportions."[52] It is worth remembering that the white population of southern states such as North Carolina might well have regarded this man as colored, on the basis of a common assumption that intermarriage with African Americans outweighed a person's Indian ancestry (I discuss this further in chapter 5). Seltzer's final report included "genealogical tables with racial diagnoses." Out of 221 people on the list, 148 or 66.96 percent were listed as either "less than ½ Indian" or "less, near border line"; 30 or 13.57 percent had their applications as "more than ½ Indian" accepted; and 17 or 7.69 percent were judged "border Line case."[53] Seltzer's assumption that people were not only seeking undeserved recognition as Indians but also displaying a lack of "family values" echoed attitudes toward Native Americans of mixed descent that were displayed throughout the assimilation period. The Collier administration had little sympathy for those not seen as keepers and purveyors of traditional Indian culture. As Lowery has shown, the blood-based definition of Indian status in the 1934 act was both a blessing and a curse for the Indians of Robeson County.[54]

Indigenous Negotiation with the 1934 Act

The New Deal prompted new responses from both "scattered" Indians and tribal members. Tribal nations had to confront the issue of blood

UNITED STATES INDIAN SURVEY

Place **Pembroke, N. C.** Date **June 4, 1936** Observer **C. C. Seltzer** Recorder **M. Mayne**

No. **6** Ser. **M** Occupation **Farmer** Race _____

Education **No read , no write** Birthplace **Robeson County** Name _____

Residence **Harpers Ferry** Father's Birthplace **Robeson County** Mother's _____

Brothers **8** Sisters **1** Sons **3** Daughters **9**

Religion _____ Reel **1** Frames **13-14** Martial State, sing., mar., div., wid. _____

Age	**52**	5	Head Circum.	**54.5**	17	
Weight	**160**	6 / 7	Head Length	**187** 18	19	Sh-Hip. 12/12 **67** 32
Stature	**168.2**	8 / 9	Head Breadth	**147** 20	21	Thoracic 15/14 **82** 33
Tragion	**154.4**		Head Height	**138**	22	Rel. Sit. Ht. 16/8, 9 **51** 34
Acromion	**136.7**		Minimum Frontal	**108**	23	Ceph. 20, 21/18, 19 **79** 35
Radiale	**105.7**		Bizygomatic	**150**	24	Length-Ht. 22/18, 19 **74** 36
Stylion	**80.0**		Bigonial	**110**	25	Breadth-Ht. 22/20, 21 **94** 37
Dactylion	**61.3**		Total Face Ht.	**118**	26	Fronto-Par. 23/20, 21 **73** 38
Span	**178.9**	10 / 11	Upper Face Ht.	**71**	27	Ceph-Fac. 24/20, 21 **102** 39
Biacromial	**37.3**	12	Nose Ht.	**53**	28	Zygo-Fr. 23/24 **72** 40
Bi-iliac	**25.0**	13	Nose Br.	**39**	29	Fronto-Gon. 26/23 **102** 41
Chest Breadth	**25.0**	14	Nose Salient	**28**		Zygo-Gon. 25/24 **73** 42
Chest Depth	**20.5**	15	Jaw L.	**102**		Facial 26/24 **79** 43
Leg	**34.3**		Bi-oc	**89**		Upper Facial 27/24 **47** 44
Sitting Ht.	**86.3**	16	Later-oc	**33**		Nasal 29/28 **74** 45 / 46
Trunk	**54.1**		Rel. Sh. Ht.			47
			Rel. Span 10, 11/8, 9	**106**	30	**Blood group type A**
			Rel. Sh. Br. 12/8, 9	**22**	31	

Fig. 3. Anthropometric Chart, box 13, E616, Applications and Other Records Relating to Registrations Under the Indian Reorganization Act of 1934, 1935–42, RG 75, NARA–Washington DC.

because of the (limited) opportunity the New Deal gave them to adopt constitutions and become self-governing entities. Meanwhile, Indians of mixed descent who did not have tribal membership were offered a chance to be officially designated as "Indian" if their blood quantum and cultural ties were seen to be adequate. In their responses, applicants also utilized the language of blood, which had become part of their own or their nations' understanding of their status (although probably not in an exactly equivalent sense), or at least of their explanations of it to the U.S. government.

The model constitution provided by the U.S. government to Indian nations contained a section that defined members as "all persons of Indian blood whose names appear on the official census rolls of the tribe as of April 1, 1935" and all children born to tribal members who were residents of the reservation at the time of their birth.[55] The Indian Office had no power to insist that Indians adopt a definition of membership that contained a blood-based requirement. Despite the assumption shared by many scholars that Native American nations were forced to adopt constitutions that defined membership by reference to blood, recent research has shown that the majority of nations did not, in fact, take up such definitions for some years after the Indian Reorganization Act was passed. As the twentieth century progressed, however, many nations began to use the language of blood to define themselves and their communities. Kirsty Gover has shown that 44 percent of nations that ratified constitutions before 1950 included blood-based requirements and that this number has grown to 70 percent at the present day.[56]

The perception of a division between the authentic Indian of "full-blood" and the inauthentic, undeserving "mixed-blood" continued to be prevalent and influential in New Deal thinking and was used, as it had been in the past, to explain and diminish Indian resistance. *The New Day for the Indians*, a pamphlet published in 1938 by "a few individuals interested in getting the facts before the public" about the workings of the New Deal, is evidence of this fact. The pamphlet was edited by ex-Office of Indian Affairs employees and "checked" by the office. It endorsed the "principle" of the 1934 act without "necessarily approv[ing] all that has been done by the Office of Indian Affairs to carry it out." It attributed Indian opposition to the New Deal to the "deception and manipulation of Indians by interested whites, or to property and class conflicts among the Indians themselves," and went on to expatiate on the "feeling between full-blood Indians and half-bloods" and the "opposition of the full-bloods to domination by the more numerous half-bloods."[57]

The response to the New Deal from people who were not members of recognized nations showed that many did define themselves as Indian even though the U.S. government (and perhaps also tribal governments) did not. Many used the discourse of blood themselves to establish their status. Like the "Cherokee-conscious" woman with whom this chapter began, many "scattered" Native Americans of mixed descent saw the 1934 act, despite its limitations, as providing a means of doing so. "It appears to be the general understanding among the Indians that section 19 . . . gives them the right to be enrolled as Federal wards if they are of ½ or more Indian blood," wrote O. H. Lipps in his final report on the enrollment of the Chippewa-Cree of North Dakota.[58] Although the Indian New Deal recycled many of the assumptions concerning Indians of mixed descent that underpinned the policies of previous decades, a strong desire felt by unclassified Indians to be officially recognized persisted, despite the lack of actual benefits that came with such a designation. "Are we too late? Or will this new bill change things?" wrote one applicant to the commissioner of Indian Affairs in 1937.[59] Another wrote to her "dear friend" Eleanor Roosevelt to see if she could get her name on the "Indian Role."[60] Many mistakenly believed that the 1934 act would confer on them a share of tribal benefits. One woman wrote to the Office of Indian Affairs to find out "how much you will have to have of Indian blood to get the rights . . . to the 'Indian' claims and Territory." She received a lengthy reply, explaining the limitations of the act for Indians of mixed descent, notifying her that the rolls of the Choctaw Nation had long been closed, and concluding: "In the circumstances, it is not clear what you have in mind [when] you speak of your 'rights to Indian claims and territory.'"[61] The files of the Office of Indian Affairs are crammed with letters in which government officials downplayed any anticipation that recognition under the act would lead to some kind of financial gain: "granting that you do prove your one-half blood status, we do not wish to raise your hopes to anticipate immediate results and benefits to be gained from the Act."[62]

A number of applications demonstrate the irony of a situation in which the federal government, which had spent the last four decades attempting to assimilate Native Americans, now refused to identify people as Indians because of the perceived extent of their acculturation. One man, who applied to be recognized as a Kawich of full descent, answered the question "Have you abandoned tribal life and adopted the habits and customs of the white community" by writing "No, except as compelled to do so by economic necessity."[63] A woman whose application was rejected because an anthropometric examination had found her to have "about equal parts of White and Indian, and a small strain of Negro," told a Siouan investigating committee that she had never heard her grandparents use Indian language or practice tribal customs because "they lost all of that."[64] Another rejected applicant noted on her application that she had not been to any schools because she was "not allowed to attend because of being Indian blood."[65] The refusal of the government to recognize her Indian status had not sheltered her from prejudice.

Many applicants did not share the government's assumption that Indianness began and ended on the reservation. "I am one of those Cherokees who were never put on the official roles [sic] of the Cherokee nation," wrote one applicant, "and for these many years, I've lived the life of a landless Cherokee." She wrote to inquire how she should "go about to establish myself with my people, and thus enjoy my rights." "Although I have never identify [sic] myself with the reservation Cherokee, I have felt and do feel all along the way that as a Cherokee, I am entitled to my Indian rights."[66] The Office of Indian Affairs felt differently: her claim was rejected, as were countless others. As in the preceding decades of assimilation policy, confusion persisted as to what—blood, culture, documentation, appearance—made a person an Indian, notwithstanding the definition of Indianness in the 1934 act. The discourse of blood continued to be a powerful and pervasive determinant in the New Deal. A new policy direction for the Office of Indian Affairs had done little to shake its hold.

CHAPTER FIVE

Colored

The Indian Nations of Virginia and
the 1924 Racial Integrity Act

In Virginia in the 1920s, 1930s, and 1940s a printed document could be found attached to some birth or death certificates. "WARNING," the document was headed, "To be attached to the backs of birth or death certificates of those believed to be incorrectly recorded as to color or race." The document began with passages from "Howe in his History of Virginia, 1845, page 349–350"; "Encyclopaedia Britannica, Eleventh Edition, Volume 14"; an 1843 petition held in the Virginia State Library; and a more modern study, *Mongrel Virginians,* published in 1926 by two members of the Department of Genetics of the Carnegie Institution in Washington DC. It concluded: "In consideration of the above and other similar evidence relating to all . . . groups claiming to be 'Indians,' the Virginia Bureau of Vital Statistics accepts the belief that there are no descendants of Virginian Indians claiming or reputed to be Indians, who are unmixed with negro blood."[1] This chapter is mainly devoted to the application of the discourse of blood in the eastern United States, where Indian populations were small, nations were not all federally recognized, policies of allotment and enrollment were not pertinent, and where Indians were believed to have had African American ancestors, and, it was argued, should be officially treated as colored.

Far from the more prominent hubs of Indian assimilation policies— Washington DC, the shores of Lake Mohonk (where the "Friends of the

Indian" met), the Philadelphia offices of the Indian Rights Association, and the western frontier states with high Indian populations—in Virginia Indigenous people were viewed as so permeated with African American blood that they no longer deserved to be called Indian. In the Jim Crow South, the Black/white dichotomy was the salient racial issue, and the Virginian Indians were classified as colored by the government officials in charge of keeping track of racial status. In the first part of this chapter I explore a drastic application of the discourse of blood by a government body denying Indian status to a group of Native American communities. While the federally recognized Indian population was identified by fractions of blood quantum, the unrecognized Virginian Indians were, for a period, officially identified by the "one-drop rule." That this policy was inflicted on their entire community, not just a segment of it, shows how pervasively the discourse of blood had come to be used to undermine the authenticity and sovereignty of Native American people by the 1920s and 1930s. This case study is also important because in this instance the refusal by the Indigenous nations of Virginia to submit to the discourse of blood was monumental and, ultimately, effective.

In the second part of the chapter I discuss the Eastern Cherokees, who drew on the discourse of blood in a very different way to cement their claim for official recognition as Indians. The Eastern Cherokees had no reported history of intermixing with African Americans, and thus escaped the intense racism that drove the treatment of the Virginian nations. Because they were perceived as having only white blood in addition to Indian ancestry, they were able to invoke notions of purity and authenticity to stabilize their legal status. The Virginian nations, on the other hand, were perceived as inauthentic, not so much because racial mixing was part of their history, but because some of that mixing was reportedly with African Americans. This perception led Indigenous peoples in Virginia during the early twentieth century to experience intense discrimination, which impacted their sovereignty.[2] Blood viewed as "Black" by public officials and the white community had uniquely deleterious consequences for Indians during the assimilation period.

Black Blood and Indian Blood

The diverse Native American nations whose lands lie in the southeast of the United States had a long history of interaction with African Americans, not just as sexual partners but also as slaves and employers, neighbors, friends, and enemies.[3] "The names of African-descended people and the fragmented stories of their lives haunt the records of Cherokees, Creeks, Choctaws, Chickasaws, Seminoles, and other south-eastern Indians," write Claudio Saunt, Barbara Krauthamer, Tiya Miles, Celia E. Naylor, and Circe Sturm, scholars who have undertaken the important work of chronicling this "multifaceted and painful past."[4]

The discourse of blood operated very differently when applied to African Americans and Native Americans, as Jack D. Forbes and other scholars have pointed out.[5] Unlike Indian blood, Black blood was governed by the rule of hypodescent, or the "one-drop rule." While any hint of African American ancestry was enough to classify someone as Black, the same cannot be said for Indian status, as we have seen. "One has not been able to say, 'I'm one-eighth African American' without giving up socially, if not legally, the seven-eighths part of one's self that is not," writes David Hollinger. "You can be one-eighth Cherokee and still be seven-eighths something else, but if you are one-eighth Black you are not likely to be counted as white at all."[6] As Sturm has formulated it:

Black/White	Black
Black/Indian	Black
Black/Indian/White	Black
Indian/White	Indian.[7]

Or, as Jack Forbes put it, "White North Americans are always finding 'Blacks' (even if they look rather un-African) and they are always losing 'Indians,' or so it would seem."[8]

In the racial hierarchy that defined U.S. society at this time, African American blood was manifestly less desirable than Native American blood. Romantic ideas of the "noble savage" contrasted with the intense racism directed at "savage" African Americans. Interracial mixing with African Americans was widely condemned. Brian Dippie argues that few issues "aroused more emotion" than sexual relationships between whites and African Americans.⁹ Phenomena such as lynching, passing as white, and obsessing over the perceived threat posed by Black men to white women demonstrated how unthinkable relationships with African American people were for many white Americans. In a number of states and colonies the horror of miscegenation was expressed by a series of antimiscegenation laws, aimed at keeping the white and Black populations separate and pure.¹⁰ Patrick Wolfe has shown that the differences in settler perceptions of Native American and African American blood stemmed from each group's imagined role in the American nation. The "one-drop rule" worked to create as many African Americans as possible by denoting people with any African American ancestry at all as Black (as Wolfe says, the more slaves the better). On the other hand Indian blood was regulated in a way that created fewer and fewer Indians: Indian status was imperiled by any hint of non-Indian ancestry (the fewer Indigenous people, the greater the prospect of taking their land).¹¹

For Native Americans with African American ancestry, these racial discourses put even greater obstacles in the way of their claim to Indian status. Because Blackness so comprehensively outweighed Indianness— "one drop" was all it took—a person with African American ancestry was correspondingly more likely to be deprived of tribal benefits, land, and recognition during the assimilation period than a person of mixed white/Indian ancestry. Allegations of Black ancestry were thus a powerful way of de-authenticating Indians. "Recently when I was speaking in a public forum about Black and American Indian relations in colonial and early America," writes Tiya Miles,

> a respected Indian elder from a Great Plains tribe impressed on me her strong desire that I cease speaking about this topic. Her fear, as she expressed it, was that documenting the intermarriage of black and Indian people would give the U.S. government just one more reason to declare Native people inauthentic and soluble and then to seize their remaining lands and any vestiges of political autonomy.¹²

Notwithstanding the extreme efforts made by the colony and state to regulate this phenomenon from the very earliest period, the long history of interracial mixing in Virginia made it easy to propagate the idea that all Virginian Indians had Black ancestry and were therefore Black.[13] At no time is this more evident than between 1924 and 1946, the period when Walter A. Plecker was in charge of the Bureau of Vital Statistics. Southern states then operated under a "Jim Crow" racial system that strictly segregated public facilities. The Supreme Court had upheld these laws as constitutional in 1896, thereby cementing the economic, educational, and social oppression of African Americans. Because the Virginian Indian nations were not federally recognized, state authorities were able to apply to them their own ideas about blood, race, and culture in ways very different from those pursued in other parts of the United States. Nevertheless, the Virginian 1924 Racial Integrity Act, as Arica Coleman has pointed out, should be viewed as part of a nationwide narrative of the use of blood as a means of denying official Indian status.[14] Plecker was unique in his passion to exercise the power that his office gave him, but he was not unique in utilizing the discourse of blood. It enabled him to view the Virginian nations as so mixed as not to be Native American at all, rather than as a separate group with their own characteristics. This attitude reflected an assumption held by many white Virginians that segregation had been achieved and could be maintained by the stringent application of the one-drop rule, buttressed by Jim Crow laws and antimiscegenation legislation. The one-drop rule made Blackness a vessel in which to deposit groups of people whose existence might otherwise call the purity of the white population into question.

Racial Integrity in Virginia

Racial integrity became a cause espoused in Virginia as a result of the actions of a small group of elite, white extremists. Virginia was a southern state with a reputation for preserving the racial status quo by the practice of what J. Douglas Smith has characterized as "a particularly genteel brand of paternalism."[15] However, the well-mannered segregation of public places and public transport was not enough for some white Virginians. In September 1922 they established the first branch of the "Anglo-Saxon Club of America."[16] Influenced by eugenic and racist tenets, the club provided a forum for the dissemination of ideas promoting the need for drastic measures to prevent Black Virginians from eventually outnumbering white Virginians. The club members successfully lobbied to have a bill introduced into the Virginia General Assembly that required the mandatory registration of all Virginians with the Bureau of Vital Statistics. This was changed to voluntary registration when several senators found the requirement to be personally insulting. The proposed legislation (titled the Racial Integrity Act) mandated a one-year prison term for "wilfully or knowingly [making] a registration certificate false as to color or race." It prohibited whites from marrying anyone save another white and required the presentation of racial certification to local registrars before a marriage license could be issued. It defined a white person as one "who has no trace whatsoever of any blood other than Caucasian," thus leaving Blackness to be defined according to the infamous one-drop rule. However, this definition of whiteness was subject to one qualification that unexpectedly impacted on the lives of the Virginian Indians. In recognition of the many elite Virginian families who claimed descent from the "Indian princess" Pocahontas and the white settler John Rolfe, the bill included the so-called Pocahontas Exception, which stated that persons "who have less than one sixty-fourth of the blood of an American Indian and have no other non-Caucasic blood shall be deemed as white persons."[17] The bill was passed in 1924.

The Racial Integrity Act thus combined two ideas concerning blood and the place of mixed-descent Indians in the community in aid of the state's quest to maintain racial integrity. First, a very small amount of Indianness was acceptable, and even desirable. Descent from an Indian "princess," a "noble savage," or other such ancestor safely in the distant past, was surprisingly of no concern in this racially obsessed state.[18] However, more recent or contemporary Indian/white mixing could not be accepted in a Jim Crow society. People with even a small amount of Native American ancestry were sufficiently impure enough to require classification as colored. Second, any drop at all of Black blood also rendered the possessor colored. Thus society divided into two groups— white or colored. The category of Indian no longer existed.

According to historian J. Douglas Smith, Virginia's Black community and its press remained "relatively quiet" while the Racial Integrity Act was debated in the legislature and the press. As the act was aimed at Virginians of mixed descent who were "no longer clearly identifiable as Black," it seemed to pose few additional problems for the already oppressed and segregated population of Virginian African Americans.[19] But there were several Native American communities who decidedly did not remain quiet. The Rappahannocks, Chickahominys, Pamunkeys, Mattaponis, and Monacans, whose lands mostly lay in the Tidewater region of the state, moved swiftly to maintain their status under the law. They found themselves sited uncomfortably on the boundary between Black and white, or teetering toward being defined as Black, with all the legal and social disadvantages that such a definition entailed.

From the perspective of Plecker, head of the Bureau of Vital Statistics, the Indigenous peoples of the Tidewater region were a troublesome reminder of just how far Virginia had strayed from maintaining a Black and white dichotomy. His solution to the problem was to declare that the Virginian nations were, in fact, Black. There had been a history of intermarriage between Indigenous groups and freed slaves in the seventeenth, eighteenth, and early nineteenth centuries, and armed with this knowledge and some incomplete census records, Plecker did all he could to establish that there was no Native American person in Virginia who was "untainted" by African American blood. If he were to fail in this endeavor, the horrifying opportunity would arise for individuals with only a small amount of Indian ancestry to claim to be white under the Pocahontas exception. Plecker referred to this as the "Indian route" to whiteness.[20] As he put it to Matthew K. Sniffen, the executive secretary of the Indian Rights Association, who had quickly seized on this issue, the Pocahontas exception "was inserted to provide for the white descendants of Pocahontas, and not for our present race of native mixed Indians."[21]

In 1924 Plecker distributed 60,000 copies of a pamphlet entitled *Eugenics in Relation to the New Family and the Law on Racial Integrity*, which called attention to communities of "negro-Indian-white intermixture" who had "practiced close inbreeding for generations until many undesirable traits have become accentuated."[22] He also advocated racial integrity in speeches and newspaper articles, but most importantly he used his position as registrar of the Bureau of Vital Statistics to embark on the task of engineering the racial makeup of the state's population. Plecker wrote to clerks of the county courts with jurisdiction over areas where he suspected that "families of mixed blood" resided, and warned them "to use every precaution not to issue marriage license[s] for one of these people to intermarry with a person of known pure white blood."[23] He also instructed doctors, local registrars, and midwives that they should "use care not to report births of children of 'Mixed' . . . parents as white." Acknowledging that it was not always easy to identify such children, he told them that if they were uncertain they should "use an interrogation mark (?) and write us privately."[24]

While Plecker's letters to (mostly male) medical doctors and white officials were usually polite, (mostly female) midwives were more often the targets of veiled and unveiled threats. "It is a very serious offense for a family to make an incorrect statement," he wrote in July 1924 to a midwife who had registered a child born in June 1924 as white. Nor was the threat of legal sanctions Plecker's only weapon. "Are you or your husband related to the Sorrels of Alto, Amherst County?" he asked her, referring to a family that he had already accused of having African American ancestry, hinting that her own racial status might be suspect. A month later Plecker wrote the woman about another birth certificate that she had signed. "We want to again warn you of the trouble you are liable to get yourself into if you do not give the correct color," he wrote. "It is my duty to see that this law is obeyed and I expect to do it. I am waiting for someone who violates this law to have them in court. If you want to be the first one, we will give you a chance."[25] Similarly, Plecker warned another woman that making false statements about race was subject to a penalty of one year in the penitentiary. "After the war it is possible that some of these cases will come into court. We might try this one," he threatened. "It would make a good one, if you continue to try to be what you are not."[26]

Members of families whom Plecker suspected to be of mixed African and Indian ancestry were the subject of blatant intimidation and disrespect. "You will have to . . . see that this child is not allowed to mix with white children," wrote Plecker to a woman whose daughter's birth certificate had been "corrected" by the City Health Department at

Lynchburg. "It cannot go to white schools and can never marry a white person in Virginia. It is an awful thing."[27] One man, who had claimed to be white and refused to give the bureau the information it had asked for to prove his claim, received a letter from Plecker that combined the threat of a jail sentence with personal insults: "Just as I expected, you declined to give the information but I did not expect you to come down quite as hard upon your mother as you did when you say that you do not know who your father was."[28]

Plecker exploited the basic function of the Bureau of Vital Statistics—the issuance of birth, death, and marriage certificates—to promote his cause, often pushing the boundaries of what was legally permitted. Thus he attached the printed warning described at the beginning of this chapter to the back of birth or death certificates. On some certificates he added specific disclaimers which stated that "the Bureau of Vital Statistics does not accept the racial classification 'Indian' on this certificate as correct," and gave detailed evidence for his belief that the holder was "under the law of Virginia . . . classified as a colored person."[29] When processing certificates, certain surnames "always arouse[d] suspicion" in Plecker's office.[30] Plecker sometimes withheld such certificates "for future reference."[31]

For Plecker, the solution to Virginia's racial problem was mainly one of recategorization. "If you choose," wrote Plecker to one man, after rejecting his birth certificate because his parents were described as "red," "you may . . . make out another certificate with the color of both parents given as colored, mulatto, or Negro. We will not accept red, Indian, or white."[32] In the same vein, Plecker wrote to one of his clerks to prevent him from using the term "mixed Indian" on birth certificates. "The word 'Mixed' without the 'Indian' would be better, but the term 'Colored' is preferred. We shall appreciate it if you will cooperate with us in our efforts to put down this 'Indian' falsehood, which has been corrupting our records until recent years."[33] However, if a family was particularly insistent, Plecker was prepared to make occasional concessions. Thus he told a midwife: "If you can secure certification more readily by using the term 'mixed' rather than 'colored' and 'mulatto,' we will accept it with the understanding that by that term you mean 'colored.' I expect you are right about it and probably it is as well not to be too insistent. That is far better than 'Indian' and infinitely better than 'white.'"[34] The perception that Indians of mixed descent were inauthentic and undeserving of Indian status thus played a powerful role not just in the contexts of enrollment, land allotment, and competency examined in earlier chapters but also in the unique racial context of the American South.

The Virginian Nations versus Plecker

The Rappahannock, Chickahominy, Pamunkey, Mattaponi, and Monacan peoples mounted a courageous and unrelenting campaign, collectively and individually, against Plecker's efforts. Whether this was because they were determined to maintain their Indian status or because they did not want to suffer the same discrimination as African Americans (which in practical terms would mean that their children would have to attend Black schools) or a combination of both, the Virginian Indians refused and resisted Plecker's efforts to reclassify them.[35] Mothers sent back certificates that did not categorize their children as white.[36] Families returned certificates with requests to change the racial classification from colored to Indian.[37] One man wrote to Plecker to tell him that "we have decided to lose the last drop of blood we have in us before we will be classed as colored."[38] Another gave Plecker five days to change his family "from colored to white" before he resorted to the "law" to stop his children from being kept out of white schools. Plecker sent a scathing reply, telling the man that his children had been excluded by the white schools because "they had you and your family there to see for themselves what you looked like," as well as accusing his wife of infidelity: "Does she say that the father was a white man and not her husband? What a mess—trying to be white!!"[39] These were not isolated objectors. Plecker reported in 1930 that the "Amherst-Rockbridge . . . people are besieging our office from a number of counties and cities demanding registration as white and are trying to force their children into white schools."[40]

Resistance was so strong that some white Virginians feared they would be subject to violence. Some registrars, according to Plecker, found themselves in physical danger. "Our Amherst County colony is up in arms and are on the verge of a race riot, threatening the life of one of our local registrars for giving out information concerning them," Plecker wrote in 1924.[41] In 1925 a Richmond woman wrote to Plecker and Governor Trinkle warning them that they might be assassinated if they persisted in enforcing the Racial Integrity Act.[42] Some of the witnesses for the state in a legal case relating to the refusal of a marriage license were "afraid [the plaintiffs] will burn [their] barn and do [them] other injury" and had to be personally convinced by Plecker to appear.[43]

As well as offering physical resistance, people attempted to subvert the system in a variety of ways. Plecker reported in 1930 that it had "become quite the custom for these people to leave their county, or even State, to marry. They are going to one county or city and securing a license, then going to another to have the ceremony performed."[44] Helen Rountree describes how the "only public record that Indian people could control was their marriage licenses: from 1924 until Plecker retired in 1946, few citizen Indian people got married in their home counties. They went elsewhere and married 'Indians.'"[45] Some tried using different surnames.[46] Printed identification cards were used by the Chickahominy people to "properly identify true members of the Tribe to prevent embarrassment by separation or confusion with Negroes when they used the train," as James R. Coates put it.[47]

Some objectors explored the possibilities of legal challenge. One family hired a lawyer to deal with the Bureau of Vital Statistics.[48] Another employed lawyers to sue the county superintendent of schools after their four children were sent home from school "on the ground that they were Negroes."[49] When Plecker and his supporters tried to get an amendment of the 1924 act through the legislature in 1925 (discussed below), he bemoaned the involvement of seven lawyers employed by the communities he was targeting.[50] Indigenous Virginians also maintained a presence at the Virginia legislature when it was in session. In patronizing terms, the press reported their presence: "it would move the heart of any Virginian to see that little group of Indians in the gallery, an old chief, a few braves, some squaws and pretty children, who, not quite understanding what it is all about, try so hard to follow the discussions, and who, losing their traditional stoicism, at times fairly radiate happiness when some legislator says a kind word in their behalf."[51] But they understood all too well. Almost as soon as the 1924 act was passed, two women challenged it when their applications for marriage licenses to marry white men were refused, Dorothy Johns (unsuccessfully) and Atha Sorrells (who was successful).[52]

The End of Racial Integrity

Plecker's campaign culminated in 1925, when he introduced to the House an amendment designed to classify all American Indians in Virginia as colored. The Virginian Indians did all they could to fight it, enlisting the help of the Indian Rights Association, talking to the press, and obtaining letters from respected anthropologists testifying to their Indianness. When E. P. Bradby, the Chief of the Chickahominy Indians–Eastern Division Inc., wrote to thank the Indian Rights Association for its support he showed his awareness of what the law would mean for the Virginian Indians: "God only knows what Dr. Plecker will try to put through this next Legislature, and if he succeeds, then there will be no more Indians in Virginia as far as the state is concerned, but we will be Indians as long as we live regardless of Laws. No law can change our blood."[53]

Fortunately, Plecker and his supporters were unable to get their new amendment passed. This failure indicates a gradual waning in support for such radical measures, a growth in opposition to the treatment of Indians under the existing law, and an increasing hesitation, even among those who supported the ideal of racial integrity, to go to such lengths to enforce it. Thus this case study shows that there were limits to how far the classification of Indians according to blood could be pushed. Plecker's extreme efforts to use blood as a recategorization tool soon aroused the opposition of other Virginians who had sympathy for the Virginian nations and were not ready to see the status of Indian reclassified as Black.

James R. Coates, for example, was a white Virginian who worked alongside Virginian nations from the 1940s onward. Coates's papers deposited in the Library of Virginia contain numerous petitions and sworn statements testifying to the Indian ancestry of individuals and groups. Thus one statement signed by Norman Cassell, an attorney and notary public, recorded that the one particular family "have been considered Indians, and so treated by their neighbors, and have associated only with white people, and the sons have married white women." The head of the family, it went on, was always "honest, sober, thrifty, industrious, well behaved, and in all respects a law abiding citizen."[54] A number of preachers, as well as a vice president of a replacement parts company and a "Dealer in General Merchandise" wrote other letters of support.[55] One local registrar refused to query birth certificates that gave the race of Virginian Indians as white because, "being in merchandise and other public business . . . the only thing I could see to do without being very injurious to my business, was to let the birth registers go on as handed in to me by the midwives as white."[56]

Nevertheless Plecker received a fair amount of support from white Virginians. Some of it was overt, from those who joined in his campaign, and some of it implicit—for example, from the states' main newspapers, which gave him sympathetic coverage, and the state government, which let him use his position to push his racial agenda. Other members of the white community aided Plecker with anonymous tips, letters, or even annotated wedding announcements—communications that Plecker immediately acted upon.[57] Schools also contacted Plecker to give information about the racial background of students.[58] One mother appears to have written to Plecker to ascertain the ancestry of a potential son-in-law.[59] An intending bride, who had written to the Bureau of Vital Statistics to inquire about the status of her fiancé, was told: "I am surprised that one of [your] respectable . . . family . . . should ask us about the racial status of [someone] with a view to obtaining a marriage licence." After describing the potential bridegroom's family as "Indian and colored," Plecker wrote: "I trust that will be clear enough and that you will immediately break off entirely with this young mulatto man."[60] A woman from Maine who had been married just over a year was asked to pass on information about her husband as follows: "What occupation is [he] following and how did he represent himself? They usually call themselves Indians when trying to practice deception. . . . Therefore, if he calls himself an Indian, that definitely establishes his Negro race. . . . Please tell us what his appearance is. Do Negro characteristics show in his hair and features?"[61]

However, even among Plecker's supporters there was a perceptible schism between those who advocated the discreet maintenance of racial categories and those who adhered to "rigid extremism" as methods of maintaining the color line. Nowhere is this more evident than in the 1924 case of *Atha Sorrells v. A. T. Shields,* which Plecker experienced as the first setback in his campaign for racial integrity. Atha Sorrells petitioned for mandamus against Rockbridge County Clerk A. T. Shields, who refused to issue marriage licence to her on the ground that he believed Sorrells to be colored and her intended to be a white man. Judge Holt proclaimed himself in "cordial sympathy" with the Racial Integrity Act. "Whether it be based upon pride, prejudice or instinct," he wrote in his reasons, "we look upon ourselves as a sceptered race and stand for its preservation in all its integrity." Shields, he held, was not wrong to refuse the marriage license if he was correct in his belief. However, the evidence that Sorrells was "colored" was not convincing. And Holt queried the act's concept of whiteness as compromised by any trace of non-white blood. "In twenty-five generations one has thirty two millions of grandfathers, not to speak of grandmothers, assuming there is no intermarriage . . . Pheonician and Ibarian, Roman and Saxon, Norman and Dane, and into it all has filtered the unknown strains of Asiatic incursions, homogenous only through the long process of time that have made us what we are." Notwithstanding this historical posturing, Holt's decision rested firmly on his opinion that Virginia's racial problem was presented by the "negro alone." But the detailed evidence of Sorrell's racial background demonstrated only "that there is no strain present in the applicant of any blood other than white, except Indian, and there is not enough of that to come within the statute."[62]

Plecker was adamant that his office were "not in the slightest degree guided by the decision of Judge Holt. That decision was based upon the evidence of the people who appeared as witnesses. . . . We consider our old records . . . as infinitely superior."[63] But it was a significant defeat. Plecker and his supporters were reluctant to risk an even greater loss of support, and did not pursue the case further on the advice of one of the lawyers involved, who stated that "in view of this ruling of our Court I feel that it would be useless for us to prosecute any more of these cases here . . . Judge Holt has indicated that in event the Commonwealth will take an appeal he will amend his written opinion and hold straight out that the statute is unconstitutional, so as to present that point directly to the appellate court."[64] Plecker accepted this advice, passing on this decision to Shields: "After going carefully over the evidence, in view of the fact that nothing new could be introduced, [the lawyers] decided . . . that it was unwise to appeal the case as the only evidence upon which we absolutely relied, that of our records was set aside by Judge Holt, and we would not care to take the risk of having the Supreme Court render a similar decision."[65]

Plecker also suffered a gradual waning of support from Virginia's governor, E. Lee Trinkle. In the beginning, Plecker and the Anglo-Saxon Club had Trinkle's support.[66] By December 1925, however, Trinkle seems to have had a change of heart. "The Indians have certainly given no trouble since I have been Governor and I hope they will continue to follow this course," he wrote to Chief Bradby.[67] He forwarded a copy of this letter to Plecker, telling him: "I am afraid sentiment is moulding itself along the line that you are too hard on these people and pushing matters too hard."[68] He also gave a copy of his letter to Plecker to Bradby, earning himself Plecker's wrath. "I am afraid," Trinkle wrote in response, "that the eternal appearance in the newspaper of some contest between yourself and the Indians makes it look as if we are probably working on them pretty hard and continually exposing their misfortune of having colored blood. I know this is humiliating if it is true and I was in hopes this could be handled in a quiet way. . . . No one could be personally more in favor of the racial integrity law than I, but I realize that movements of this kind cannot always be perfectly accomplished in this short period and that often times the best results can be reached by extreme caution."[69] In 1925 Trinkle posed with a Pamunkey chief and his daughter for a photograph that accompanied an article in the *Richmond Times-Dispatch* about a football game between Haskell Institute, a prominent Native American school, and the College of William and Mary. Trinkle's presence, and the headline, "Chief Cook Loses Stoicism as Haskell Scalps the Palefaces," made a very public display of state-sanctioned Indianness. Plecker was not amused.[70]

Legislatively, there was a gradual reduction of the "stringent whiteness" required by the Racial Integrity Act as time went on.[71] In 1930 the act was amended to define a "colored person" as a person in whom there is any "ascertainable Negro blood," and to allow people with "one-fourth or more of American Indian blood" to call themselves American Indians. Those of mixed Indian and African American ancestry who had "one-fourth or more of Indian blood and less than one-sixteenth Negro blood" were also permitted to call themselves Native Americans, as long as they were "domiciled" on an Indian reservation.[72] In 1942, responding to lawyers' demands, the attorney general ruled that they should be provided with photostatted copies of birth certificates that did not contain any racial information on the back—whether it be the "warning" discussed earlier in the chapter, or personalized information about the holder. "This is the worst backset [sic] which we have received since Judge Holt's decision," Plecker wrote to John Powell. "Now the whole crowd can come pouring in demanding that we give Photostat copies of the certificates without comments . . . we are now compelled to declare them Indian or white as the case may be." Plecker admitted that he knew his actions had bordered on the illegal. "In reality, I have been doing a good deal of bluffing, knowing all the while that it could not be legally sustained." He nevertheless believed that he was correct in the racial classifications he was enforcing; accordingly he was "somewhat indignant over the charge . . . that we were falsifying our records."[73]

The Virginia legislature, and many of the white population for that matter, were not convinced by Plecker's methods of safeguarding "Racial Integrity." The *Indian Truth*, the newsletter of the Indian Rights Association, reported in 1926 that the amendments to the 1924 act designed to validate Plecker's dealings with the Virginia nations "caused more debate than any other subject considered by the General Assembly, and incidentally . . . helped the Indian cause," but were now "indefinitely postponed." The *Truth* quoted an "intelligent observer" from Richmond, who was of the opinion that "most of our people resent the advertising given Virginia, and especially the unwarranted attack made on our Indians. They constitute as a whole a desirable part of our citizenship, having no criminals or paupers—something that cannot be said of either our White or Negro population."[74]

Even more tellingly, Plecker's own reports and personal papers occasionally reveal the increasing marginalization of his views, which were at times greeted with apathy and at other times with scorn. "The most striking feature of the situation," he wrote in his annual report for 1926, "is the inertia of the mass of the population and their failure to realize that there is danger of the ultimate disappearance of the white race in Virginia, and the country, and the substitution therefore of another of brown skin."[75] Plecker admitted to a sympathizer from New Orleans that he had presented his views to the Association of Registration Executives "two or three times, and I am usually laughed down, and everybody considers the thing entirely beyond their reach and that I am simply an old crank trying to accomplish the impossible."[76] A growing reluctance among the white population to force the absorption of the Virginian Indians into the Black population can thus be discerned—not necessarily from any sense of social injustice, but more from an unwillingness to collaborate in such an extreme project, initiated by a person who could easily be seen as a fanatic. One may also speculate that many Virginians were worried that Plecker's extreme measures might reveal uncomfortable truths about their own family backgrounds. Plecker ran the risk of "offending and antagonizing individuals," and no doubt did so. "We cannot consider the individual but the State," he wrote to a school superintendent who had been offended by a claim that "fifty of the most influential families of Russell County had been found to have Negro blood."[77] As we saw earlier, Plecker himself also complained that apathy played a part in this gradual reduction of support for racial integrity.

Sympathizers outside the state were soon alerted to the situation, and joined in the protests. In May 1925 Frank G. Speck, an anthropologist from the University of Pennsylvania who had worked and developed a sympathetic relationship with the Virginia nations, passed on to Matthew Sniffen, secretary of the Indian Rights Association, correspondence from Plecker to Chief George L. Nelson of the Rappahannocks, illustrating what he termed "Plecker's attempted buy-out."[78] After visiting Virginia and talking to the Virginian nations, Sniffen responded by publishing a critical piece in the IRA's newsletter, the *Indian Truth*. "These people are industrious, peaceable, self-supporting tax-payers and citizens, and an asset to the communities in which they live," he wrote. "They are entitled to proper consideration by the State officials, and their claim of Indian descent should be carefully investigated before they are refused the classification which they demand."[79] Plecker wrote to tell Sniffen and the IRA not to become involved: "You will confer a favor upon the State and our office if you will keep hands off until called upon for assistance by those who are required by law to settle the question and guard the safety of the State. If you cannot show that my position is wrong, I think you are due me an apology through the columns of your paper."[80]

However, the *Indian Truth* continued to publish reports on the Virginian nations' campaign through 1928, and Plecker's debate with Sniffen was reported in the Virginia newspapers.[81] George Nelson wrote to Sniffen to say "we have been having some hot shots fired at the Indians since your publication of the Truth. I think it hit Dr Plecker pretty hard and it started a series of articles in the *Richmond News-Leader* and *Richmond Times-Dispatch*. Yet the Indian has answered every one of them through the same papers and given them just as good as he sent."[82] Sniffen also maintained correspondence with a number of other Virginia chiefs, including E. P. Bradby, who complained that when babies were born to the Chickahominys and parents attempted to register them as Indians they received "after a long time a paper carrying no race whatever." "Dr Plecker," Bradby said, "is just writing us up to suit him-self."[83]

Speck continued to advise the Indians and, perhaps more importantly, to undermine Plecker's authority. "I note that Plecker is still on the active list," Sniffen wrote to Bradby in October 1925. "He is evidently possessed of a mania for persecution. It will do no good to reason with him nor to appeal to his justice or mercy. It is a case of Pilate."[84] Despite their verbal support, neither Speck nor Sniffen would travel to Virginia to speak on behalf of the Indians before the legislature, believing their position as northerners would prevent them from wielding any influence.[85] But they and the chiefs all congratulated each other on the occasion when amendments to the 1924 act were defeated.[86]

There was both support and opposition from diverse African American organizations. In 1925 the National Association for the Advancement of Colored People charged Plecker with using the "government franking privilege to spread propaganda derogatory to the Negro race," after he had distributed *Eugenics in Relation to the New Family* across the state of Virginia—a pamphlet that outlined the Racial Integrity Act.[87] Surprisingly, however, Plecker's efforts also led to an unholy alliance with some other African American organizations.[88] For "negroes and mulattoes who are frankly and honestly living as such" Plecker had "the highest regard," he told a representative of the Commission on Inter-racial Relations.[89] And the regard was occasionally mutual. Ame Garvey, wife of Marcus Garvey, visited Plecker's office to deliver an address in which she stated: "Our organization of more than 4,000,000 negroes is heartily in sympathy with Virginia's effort to keep the races pure."[90] On the other hand, the *Norfolk Journal and Guide*, an African American paper, recorded one writer's support for the idea that all the races "will blend finally in the American race type and color. . . . We do not favor race separation by forcible expatriation and we prefer to leave the mixing of the races to take care of itself, being a matter which we were not consulted about in the beginning and shall not be consulted about in the ending. . . . The Almighty God of the Republic who purposed to make 'a new people and a new nation,' on this Continent will take care of the matter."[91]

As late as 1943, Plecker's efforts came to the attention of John Collier, commissioner of Indian Affairs. Collier must also have voiced his opposition to Plecker since he received an antagonistic reply from Plecker. "I had no thought of the 'several hundred thousand Indian citizens' referred to by you, but am intensely interested in the groups of Negroid-pseudo-Indians now trying to register births either as Indians or as white," Plecker wrote, before giving his usual spiel on census records and genealogical research. "Our own indexed birth and marriage records, showing race, reach back to 1853. Such a study has probably never been made before." Chillingly, he added: "Your staff member is probably correct in his surmise that Hitler's genealogical study of the Jews is not more complete." Plecker did not hesitate to question the authority of the Indian Office: "Would it not be in order for the Office of Indian Affairs to check up with the Bureau of Ethnology and the Census as to the racial composition of the 'Indians' of Virginia and other eastern States? No one questions the fact that true Indians exist in the West," he pointed out, hinting that perhaps they should.[92]

White Virginians opposed Plecker's campaign not because they objected to his blood-based categorization of the non-white population of Virginia, but rather because they felt sympathy for Indian people. As John S. Fulton, MD, wrote bluntly to Plecker: "I am frank to say mixed Indian blood does not pain my gorge a tenth as much as the black pigment."[93] Many white Virginians were happy to have a tri-racial, rather than a biracial, society, and some clearly felt that the idea of "racial integrity" was more about keeping Black and white bloodlines separate than it was about maintaining the racial categories that defined Virginian society. Plecker's ideas drew their momentum from common ideas held across the country about undeserving mixed-blood Indians, which have been noted in previous chapters. But although Virginia remained a racially segregated state there was a reluctance to remove Indian status altogether.

The Eastern Band of Cherokees

The treatment of the Virginian Indians was a unique occurrence directed by one powerful individual who, for a brief period, had the support of the state legislature. The Eastern Cherokees, another southeastern Indian nation based in North Carolina, drew upon and experienced the discourse of blood very differently, using it proactively to their own ends in their fight to escape the color line. This nation had evaded the forced removal of the bulk of the Cherokee population in 1838 and had received federal recognition through early interactions with the federal government. It was perceived by white Americans—anthropologists and government officials alike—as conservative, morally upright, and pure of blood.[94] As a result, Eastern Cherokees were able to present themselves as deserving of Indian status. An 1892 extra census bulletin described the Eastern Cherokees in glowing terms as blending racial purity with modest acculturation. "Although many are full-blood Cherokees," the bulletin read, "[they] are citizens of the United States and are voters and taxpayers in North Carolina." The bulletin went on to describe the Eastern Cherokees as an "enterprising, moral . . . law-abiding . . . and almost entirely self-supporting" group who had retained their

Indianness. "While in many respects [they] are progressive," the bulletin continued, "[they] still they preserve some traditions and customs of their old Indian life."[95] Photographs were included in the bulletin to show that the Eastern Cherokees retained the "physical features of their race."[96] This perception of their resilient Indianness survived into the twentieth century. "Owing to their isolated location, they have had but little to do with the outside world and have therefore retained, to a large extent, their primitive customs," wrote the secretary of the Interior to a member of Congress sometime between 1907 and 1916. "In fact, in all material respects they conduct themselves in accordance with the time honoured customs of their ancestors. A large proportion of them are full blood Indians. It is probable that the degree of Indian blood of at least 3,000 of them exceeds one half."[97] They were still described as "the most pure-blooded and most conservative of the [Cherokee] nation" in a 1947 doctoral thesis, and other scholars drew on the work of anthropologist Leonard Bloom, who also believed "that these people were among the more conservative and least amenable to acculturation of the citizens of the Cherokee Nation."[98]

Despite the view that the Eastern Cherokees had "pure" blood, cross-cultural relationships were, of course, part of their history as with any other group of people. In 1889 the North Carolina General Assembly incorporated the Eastern Band, making them a body recognized by the state, and in 1895 an act proclaimed that no person of less than 1/16 Cherokee blood should be recognized as a member.[99] Throughout this period and into the early twentieth century a proactive tribal council worked hard to apply this strict blood quantum requirement to tribal membership. In 1910 tribal leaders John G. Welch and Joseph A. Saunooke, together with the special Indian agent, Chas. L. Davis, composed a form letter to potential applicants for enrollment with the Eastern Band. It informed applicants that they would have to show "beyond doubt that they possess Cherokee Indian blood," especially if they "show[ed] no physical indication of it."[100] The tribal council tried to limit membership to persons with the amount of "blood [of] 1/16 or more" but "with no success." It challenged the right of several families to be on the rolls because they could not demonstrate "the primary requisites essential to such membership, such requisites (which must exist concurrently) being Cherokee blood, tribal recognition, pecuniary interest, and a proper degree of Cherokee affiliation and association."[101]

In 1924 the title to the lands of the Eastern Cherokees was transferred to U.S. government trusts, and they became wards. The government undertook to create a new membership roll, and the "Baker Roll," completed in 1928, nearly doubled the tribal population. The tribal council challenged the membership of 1,229 of these enrollees without success, and continued to lobby for a more restrictive definition of Eastern Cherokee tribal membership.[102] Joseph Howell (who had earlier investigated the actions of the Dawes Commission) acted for the tribal council and fully supported their efforts to reject Cherokees with less than $1/16$ blood. "Many of the applicants seem to indulge the belief that, because they are recognized as of Cherokee Indian blood, in greater or less degree, it must follow they are entitled to enrollment," he wrote in his brief. "This theory is altogether too broad to stand the test of examination. It is well known that there are scattered throughout the States of the Atlantic Seaboard, from the time of Pocahontas (from whom many proudly claim descent), down to the present, numerous persons who have the racial characteristics of Indians but, for generations have had no tribal relations, due to the absorption and assimilation of that race by reason of education, inter-marriage and environment."[103] Howell continued: "The writer of this brief has sat with the Council of the Eastern Band of Cherokees, and heard one member after another, *nearly all of whom were full-bloods*, express, through an interpreter, their grief and disappointment growing out of the failure of Congress to carry out the plan they had agreed to for the determination of the blood question." On behalf of the council, Howell protested strongly against the bureau's instructions to enrollment officers that there must be "an appreciable and recognizable degree of Eastern Cherokee Indian blood." Howell thought the $1/16$ rule was just and would not rule out any person with a remotely justifiable membership in the nation. To illustrate the leniency of the rule he wrote that there would "have to be five alien marriages, out of the Cherokee strain, to produce a Cherokee of less than $1/16$ Cherokee blood. . . . Along this line, it is startling to think that if one full-blood Indian should arise on one side of the room, it would require 32 persons, of less than ¹⁄₁₆ Cherokee blood, to stand upon the other side to match and equal his Indian blood. Think of the absurdity of the proposition that it might require 32 persons to make one Indian."[104]

The situation of the Eastern Cherokees was very different from that of the Virginian nations because the Eastern Cherokees were believed to have had fewer relationships with the African American population. Applicants for enrollment who were examined and rejected were most often "recognized as white people in the community."[105] The Eastern Cherokees, with a tribal council acknowledged by the state of North Carolina, assisted in the official recognition of their nation by drawing on the stereotype of the deserving full-blood Indian. Far from being victimized, as were the Virginian nations, their image as a racially pure, culturally contained group, as well as being led by a hands-on, conservative tribal council, prevented their authenticity from being called into question. Katherine M. B. Osburn has shown that the Mississippi Choctaws also consistently stressed their "full-blood" status in the documents they brought before Congress, demonstrating their authenticity by adopting the language of blood to their political advantage.[106] The discourse of blood could thus be both a means of authentication for a tribal nation or a path to its disenfranchisement as a distinctive racial body. Any hint of interracial relationships between Native American people and African Americans was enough to threaten Indian status and authenticity.[107] Native Americans could use the discourse of blood as a means to demonstrate their Indianness. With this in mind, the decision of many Indian nations to define their membership by blood quantum in the post-1934 era makes sense. The perception of them as authentic and deserving had become inextricably linked to blood—and control of this perception could increase the possibility of sovereignty.

In the twentieth century, as we have seen, it became extraordinarily difficult for an Indian community to prove that they did not have a history of interracial relationships. Native American nations were therefore in a terrible bind—relationships with other ethnicities were unavoidable, but at the same time led to a diminution of government protection. Interracial relationships did not and had never, though, lead automatically to a loss of tribal cohesiveness. Arthur H. Estabrook and Ivan E. McDougle, the authors of *Mongrel Virginians*, characterized the Virginian nations as "ambiguous of race"—but in fact nothing could have been further from the truth. The effect of the racial integrity law on the Virginian nations was, according to Helen Rountree, to generate pride in their ethnic status:

> True, many of them left their kinsmen to find easier lives with more opportunity; some returned in later years; others stayed away permanently. But the ones who stayed became welded together to a degree not experienced before. . . . They stepped up their visiting of one another and of other eastern Indians . . . and for a time there was even talk of a new Powhatan Confederacy.[108]

The Pamunkeys gained federal recognition in 2015. The Eastern Band of the Cherokee Nation elected to incorporate under the Indian Reorganization Act in the 1940s and is a federally recognized nation with a reservation and a successful casino.[109]

Conclusion

Writing Blood into the Assimilation Period

From the sixteenth century onward, argues Aileen Moreton-Robinson, racial markers such as blood quantum helped to divide "humans into three categories: owning property, becoming propertyless, and being property."[1] For the bulk of the assimilation period, Native Americans of mixed descent were not dealt with specifically by the legislation that oversaw the division of reservations into allotments. They were not explicitly prevented from owning Indian lands or receiving tribal benefits or from calling themselves Menominee, Cherokee, or Anishinaabeg, or by the name of whatever nation they had connections with.[2] The U.S. government began the process of assimilation by utilizing an inclusive definition of Indian status that ostensibly paid no heed to whether or not an individual had mixed ancestry as long as they were recognized by a tribal nation. The U.S. government's increasing reliance on the discourse of blood, however, did have an impact on people who were understood to be Indians of mixed descent. In contrast to authentic and deserving "full-bloods" they were seen to be crafty, inauthentic, and unworthy of government protection and the special benefits and rights that came with Indian status. Not all people of mixed descent were victims of this binary. Some were genuinely no longer recognized as part of the kinship networks of tribal nations. But the possibility existed for some people to fall through the cracks of the enrollment process and not be enrolled.

Some lost the legal protection of their lands. Some were thought not to be really Indian, especially if they had African American ancestry, and thus faced the disdain of white American society for those it called "colored." The New Deal, although it offered an opportunity to disenfranchised people to regain Indian status if they had a blood quantum of more than half, was infused with the same prejudices about who was worthy of recognition as an Indian.

Not many people during the assimilation questioned the use of "blood" as a means to define Indianness. Some did, however, observe the prejudice inherent in the use of the terms "full-blood" and "mixed-blood." In 1914, for example, Seneca archaeologist Arthur C. Parker, editor-general of the *Quarterly Journal* of the Society of American Indians, noted that there were prevailing stereotypes about "full-bloods" and "mixed-bloods." "All through official reports and even in private writings we are impressed with the expression 'the full blood,'" he wrote. "There are many qualifying phrases, such as 'the ignorant full blood,' 'the restricted full blood,' the 'non-progressive full blood' or the 'pagan full blood.'" Going further, Parker described "another class of critics [who have] an aversion to mixed bloods. To some, mixed bloods are of decidedly criminal tendencies. The 'half breed' of the motion picture film is always pictured as a moral degenerate."[3] Parker was one of the few people who noted in print that the discourse of blood carried with it the spurious idea that people of mixed descent and full descent each had peculiar personal characteristics. He recognized the power of popular culture in supporting these views (a dimension that this book leaves unexamined). He noticed the adjectives that were so often attached to such racial classifications such as "mixed-blood" and "full-blood." In contrast, most government administrators in the assimilation period were happy to push pens and make decisions, without ever, as far as we know, publically questioning the categories they were applying to richly varied populations who had their own markers of kinship and belonging.

If one looks, as Parker wished, beyond the stereotype of the shrewd, inauthentic, undeserving "mixed-blood," it is possible to see another story: how the category of "mixed-blood" was a vehicle of land theft. In

1912, for example, the Dawes Commission summarized its work in Indian Territory between 1894 and 1912 as follows: "Applications were made for the enrollment of over 200,000 persons, of which number 101,221 were enrolled and found entitled to allotments."[4] The commission also conceded that unallotted land as of June 30, 1910, when allotment was completed, totaled 1,815,189.22 acres.[5] Who were the 80,000 people who were not enrolled that could have taken their share of the 1.8 million acres? Some no doubt had tenuous tribal connections. But some of those who missed out would have been people designated as being of mixed descent, victims of the stereotype of the mixed-descent Indian as undeserving, corrupt, and cunning. If the government had allowed Indigenous nations to define their own membership or even used a more cultural definition of Indian status instead of the discourse of blood, many nations today might have greater assets.

The U.S. government's use of the discourse of blood played a crucial role in the rationalization of the theft of native land, and in the long negotiations on assimilation practices that took place in diverse local contexts across the United States. It enabled the government to use the protection of "real" Indians as a cover for the removal of rights from mixed-descent Indians. Blood was used to promote division in Native communities and to undermine the authority of tribal governments. The discourse could be used in efforts to destabilize the sovereignty of Indigenous nations by implying that they were not really Indigenous any more, that their status was somehow suspect, that they had been absorbed or assimilated, and therefore no longer deserved to be treated as separate communities with their own cultures, needs, and legal status. Blood reconciled the real goal of allotment policy—the acquisition by white Americans of as much Indian land as possible—with the comforting knowledge that "real" Indians still had their reservations. "Mixed-bloods" were not deserving of their lands, therefore they could be taken without guilt. From the perspective of the U.S. government the category of the "mixed-descent Indian" was, then, a conduit of loss—of land, tribal recognition, and authenticity.

For Native American people, though, blood could be a means of varied responses to the challenges of assimilation and the incursions of capitalism. It could be used as a tool to establish authenticity, or as a proof of qualification for release from government control. In the present day, blood can be used to anchor tribal membership in the past. In the second half of the twentieth century, blood was increasingly used to define Indianness—both by the U.S. government and Indigenous nations. After analyzing 245 historical and current tribal constitutions, Kirsty Gover discovered "a striking increase in the tribal use of blood quantum rules over time, from 44 per cent of pre-1941 constitutions to 70 per cent today." Blood's discursive iterations shifted in the termination period, and then took on yet newer meanings during post–WWII period as Native American nations fought for sovereignty and self-determination. Gover concludes that after 1970 "descent and blood rules appear[ed] to function as reparative devices, 'repairing' the historic continuity of the communities."[6]

Blood's shifting meanings and continuing resonances make it imperative that historians read the archives of the assimilation period with a clear sense of its nuances. The terms used in the records by both white Americans and Native Americans stand for a complex and fluctuating range of assumptions about ethnic status, skin color, and specific cultural ties or behaviors. Blood quantum was often recorded incorrectly, decided on a glance, claimed by applicants for a particular purpose, and often had little to do with Indigenous ideas about identity, kinship, and tribal membership. At the same time, as Tracey Banivanua Mar has described, "identity [could be] a space, both tiny and momentous, of myriad and complex acts of resistance."[7] How should historians deal with this terminology when using archival sources? How can they ensure that they do not repeat its biases, misconceptions, and errors? They must not, as Malinda Maynor Lowery puts it, take for "granted that the past observer understood the dimensions of belonging and culture that marked someone as an Indian."[8] They must also remember, as Rose Stremlau writes, that the terms "full-blood" and "mixed-blood," when used by Native Americans, tell us "more about their own understanding of inherent racial differences and the workings of white supremacy than about [Indigenous] beliefs about race or belonging"[9] Historians must pay attention to the intricate makeup and beliefs of Indigenous peoples and families and work hard not to recycle nineteenth- and early twentieth-century prejudices based on out-of-date ideas of ethnicity that once served the U.S. government in its efforts to undermine tribal sovereignty. Similarly, historians must respect and listen to what Native American nations have to say about their own requirements for membership and consider how their research might assist or detract from their sovereignty. This book was not written in support of false claimants to Native American tribal status but rather to point out that the United States was, in complex and unique ways, one of a number of settler colonial societies who attempted to reduce an Indigenous population by redefinition.

It is time to add the discourse of blood with its devastating impacts to the other assaults—removal of children, boarding schools, forbidden languages, land loss, poverty—endured by Indigenous peoples during the assimilation period. We must also add the story of Native American peoples' unrelenting resistance and negotiation with this so-called racial science. The course of physical, metaphorical, and ideological incidents, encounters, collaborations, and bargains prompted by the discourse of blood constitutes a narrative that needs to be recognized as central to Indigenous history in this era. Most importantly it is time to hand control of the discourse of blood back to Native American communities, for them to do with as they wish.

ACKNOWLEDGMENTS

This book was written and researched with the support of an Australian Research Council Postdoctoral Fellowship, a Monash Fellowship, and a Barra Foundation International Fellowship. Many archivists and librarians assisted my research. In particular, I want to thank George Briscoe, who helped me navigate the overwhelming holdings of the National Archives and Records Administration in Washington DC, and Scott Forsythe, who guided me through NARA's considerable holdings in the Chicago office (and so kindly assisted me in my search for a mid-morning cup of coffee).

Four wonderful research assistants—Sianan Healy, Prue Flowers, Jordy Silverstein, and, only too briefly, Leigh Boucher—acted as mediators between myself and libraries and archives in Melbourne and across the world, prompted me with their critical and engaged questions about the project, and tempered this intellectual work with humor and friendship. There were times when I had to remind myself (and others) that our meetings, which often took place in cafés rather than my office, were actually part of the hard work of writing a book. All four are now embarked on their own successful careers, and I know that one day I will count myself extremely lucky that I was able, even for a short time, to draw on their talents and even luckier to now count them as friends.

I am grateful to Paul Spruhan, who kindly shared his knowledge and groundbreaking research on blood quantum, and Margaret Jacobs whose long-distance support and incredible scholarship opened my eyes to ways of doing comparative settler colonial history that I could not have imagined. As she has been since the very beginning of my career as an historian, Patricia Grimshaw has been an inspiration, mentor, friend, and cheerleader. Patrick Wolfe was generous and supportive of this project in its early days. Then as I was making the final changes to the manuscript I was suddenly mourning the loss of this talented scholar. His work has had an enormous influence on me, right from the second year of my undergraduate degree, when his lectures first opened my mind to the intricate cruelties of settler colonialism's "logic of elimination." During the writing of this book, Lynette Russell helped me out of a career crisis with characteristic generosity and efficiency. Bain Attwood read the entire manuscript and offered an astute critique that developed the argument considerably. Glenn Moore brightened many a day with his nifty emails. My conversations with Taylor Spence about the history of settler colonialism and beyond have been, and are still, a pleasure and an inspiration. Michael McDonnell and Philip Deloria swooped in at the last minute with wonderful advice. Also in the final stages Leonie Stevens gave invaluable, expert, and life-saving assistance with all matters, as she termed it, footnotery. Kalissa Alexeyeff, Tracey Banivanua Mar, Leigh Boucher, Jane Carey, Philip Deloria, Penny Edmonds, Pat Grimshaw, Mike McDonnell, and Peter Sherlock read chapter drafts and brought their own expertise to bear on my ideas, as did the many members of my various Monash University research groups. Monash University provided a supportive environment in which to write, and my colleagues there—especially Susie Protschky, Kate Murphy, Charlotte Greenhalgh, Rachel Standfield, Lynette Russell, Adam Clulow, Leah Garrett, Taylor Spence, Christina Twomey, Clare Corbould, Al Thompson, and Megan Cassidy Welch—have contributed to this book in all kinds of ways. I am also grateful for the time and effort given by the anonymous reviewers of the manuscript.

I finished the first draft of this book ten days before my eldest daughter was born, and waddled my way to the post office to send it off to Matt Bokovoy at the University of Nebraska Press on a sunny morning that I remember with the clarity of a time ripe with new beginnings and endings. I am embarrassed to think how much time passed between that moment and this, and I thank Matt for his faith in the project, his editorial input, and for his patience with an author whose attention was so often pulled away by family obligation. Perhaps one day I can entice him down under to try out some of our excellent beaches.

Finally, for their continuing love and encouragement, I thank my wonderful family and friends, who have so dealt so kindly with me as I have agonized my way through this project. As always, I appreciate Gail Murphy's support and the pride that she takes in all my achievements. Samantha Benton has talked through the personal, ethical, and intellectual issues raised by the writing of this book during forest walks that have been my saving grace. I would be have been similarly lost without Lynder "Winnie" Jewell's and Emma Bannock's texts, phone calls, dinners, "gongs," and unflagging humor. I have been blessed to have these three women as my companions on the journey all the way from our misty mountain childhoods to the stark, grown-up realities of today, and they continue to astound me with their courage and strength. Kalissa Alexeyeff, Tracey Banivanua Mar, and Ann Standish have been a precious island in the chaos. In those moments when academia seemed impossible, these three kind, brave, and clever women showed me through example and advice not only why it is that we do what we do but what are the best ways to go about it (and you all know exactly how I expect you to celebrate this book now it is finally published). Cindy Van Es and Jihan Stevens helped me write this book in all kinds of practical ways. More than that, it has been a privilege and a pleasure to share the journey of motherhood with them. Terri Bahri, Fred Ellinghaus, Alan Hanley, Anthony Michaels, and my talented cousin Carli Ellinghaus undertook many hours of childcare that enabled me to return to work post-motherhood. The time, energy, and love that they bestowed on my children helped me turn my attention to my computer with ease. Without them, this book would never have been completed. Most of all: Thank you, Dad.

Last but in no way least, I am grateful to Kristian Hanley and our beautiful daughters. This book, it is strange to think, is older than my girls, and Dahsha and Marlo's young lives have taken place alongside it and delayed it considerably (for which I resent them not at all). I dedicate it to them, for all those things that I cannot put into words.

NOTES

INTRODUCTION

1. Readers will note that when it is necessary to refer to the diverse Indigenous peoples of the United States as a single group, I have followed the common convention of using the terms Indian, Native American, and Indigenous interchangeably. The Australian federal government Parliamentary Counsel, Drafting Direction No 2.1 on English usage recommends capitalizing "Indigenous" when referring to the original owners of the Australia and extending this, where appropriate, to other national contexts. I have done so also in recognition of Native American sovereignty. Also in recognition of Indigenous sovereignty I have used "nation" rather than tribe wherever possible (although, to prevent confusion, I have made an exception in the case of the Five Tribes—the Cherokees, Chickasaws, Choctaws, Seminoles, and Muscogees [Creeks]). I have sparingly used the word "identity" to refer to any individual's or community's ethnic self-identification. When used in the present day in reference to Indigenous people, "identity" has connotations that arise from the social movements of the postwar period. The word was rarely used in the assimilation period. Instead, I have used the term "status" in referring both to legally and communally recognized membership of an Indian nation or community.

2. Laurence F. Schmeckebier, *The Office of Indian Affairs*, 144. Commissioner of Indian Affairs, Thomas Morgan, briefly addressed the question "What is an Indian" in one section of his 1892 report to the secretary of the Interior. "One would have supposed that this question would have been . . . adjudicated long before this," he wrote, but "the Government has gone on legislating and administering law without carefully discriminating as to those over whom it had a

right to exercise such control." Morgan noted that the government had accepted signatures on treaties from Indians of mixed descent, included them on censuses, paid them a share of tribal monies held in trust, and allotted them lands. Denying people of mixed descent Indian status, he argued, might therefore "unsettle and endanger the titles to much of the lands that have been relinquished by Indian tribes and patented to citizens of the United States" and thereby raised the question of whether "real Indians" might have an "equitable claim against the United States for misappropriation of their funds." Accordingly, he advised that the government should not make any distinction between Indians of full and mixed descent, and that the term "Indian" should be given "a liberal and not a technical or restrictive construction." U.S. Congress, House, *Sixty-First Annual Report of the Commissioner of Indian Affairs to the Secretary of the Interior, 1892* (Washington DC: Government Printing Office, 1892), 31, 36–37.

3. Russell, "The Racial Paradox of Tribal Citizenship," 170.

4. "Qualifications of Applicants," Code of Federal Regulations Title 43, Pt. 2531.1 (1887).

5. Cohen, *Handbook of Federal Indian Law*, 5.

6. McCorquodale, "The Legal Classification of Race in Australia," 7–24. See also Gardiner-Garden, *Current Brief No. 10*.

7. See, for example, Hosmer, "Reflections on Indian Cultural 'Brokers,'" 493–509, and Wilson, "Blood Quantum," 119.

8. As Pauline Turner Strong and Barrik Van Winkle argue, because blood allows the distance between ancestors to be calculated and quantified, it becomes a "discourse of precise, objectified relatedness and distance [which] articulates with discourses of authenticity, purity, contamination, and conflict." Strong and Van Winkle, "Indian Blood," 554. See also Raibmon, *Authentic Indians*.

9. Baker, *Anthropology and the Racial Politics of Culture*, 115.

10. Garroutte, *Real Indians*, 42.

11. McMullen, "Blood and Culture." On the other hand, Laura L. Lovett has identified a tendency for people of African American descent to claim prestige from having a Native American ancestor. Lovett, "African and Cherokee by Choice," 203–29.

12. Sturm, "Blood Politics, Racial Classification, and Cherokee National Identity," 224.

13. Linke, *Blood and Nation*, vii. See also Meyer, *Thicker Than Water*; Johnson, Jussen, Sabean and Teuscher, *Blood and Kinship*; and Hanson, "Blood and Purity in Leviticus and Revelation," 215–30.

14. Sweet, *Bodies Politic*, 272; Chaplin, "Natural Philosophy and an Early Racial Idiom in North America," 230–31.

15. Martínez, "The Black Blood of New Spain," 479–520; Aubert, "The Blood of France," 439–78.

16. Villella, "Pure and Noble Indians," 633–63; McDonald, "Intimacy and Empire," 134–56.
17. For a comprehensive discussion of the use of blood quantum in the colonial period see Spruhan, "A Legal History of Blood Quantum," 4–8. See also Higginbotham Jr. and Kopytoff, "Racial Purity and Interracial Sex," 1967–2029; Nash, "The Hidden History of Mestizo America," 10–32, 16; and Forbes, *Africans and Native Americans*.
18. Spear, "Clean of blood, without stain or mixture," 95–108.
19. Wolfe, *Traces of History*, 38–39.
20. See, in particular, Barker, "IndianTM USA," 25–79; Biolsi, "The Birth of the Reservation," 28–53; Bragi, *Invisible Indians*; Brownell, "Who Is an Indian?," 275–320; Dennison, *Constituting a Twenty-First-Century Osage Nation*; Dickson-Gilmore, "Iati-Onkwehonwe," 27–43; Doerfler, *Those Who Belong*; Garroutte, *Real Indians*; Gover, *Tribal Constitutionalism*; Hamill, "Show me Your CDIB," 267–82; Lawrence, *"Real" Indians and Others*; Lowery, *Lumbee Indians in the Jim Crow South*; Lyons, *X-Marks*; Meyer, "American Indian Blood Quantum Requirements," 231–49; Mihesuah, "American Indian Identities," 13–38; Perdue, *"Mixed Blood" Indians* and "Race and Culture," 701–723; Simpson, "Paths toward a Mohawk Nation," 113–36; Strong and Van Winkle, "Indian Blood"; Sturm, *Blood Politics*; Villazor, "Blood Quantum Land Laws," 801–37; and Weaver, "Indigenous Identity," 240–55.
21. Tallbear, "DNA and Native American Identity," 74.
22. Spruhan, "Indian as Race/Indian as Political Status," 27–49; "A Legal History of Blood Quantum"; "The Origins, Current Status, and Future Prospects of Blood Quantum," 1–17.
23. "It was a time when the tendency to use racial biology to define Indian identity rather than culture was cemented." Forbes, "Basic Concepts for Understanding Native History and Culture," 29.
24. Chang, *The Color of the Land*, 71–105.
25. May, *African Americans and Native Americans in the Creek and Cherokee Nations*; Miles and Holland, *Crossing Waters, Crossing Worlds*; Miles, *Ties That Bind*; Saunt, *Black, White, and Indian*; Naylor, *African Cherokees in Indian Territory*; Osburn, "Any Sane Person," 451–71; Sturm, *Blood Politics*; Yarborough, *Race and the Cherokee Nation*.
26. Gross, *What Blood Won't Tell*; Gonzales, "Racial Legibility," 57–68.
27. Basson, *White Enough to Be American*; Foster, *We Know Who We Are*; Graybill, *The Red and the White*; Gross, *What Blood Won't Tell*; Hagan, "Full Blood, Mixed Blood, Generic, and Ersatz," 309–26; Hyde, *Empires, Nations, and Families*; Ingersoll, *To Intermix with Our White Brothers*; Murphy, *Great Lakes Creoles*; Nash, "The Hidden History of Mestizo America," 941–64; Penn, *As We Are Now*; Peterson and Brown, *The New Peoples*; Snipp, "An Overview of American Indian

Populations," 38–48; Shoemaker, *American Indian Population Recovery*; Unrau, *Mixed-Bloods and Tribal Dissolution*.

28. Meyer, "American Indian Blood Quantum Requirements," 231.

29. Spruhan, "A Legal History of Blood Quantum," 3.

30. Stoler says other kinds of colonial "unwrittens" existed as well: "what was unwritten because it could not yet be articulated, and what was unwritten because it could not be said." Stoler, *Along the Archival Grain*, 3.

31. Cathleen Cahill notes that the Office of Indian Affairs workforce expanded "from just over 500 employees in the field in 1869 to nearly 4,000 by 1897 and 6,000 by 1912." The Indian Office also received dramatically increased budget appropriations across the allotment period. Cahill, *Federal Fathers and Mothers*, 2.

32. Cahill, *Federal Fathers and Mothers*, 6.

33. Malcomson, *One Drop of Blood*, 110.

34. Stremlau, *Sustaining the Cherokee Family*.

35. McMullen, "Blood and Culture," 268.

36. Stocking Jr., "The Turn-of-the-Century Concept of Race," 6; Meyer, "Race and Identity in Indian Country," 800; Baker, *Anthropology and the Racial Politics of Culture*; Bieder, "The Representations of Indian Bodies," 165–79.

37. See Hinsley, *Savages and Scientists*.

38. Genetin-Pilawa, *Crooked Paths to Allotment*, 2.

39. Stoler, *Along the Archival Grain*, 1.

40. Wolfe, "Settler Colonialism and the Elimination of the Native," 387–409, and *Traces of History*, 173–201.

41. J. Kēhaulani Kauanui argues similarly in her history of the Hawaiian Homestead Act. "Blood quantum," she argues, "is a manifestation of settler colonialism that works to deracinate—to pull out by the roots—and displace indigenous peoples." Kauanui also compares the Homestead Act with the Allotment Act, noting that whereas the General Allotment Act "worked to systematically break up tribal land holdings, Hawaiian lands had already been privatized in 1848. Allotment under the HHCA proved to be a different form of Native assimilation. Unlike the explicit push to *detribalize* Indians through the Dawes plan—with individual land title vulnerable to alienation—the initial aim of the HHCA Proposal was to rehabilitate urban Kanaka Maoli by *returning* them to land 'for their own good.'" J. Kēhaulani Kauanui, *Hawaiian Blood*, 9, 87.

42. Miller, *Invisible Indigenes*, 7.

43. Anderson, *The Cultivation of Whiteness*; Beresford and Omaji, *Our State of Mind*; Birch, "A Mabo Blood Test?," 32–42; McGregor, *Imagined Destinies*; Moran, "White Australia, Settler Nationalism and Aboriginal Assimilation," 168–93; Wolfe, "Land, Labor and Difference," 866–905 and *Settler Colonialism and the Transformation of Anthropology*. Biological absorption also forms an important

part of the scholarly discussions about whether assimilation policies were genocidal. See, in particular, Moses, *Genocide and Settler Society*. For a critique of biological absorption see Rowse and Smith, "The Limits of 'Elimination' in the Politics of Population," 90–106.

44. I explored these ideas in greater detail in *Taking Assimilation to Heart*.

45. See Garoutte, "The Racial Formation of American Indians," 224–39; Wolfe, "Settler Colonialism and the Elimination of the Native," 387–409; Trosper, "Native American Boundary Maintenance," 256–74; Meyer, "American Indian Blood Quantum Requirements"; Lawrence, *"Real" Indians and Others*. Other scholars do not see government definitions of Indian status as a deliberate strategy. See Dippie, *The Vanishing American*, David D. Smits, "'Squaw Men,' 'Half-Breeds,' and Amalgamators," 157–92; Harmon "When Is an Indian Not an Indian?," 95–123.

46. See, for example, Jaimes, "Federal Indian Identification Policy," 123–38; Limerick, *The Legacy of Conquest*; and Allen, "Blood (and) Memory," 97. In the 2000s, exactly how blood quantum operated as part of assimilation policy became part of the public controversy excited by Professor Ward Churchill, formerly of the University of Colorado, Boulder. In the wake of a scandal prompted by an essay in which he argued that 9/11 was a natural consequence of American foreign policy, Churchill was accused of shoddy scholarship in several areas. One was in regard to his claims about blood and the 1887 General Allotment Act. In a number of publications, Churchill seemed to say that the act contained a requirement for allottees to be of "one-half or more degree of Indian blood." See LaVelle, "The General Allotment Act 'Eligibility' Hoax," 251–302.

47. Russell, "The Racial Paradox of Tribal Citizenship," 170.

48. From the very beginnings of the American nation, individual commentators discussed the possibilities of amalgamation with Indians. Thomas Jefferson's *Notes on the State of Virginia* (1800) and anthropologist Lewis Henry Morgan's *The Indian Journals* are probably the most famous and often quoted, but there were many more. In 1705 Robert Beverley, a native Virginian who inherited significant landholdings in the state, and brother-in-law of William Byrd, another famous Virginian historian, wrote a history of his home in which he lamented that intermarriage with Indians had not been undertaken more extensively: "consequently the Abundance of Blood that was shed on both sides wou'd have been saved; the great Extremeties they were so often reduced to, by which so many died, wou'd not have happen'd; the Colony, instead of all these Losses of Men on both Sides, wou'd have been encreasing [*sic*] in Children to its Advantage; . . . and, in all Likelihood, many, if not most, of the *Indians* would have been converted to Christianity by this kind Method; the Country would have been full of People, by the Preservation of

the many *Christians* and *Indians* that fell in the Wars between them. Besides, there would have been a Continuance of all those Nations of *Indians* that are now dwindled away to nothing." Rev. Jedidiah Morse, in his report to the U.S. government on the state of "Indian Affairs" in 1820, noted that intermarriages and relationships that "amount[ed] to the same thing" had taken place to "a great extent" between whites and the Cherokees, Choctaws, and Chickasaws. The children of these marriages, Morse believed, were of "promising talents and appearance" and required only education to make them eligible partners for whites. "Let intermarriage with them become general," Morse argued, "and the end which the Government has in view will be completely attained. They would then be literally of one blood with us, be merged in the nation, and saved from extinction." Elwell S. Otis, in his book-length discussion of *The Indian Question* published in 1878, concluded his study with a hesitant promotion of biological absorption. Although the child of a relationship between white and Indian would be "an inferior being, both in mind and morals," Otis felt confident that the small size of the Indigenous population would mean that there would be "no decided effect . . . upon our national character." Otis noted that "there are but few instances in history, where clans, tribes, or people, of a distinct stock, have been so partial to their own lineage or descent, as to be checked from affiliating with, and intermarrying among those of a different origin and nature, in case both are thrown into close neighborhood." Thus, the "gradual absorption of our Indian stock will assuredly continue, and it is probable, that it will be finally merged in the great body of our white population." Charles Carroll, who published a contentious five-hundred page anti-amalgamation book in 1902, maintained that sexual relationships between whites and African Americans were turning the entire American population "into Indians"—according to Carroll, who quoted a professor of anthropology at the University of Chicago on the matter, Indians were simply the progeny of early Black/white relationships. Thus, as interracial mixing went on, he saw the whites becoming darker and the African Americans lighter. Another, later, anti-Black/white miscegenation text published in 1930 also saw Indianness as an intermediate point between Black and white. A. H. Shannon saw the issue of Indian-white mixing as tangential to the larger one of white-Black mixing. While a 'ragged fringe of immorality' had existed between whites and Indians, of more concern were the progeny of white-Indian-African American ancestry who were trying to claim whiteness, using their Indianness as a kind of stepping stone. Beverley, *The History and Present State of Virginia*, 38–39; Morse, *A Report to the Secretary of War of the United States on Indian Affairs*, 74–75; Otis, *The Indian Question*, 281–83; Carroll, *The Tempter of Eve*, 451–53.

Shannon, *The Negro in Washington*, 118. The idea of amalgamation appeared, of course, in other settler societies. See Salesa, *Racial Crossings*.

49. U.S. Congress, House, *Annual Report of the Commissioner of Indian Affairs, 1905*, 5.

50. *Annual Report of the Commissioner of Indian Affairs, 1905*, 5.

51. The total Native American population was recorded as 265,683. Of the 93,423 people recorded as being of "mixed-blood," 88,030 were recorded as "White and Indian" (a category which included "Mexican and Indian," 2,255 were "Negro and Indian," 1,793 were "White, Negro and Indian," eighty were "Other mixtures" and 1,265 were "Mixture unknown." U.S. Bureau of the Census, *Indian Population in the United States and Alaska, 1910* (Washington DC: United States Government Printing Office, 1915), 31, 32, 35, quoted in Reddy, *Statistical Record of Native North Americans*, 113, 114, 134.

52. See, for example, Debo, *And Still the Waters Run*, 64, 167; Malcomson, *One Drop of Blood*, 108; Olson and Wilson, *Native Americans in the Twentieth Century*, 80; Unrau, *Mixed-Bloods and Tribal Dissolution*, ix.

53. Only a few scholars have focused on such people. In 1958 Verne Dusenberry wrote poignantly about the "dispossessed métis" or "The Landless Indians" of Montana. Dusenberry, "Waiting for a Day That Never Comes," 120. More recently they have been described as "unenrolled American Indians" by Resa Crane Bizzaro and "outalucks" by Eva Marie Garroutte. Bizarro, "Shooting Our Last Arrow," 61–74; Garroutte, *Real Indians*, 14.

54. August A. Breuninger to President Woodrow Wilson, 6 February 1917; E. B. Meritt to August A. Breuninger, 26 February 1917; August A. Breuninger to Commissioner of Indian Affairs, 5 March 1917, 17694–1917, box 218, General Services 53 Enrollment—Citizenship—Degree of Indian Blood, Central Classified Files 1907–39, RG 75, NARA–Washington DC. Breuninger's grandmother was a Menominee woman who had married a German man. When Breuninger was a child his father left the Green Bay mission where he was raised and went to live in Arkansas. In 1910 Breuninger testified to the Senate Committee on Indian Affairs about his difficulties in getting enrolled with the Menominees and in 1911 he suggested the founding of an Indian University. U.S. Congress, Senate, *Condition of Indian Affairs in Wisconsin*, 851–54; Crum, "The Idea of an Indian College or University in Twentieth Century America," 20–23. In the 1920s Breuninger was declared insane and briefly committed to an asylum because his attempts to file suits against the secretary of the Interior and the commissioner of Indian Affairs on behalf of "exiled half-breeds [had] led the authorities to consider him a paranoiac." Pamphlet: "Un-a-Quah Free: Americanism Still Lives!" Folder 208, Papers of Lucullus Virgil McWhorter, 1845–1945, Washington State University Libraries Manuscripts, Archives and Special Collections, Pullman, Washington State.

55. Office of Indian Affairs, *Indian Land Tenure, Economic Status, and Population Trends*, 11–12.
56. Office of Indian Affairs, *Indian Land Tenure, Economic Status, and Population Trends*, 12.
57. Lyons, *X-Marks*, 37.
58. Hyde, "The Blue Flower and the Account Book," 3.
59. Tallbear, "The Political Economy of Tribal Citizenship in the United States," 72.
60. Dennison, "The Logic of Recognition," 23.
61. Barker, "IndianTM USA," 46.
62. Paying attention to the macro, settler colonial, and therefore transnational context in which the discourse of blood operated is important. But of course, one of the critiques of the settler colonial framework is that it glosses over local differences in favor of theorizing uniformity. Corey Snelgrove, Rita Kaur Dhamoon, and Jeff Corntassel have written of their concerns that settler colonial studies can de-center Indigenous peoples and the issues that matter most to them. Australian scholar Tim Rowse argues that the scholarly focus on settler colonial efforts to eliminate and erase Indigenous populations and undermine the authenticity of Indigenous identities results in analyses that see all "representations of Indigenous Australians and all self representations by them [as] subject to the suspicion that they are best understood as the tactical moves of a deeply cunning settler colonial governmentality." Snelgrove, Dhamoon, and Corntassel, "Unsettling Settler Colonialism," 9. Rowse, "Indigenous Heterogeneity," 298, 300.
63. Kauanui, *Hawaiian Blood*, 9.
64. I am drawing here on Audra Simpson's concept of refusal, which she uses to describe Haudenosaunee insistence upon their sovereignty and integrity of governance by refusing "the 'gifts' of American and Canadian citizenship." Simpson, *Mohawk Interruptus*, 7.
65. Simpson, "On Ethnographic Refusal," 67–80. Simpson also uses the phrase to mean "a refusal, or a denial within the space of ethnography." She gives the example of a moment when, in her interviews, someone refused to engage with a question or issue: "it was enough that he said what he said. 'Enough' is certainly enough. 'Enough,' I realized, was when I reached the limit of my own return and our collective arrival." Simpson, "On Ethnographic Refusal," 77–78.
66. They were not alone. Other scholars have detailed moments when Indigenous people resisted categories imposed upon them by settler governments in diverse times and places. Thomas Biolsi, for example, describes an 1885 census of Lakota people at the Rosebud Agency that contains, as well as names "such as 'Black Elk,' 'Walking Bull,' and 'Dull Knife,' . . . names such as 'Bad Cunt,' 'Dirty Prick,' and 'Shit Head.' . . . Lakota people were filing past the census enumerator, then

getting back in line—or lending babies to people in line—to be enumerated a second time using fictitious and rather imaginative names." Biolsi, "Birth of the Reservation," 28. Rose Stremlau has described the unwavering resistance of the Nighthawk Cherokees to the efforts of the Dawes Commission to enumerate them and their families. Stremlau, *Sustaining the Cherokee Family*, 107–9, 146–47, 152, 165–74. Beyond the borders of the United States, Angela Wanhalla has detailed the Ngāi Tahu of Southern New Zealand's suspicion, resistance, and manipulation of an 1890 census that sought to impose government-defined categories of "Māori" and "half-castes." Wanhalla, "The Politics of 'Periodical Counting,'" 198–217. Brian Edward Hubner recounts Iroquois, Huron, and Mohawk people refusing to speak to census enumerators: "This is the Whiteman's Law," 201–2. Robin Jarvis Brownlie describes First Nations people hiring lawyers in order to be enfranchised (a legal status similar to competency) in *A Fatherly Eye*, 140. In Australia in the 1960s, Aboriginal people lobbied for inclusion on their own terms in the national census. Clark, *Aborigines & Activism*, 180–202.

67. Million, *Therapeutic Nations*, 25.
68. Simpson, "On Ethnographic Refusal," 78.
69. Corntassel, "Who Is Indigenous?," 75.
70. Lyons, *X-Marks*, 60 (emphasis in original).
71. Grande, San Pedro, and Windchief, "Indigenous Peoples and Identity in the 21st Century," 107.
72. Mihesuah, "American Indian History as a Field of Study," 144.

1. FRAUD

1. I use the Native-referent term "Anishinaabeg" (sometimes spelled Anishinaabek) to refer to the peoples of the White Earth Reservation. In the past, these peoples have been referred to by mainstream America as "Chippewas" and today are often known as "Ojibwes."
2. William M. Campbell to Henry M. Rice, 14 September 1895, E1298 Letters Sent by the Chairman, 1893–1900, Chippewa Commission Records, RG 75, NARA–Great Lakes Region [hereafter Chippewa Commission Records], (emphasis in original).
3. E1303 Proceedings in Enrollment Cases, 1897–1899, Chippewa Commission Records, 3.
4. [Applicants] to D. S. Hall, 15 December 1891, E1297 Correspondence, 1889–1900, Chippewa Commission Records.
5. Vezina v. United States et al., No. 4725 Circuit Court of Appeals, Eighth Circuit, 245 F. 411, 1917.
6. Adams, *Assault on a Culture*; McDonnell, *Masters of Empire*; Witgen, *An Infinity of Nations*; Stark, "Marked by Fire," 119–49.
7. Meyer, *The White Earth Tragedy*, 39–40, 103.

8. Witgen, "The Rituals of Possession," 646. Jacqueline Peterson, in "Prelude to Red River," 41–67, shows that by the 1820s intermarriage between Indians and whites had resulted in a sizeable network of Métis towns, villages, and trade relationships in the Great Lakes region.

9. Bohaker, "Nindoodemag," 23–52. See also McNally, *Ojibwe Singers*.

10. Miller, *Ogimaag*.

11. Treuer, *Warrior Nation*, 75.

12. U.S. Congress, House, *Final Report of the United States Chippewa Commission*, 97.

13. U.S. Congress, House, *Final Report*, 98.

14. U.S. Congress, House, *Final Report*, 105, 108.

15. U.S. Congress, House, *Final Report*, 112.

16. U.S. Congress, House, *Final Report*, 190.

17. U.S. Congress, House, *Final Report*, 170.

18. U.S. Congress, House, *Final Report*, 94.

19. U.S. Congress, House, *Final Report*, 112.

20. Thomas J. Morgan to D. S. Hall, 10 December 1891, E1297, Chippewa Commission Records.

21. U.S. Congress, House, *Annual Report of the Commissioner of Indian Affairs, 1895*, 29.

22. Meyer, *The White Earth Tragedy*, 95–96.

23. Meyer, *The White Earth Tragedy*, 96.

24. Chairman, Chippewa Commission to commissioner of Indian Affairs, 9 December 1890, E1297, Chippewa Commission Records.

25. T. J. Morgan to D. S. Hall, 10 December 1891, E1297, Chippewa Commission Records.

26. Doerfler, *Those Who Belong*, 4.

27. Geo. H. Shields to Hon. Geo Chandler, 18 February 1891, E1297, Chippewa Commission Records.

28. In all but one of the eleven cases the applicants were described as being of mixed descent. Three were enrolled, five were turned away, two were referred to the commissioner of Indian Affairs, and one decision went unrecorded. T. J. Morgan to D. S. Hall, 10 December 1891, E1297, Chippewa Commission Records. A letter from the Department of the Interior is evidence that some of these decisions were not final. C. F. Larabee, Department of the Interior, to D. S. Hall, 25 May 1898, E1297, Chippewa Commission Records.

29. D. J. Hall to T. J. Morgan, 13 November 1891, E1298, Chippewa Commission Records.

30. Chairman to commissioner of Indian Affairs, 8 March 1893, E1298, Chippewa Commission Records.

31. D. J. Hall to T. J. Morgan, 13 November 1891, E1298, Chippewa Commission Records.

32. William M. Campbell to Frank C. Armstrong, acting commissioner of Indian Affairs, 20 June 1894, E1298, Chippewa Commission Records.

33. Chairman to commissioner of Indian Affairs, 8 March 1893, E1298, Chippewa Commission Records.

34. Frank C. Armstrong to the Secretary of the Interior, 5 October 1893, E1298, Chippewa Commission Records.

35. Thomas Smith, acting commissioner of Indian Affairs to M. R. Baldwin, 22 May 1896, E1298, Chippewa Commission Records.

36. For example, in answer to Chairman Hall's inquiry about a particularly difficult case, the Department of the Interior replied: "If [the applicant] has never heretofore been enrolled with any of the bands of Chippewa Indian of Minnesota, the evidence should establish: First, that she is a Chippewa Indian of Minnesota; that her parents (or one of them) were *recognized* members of some band of Chippewas of the State prior to January 14, 1889, living with them and drawing annuities with them; that he or she actually removed to the White Earth Reservation with the *bona fide* intention of making his or her permanent home." C. F. Larabee, Department of the Interior to D. S. Hall, 25 May 1898, E1297, Chippewa Commission Records.

37. Chairman, Chippewa Commission to T. J. Morgan, commissioner of Indian Affairs, 30 July 1892, E1300, Letters Sent by the Chairman to the Secretary of the Interior, May–December, 1892, Chippewa Commission Records.

38. William M. Campbell to D. M. Browning, 24 February 1894, E1298, Chippewa Commission Records.

39. *Annual Report of the Commissioner of Indian Affairs, 1895*, 29.

40. Doerfler, *Those Who Belong*, 29. See also Meyer, *The White Earth Tragedy*, 118–19, 180–81.

41. Doerfler, *Those Who Belong*, 12.

42. Box 2, Testimony Volume 3: Cove, Minnesota, 5 June 1914, RG 118, Records of the U.S. Attorney, U.S. Department of Justice, District of Minnesota, Records Related to the White Earth Cases, 1911–1919, NARA–Great Lakes Region [hereafter U.S. Attorney, Records Related to White Earth Cases].

43. Doerfler, *Those Who Belong*, 24.

44. Doerfler, *Those Who Belong*, 12–13.

45. Meyer, *The White Earth Tragedy*, 155.

46. Indian Rights Association, *Twenty-Eighth Annual Report, 1920*, 29–30.

47. Fritz, "The Last Hurrah of Christian Humanitarian Indian Reform," 147–62.

48. Meyer, *The White Earth Tragedy*, 160–61.

49. Secretary of interior to attorney general, 31 March 1910, E1293 Records of Special Agent John H. Hinton, Correspondence, 1910–1914, White Earth Reservation Records, RG 75, NARA–Great Lakes Region [hereafter White Earth Reservation Records].

50. J. H. Hinton to [applicant], 11 February 1913, E1293, White Earth Reservation Records.

51. J. H. Hinton to [applicant], 17 April 1913, E1293, White Earth Reservation Records.

52. Fritz, "The Last Hurrah of Christian Humanitarian Reform," 156.

53. Geo. Wickersham to secretary of interior, 19 March 1910, E1293 White Earth Reservation Records.

54. J. H. Hinton to commissioner of Indian Affairs, 18 June 1910, E1293, White Earth Reservation Records.

55. Volume Four: Testimony on behalf of the plaintiff, taken before C. E. McNamara, Notary Public, at the Federal Building, the City of Minneapolis, Minnesota, December 5th, 1914; E. C. O'Brien and Charles W. Smith, appearing on behalf of the plaintiff; and R. J. Powell appearing on behalf of the defendants, RG 118, Records Related to the White Earth Cases.

56. United States District Court, District of Minnesota, Sixth Division, United States of America, plaintiff, vs. John C. Cabanne, Defendant, RG 118, U.S. Attorney, Records Related to White Earth Cases.

57. United States v. First National Bank of Detroit, Minnesota; United States v. Nichols-Chisholm Lumber Company; United States v. Nichols-Chisholm Lumber Company, Nos. 873, 874, 875, Supreme Court of the United States, 234 U.S. 245; 34 S. Ct. 846; 58 L. Ed. 1298; 1914.

58. Beaulieu, "Curly Hair and Big Feet," 281–314.

59. Bokovoy, *The San Diego World's Fairs and Southwestern Memory*, 87.

60. Aleš Hrdlička, "Physical anthropology of the Lenape or Delawares, and of the eastern Indians in general."

61. Upham, "Holmes Anniversary Volume," 182.

62. Jenks, *Indian–White*, 7.

63. Albert E. Jenks, on Direct Examination, 7 July 1914, Abstract of Testimony of Dr. Jenks, U.S. Attorney, Records Related to White Earth Cases.

64. Albert E. Jenks, on Direct Examination, 7 July 1914, Abstract of Testimony of Dr. Jenks, U.S. Attorney, Records Related to White Earth Cases. Aleš Hrdlička had a similar opinion conflicting with that of eugenicists. See Bokovoy, *The San Diego Fairs and Southwestern Memory*, 101–4.

65. Bokovoy, *The San Diego World's Fairs and Southwestern Memory*, 102–3; Spencer, "Aleš Hrdlička, M.D., 1869–1943."

66. Smithers, "The Dark Side of Anti-Racism," 67.

67. Meyer, *The White Earth Tragedy,* 167.
68. U.S. Congress, House, *Report in the Matter of the Investigation of the White Earth Reservation,* 1:v.
69. U.S. Congress, House, *Report,* xxii.
70. U.S. Congress, House, *Report,* xv.
71. U.S. Congress, House, *Report,* xxiii–xxiv.
72. U.S. Congress, House, *Report,* xi.
73. Meyer, *The White Earth Tragedy,* 170.
74. Doerfler, *Those Who Belong,* 29; Vizenor, *Survivance*; Simpson, *Mohawk Interruptus,* 7.
75. Vizenor and Doerfler, *The White Earth Nation,* 64.

2. CHAOS

1. J. W. Howell, Report Relating to the Enrollment of Citizens and Freedmen of the Five Civilized Tribes, 1909, E57, RG 75, National Archives and Records Administration—Southwest Region, Fort Worth, 37–38. Carter reports that the commission subsequently relied on the case as confirmation of its position that it could not consider any application that was pending on October 31, 1902, even if the person was on a tribal roll. Carter, *The Dawes Commission and the Allotment of the Five Civilized Tribes,* 119–20.
2. *Report of the Commissioner to the Five Civilized Tribes, 1912,* 6.
3. *Report of the Commissioner to the Five Civilized Tribes, 1910,* 5.
4. Smithers, *The Cherokee Diaspora,* 174–75.
5. Chang, *The Color of the Land*; Debo, *And Still the Waters Run*; McDonnell, *The Dispossession of the American Indian*; Sober, *The Intruders.*
6. Carter, *The Dawes Commission,* 39–105; McLaughlin, *After the Trail of Tears.* See also Chang, *The Color of the Land,* 138.
7. U.S. Senate, *Allotting Indian lands in Indian Territory,* 6.
8. It did, however, mention blood in a paragraph making arrangements for the coal and asphalt revenue earned by mines owned by the Choctaw and Chickasaw tribes, showing that blood was already becoming a ubiquitous way of thinking about who deserved access to tribal revenues. *An Act for the Protection of the People of the Indian Territory, and for other purposes.*
9. U.S. Census Bureau, *Statistics of the Indian Population,* 12.
10. U.S. Census Bureau, *Statistics of the Indian Population,* 32.
11. Armstrong, *Report of a Trip Made in Behalf of The Indian Rights Association to Some Indian Reservations of the Southwest,* 26.
12. Porter and Wright, *Extra Census Bulletin,* 8.
13. *Report of the Commissioner to the Five Civilized Tribes, 1912,* 53–54.
14. *Report of the Commissioner to the Five Civilized Tribes, 1913,* 94.

15. *Report of the Commissioner to the Five Civilized Tribes, 1913,* 62.
16. Miles, *Ties That Bind,* 192. In addition to Miles's work, see Brooks, "Confounding the Color Line," 125–33; Chang, "Where Will the Nation Be at Home?," 80–99; Grinde Jr. and Taylor, "Red vs Black," 211–29; Lovett, "African and Cherokee by Choice," 203–29; Malcomson, *One Drop of Blood,* 66–114; May, *African Americans and Native Americans in the Creek and Cherokee Nations;* McMullen, "Blood and Culture"; Naylor, *African Cherokees in Indian Territory;* Micco, "Blood and Money," 121–44; Ray, "A Race or a Nation?," 387–463; Saunt, *Black, White, and Indian* and "The English Has Now a Mind to Make Slaves of Them All," 47–75; Sturm, *Blood Politics* and "Blood Politics, Racial Classification, and Cherokee National Identity." Historians have also focused on how differences in ancestry broadly dictated how Indians reacted to the allotment process. Erik Zissu and Circe Sturm investigate how Five Tribes Indians used and responded to discourses of "blood." Zissu, *Blood Matters;* Sturm, *Blood Politics.* Andrew Denson also touches on the topic in *Demanding the Cherokee Nation,* 201–18. David Chang shows how the Creek Nation fared under the Dawes Commission's efforts to make land ownership dependent on race. Chang, *The Color of the Land.*
17. Mulroy, "Mixed Race in the Seminole Nation," 114.
18. Van Riper, "The American Administrative State," 23.
19. *Report of the Commission to the Five Civilized Tribes, 1905,* 8.
20. Carter, *The Dawes Commission,* 71.
21. *Sixth Annual Report of the Commission to the Five Civilized Tribes, 1899,* 10.
22. *Annual Report of the Commission to the Five Civilized Tribes, 1896,* 89.
23. *Report of the Commission to the Five Civilized Tribes, 1907,* 6.
24. *Report of the Commission to the Five Civilized Tribes, 1905,* 9. This was not the only time the commission made this confession. "It must not be assumed that the report of the testimony and field judgments is absolutely full and correct," wrote Commissioners Needle and Breckinridge in transmitting the details of eighty-one cases to the commission. "Mistakes and omissions were unavoidable, and review and verification at the time impossible, from the very nature of field work." Commissioners Needle and Breckinridge to Commission to the Five Civilized Tribes, 19 October 1901, E65A Records of the Chief Clerk of the Cherokee Enrollment Division, 1900–1901, Cherokee Enrollment, RG 75, NARA–Fort Worth. Sometimes the commission's lack of rigor reportedly worked to the advantage of people with shaky claims, or to some at least it seemed that way. William Chisholm, who lived in the Cherokee Nation from 1894 to about 1919, was in Tahlequah when some "Cherokees were filing claims for allotments. W. W. Hastings was in the office at that time. Two girls

came in and proved their right to land all right, but they were red-headed and freckled-faced and Hastings couldn't help but ask them what degree of Cherokee blood they were. They said 'full-blood' and he just winked and signed them up as such." Interview with William Chisholm, [n.d] Vol. 17, Interview ID 7390, Indian Pioneer Papers, Western History Collections, University of Oklahoma, Norman, Oklahoma, 454–55 [hereafter Indian Pioneer Papers].

25. Carter, *The Dawes Commission*, 125, 70, 82, 145.

26. Howell, *Report*, 125.

27. Howell, *Report*, 135–36.

28. Howell, *Report*, 178–79.

29. *Sixth Annual Report of the Commission to the Five Civilized Tribes, 1899*, 11.

30. Quoted in Kent Carter, *The Dawes Commission*, 44.

31. Stremlau, *Sustaining the Cherokee Family*.

32. Proceedings before George Reed, Clerk to the Commission of Indian Affairs, 12 November 1910, Folder 4, box 1, E58A Transcripts of Testimony Given to W.C. Pollock, 1910–1911, Five Civilized Tribes Agency, RG 75, NARA–Fort Worth.

33. Howell reported this happening in one case in Indian Territory in 1878. Howell, *Report*, 103.

34. *Letter from Albert J. Lee*, 2.

35. Howell, *Report*, 128–29. "Joe and Dillard Perry Cases," E90B1 Dockets of Special Enrollment Cases 1905-1907, Muskogee, RG 75, NARA–Fort Worth. Kent Carter reports that the Perrys were put back on the rolls in 1908 after a U.S. Supreme Court ruling on a separate but related case. Carter, *The Dawes Commission*, 100.

36. Howell, *Report*, 23, 65, 73, 149.

37. Stremlau, *Sustaining the Cherokee Family*, 33, 119.

38. Howell, *Report*, 39.

39. Interview with James P. Sneed, [n.d.], Vol. 85, Interview ID 5850, Indian Pioneer Papers, 383.

40. File 60, Folder One, E74 Applications for Enrollment Through Intermarriage, Records Relating to Cherokee Citizenship, RG 75, National Archives and Records Administration—Fort Worth.

41. Interview with Mary Grayson, May 20, 1937, Indian Pioneer Papers, Vol. 35, Interview ID 5995, 458. For more on the Grayson family see Saunt, *Black, White, and Indian*.

42. Interview with Jobe McIntosh (Creek), Vol. 29, Interview ID T-548, Doris Duke Collection, Western History Collections, University of Oklahoma, Norman, Oklahoma, 26 [hereafter Doris Duke Collection].

43. Interview with Mrs. Hattie Pierce Nelson, July 22, 1937, Vol. 66, Interview ID 6849, Indian Pioneer Papers, 286.

44. Protest of the Choctaw Indians Against Re-opening the Choctaw and Chickasaw Tribal Rolls, n.d., Choctaw National Records, Oklahoma Historical Society, Oklahoma City [hereafter Choctaw National Records.]

45. J. B. Mayes to National Council, 10 November 1891, Cherokee National Records, Oklahoma Historical Society.

46. An interview with Cook McCracken, n.d., Vol. 57, Interview ID 5131, Indian Pioneer Papers, 14.

47. An interview with Mrs Mary J. Barker, 24 February 1938, Vol. 4, Interview ID 13113, Indian Pioneer Papers, 8.

48. Stremlau, *Sustaining the Cherokee Family*, 13.

49. Carter, *Dawes Commission*, 51.

50. "Affidavit of Witness," Letters and Documents Relating to Citizenship in the Creek Nation, 1896–1910, CRN 4, Oklahoma Historical Society.

51. Carter, *Dawes Commission*, 71; C. Price, Commissioner to Delegates, Choctaw Nations, 27 April 1882, Volume 47 March–April 1882, E96 Letters Sent "Land," RG 75, NARA–Washington DC [hereafter E96 Letters Sent]. See also Katherine M. B. Osburn, "Any Sane Person," 451–71; Yarborough, "Dis Land Which Jines Dat of Ole Master's."

52. See, for example, A. Price, commissioner of Indian Affairs to [father of inter-married man], 8 July 1881, and A. Price, Comm., to [white woman married to Chickasaw man], 9 July 1881, Volume 42, June–August 1881, A. Price, commissioner of Indian Affairs to [man marrying the white widow of a Chickasaw man], November 3, 1881, Volume 51, August–October 1882, E96 Letters Sent "Land," RG 75, NARA–Washington DC.

53. Burton, *Indian Territory and the United States*, 7–8.

54. Carter, *Dawes Commission*, 108.

55. McLaughlin, *After the Trail of Tears*, 357.

56. McLaughlin, *After the Trail of Tears*, 356.

57. OHS microfilm DC roll 4, quoted in Carter, *Dawes Commission*, 114.

58. Carter, *Dawes Commission*, 121; Stremlau, *Sustaining the Cherokee Family*, 153–57.

59. Robin Stann, interviewed by L. W. Wilson, journalist, 12 November 1937, Vol. 86, Interview ID 12117, Indian Pioneer Papers, 2.

60. Carter, "Snakes & Scribes."

61. Zellar, *African Creeks*, 226; see 194–230 for a full discussion of the Creek Nation's attempts to negotiate with the Dawes Commission and how that impacted on Creek freedpeople.

62. Protest of the Choctaw Indians Against Re-opening the Choctaw and Chickasaw Tribal Rolls, n.d., Choctaw National Records.

63. Schreier, "Indian or Freedman?," 460, 470.

64. Osburn, "Any Sane Person," 451–71.

65. Stremlau, *Sustaining the Cherokee Family,* 145.

66. Carter, *Dawes Commission,* 147. See, for example, U.S. Senate, *Allotting Indian lands in Indian Territory;* U.S. Senate, *Protest of Keetoowah Cherokees;* U.S. Senate, *Rights of Mississippi Choctaws in the Choctaw Nation.*

67. Stremlau, *Sustaining the Cherokee Family,* 146–47.

68. Stremlau, *Sustaining the Cherokee Family,* 107–8. See also Deer and Knapp, "Muscogee Constitutional Jurisprudence," 125–81;. Harring, "Crazy Snake and the Creek Struggle for Sovereignty," 365–80; Holm, "Indian Lobbyists," 115–34; Littlefield Jr. and Underhill, "The 'Crazy Snake Uprising' of 1909," 307–24; and *Memorial from the Keetoowah Society.*

69. Carter, *The Dawes Commission,* 55, 135, 147, 80–84

70. Hoke Smith to Henry Dawes, "General Letter of Instructions," 28 November 1893, quoted in Carter, *The Dawes Commission,* 3.

71. For example, Commissioner McKennon's testimony to the House of Representatives Committee on Indian Affairs in 1896 described corruption so great that the commission was "compelled to report that these governments in all their branches are wholly corrupt, irresponsible, and unworthy to be longer trusted with the care and control of the money and other property of Indian citizens, much less their lives, which they scarcely pretend to protect." This alleged tribal corruption removed any obligation the government had to uphold the treaties it had signed with the Five Tribes. "There is no alternative left to the United States but to assume the responsibility for future conditions in this Territory," McKennon argued. "The pretense that the Government is debarred by treaty obligations from interference in the present condition of affairs in this Territory is without foundation. The present conditions are not 'treaty conditions.'" Indeed, he said, the treaties themselves obligated the government to undermine the tribal governments: "There is not only no treaty obligation on the part of the United States to maintain, or even to permit, the present condition of affairs in the Indian Territory, but on the contrary the whole structure and tenor of the treaties forbid it. If our Government is obligated to maintain the treaties according to their original intent and purpose, it is obligated to blot out at once present conditions." U.S. Congress, Senate, *Argument Made By Judge McKennon,* 4–5, 63.

72. *Report of the Commission to the Five Civilized Tribes, 1905,* 5–6.

73. Sturm, *Blood Politics,* 173.

74. U.S. Congress, Senate, *Report of the Commission Appointed to Negotiate with the Five Civilized Tribes,* 68–69.

75. *Report of the Commissioner to the Five Civilized Tribes, 1913,* 5.

76. Debo, *And Still the Waters Run,* 179.

77. An interview with Lillie Gordon Franks, October 29, 1937, Vol. 32, Interview ID 12005, Indian Pioneer Papers, 53.

78. Bonnin, Fabens, Sniffen, *Oklahoma's Poor Rich Indians*, 14.
79. *Report of the Commissioner to the Five Civilized Tribes, 1908*, 3–4.
80. Dana Kelsey reported that one "average" Indian Territory "school reported that less than 25 per cent of even the larger boys had any intelligent idea of their lands." Kelsey made it an "important feature" of schoolroom work to teach allotted children about their allotments, and schools even collected data about individuals' tracts of land, what parts of it were restricted or unrestricted, its location, the acreage of timber or agricultural land, its value, the present use being made of the land, and its rental value or agricultural potential. This information also provided "valuable material for use in arithmetic and language, besides giving the pupils knowledge of immediate and vital importance." *Report of the Commissioner to the Five Civilized Tribes, 1912*, 92.
81. *Report of the Superintendent for the Five Civilized Tribes, 1916*, 9.
82. Moorehead, *Our National Problem*, 16
83. Interview with Ben Hartness (Cherokee), Vol. 15, T-460-2, Doris Duke Collection, 1–2.
84. *Report of the Commissioner to the Five Civilized Tribes, 1912*, 54.
85. *Report of the Commissioner to the Five Civilized Tribes, 1913*, 93.
86. General Services File 53 Enrollment—Citizenship—Degree of Indian Blood, Central Classified Files 1907–1939, RG 75, NARA-Washington DC [hereafter General Services File 53, NARA-Washington].
87. C. F. Larrabee, acting commissioner to Charles G. Covert, 7 November 1907, File 86886-07, General Services File 53, NARA-Washington.
88. The Five Tribes continued to police their citizenship throughout the twentieth century. For a discussion of their efforts in the second half of the twentieth century, see Miller, *Claiming Tribal Identity*.
89. *An Act Making Appropriations for the Current and Contingent Expenses of the Bureau of Indian Affairs, 1920*, 9. The Five Tribes, the "Chippewa" of Minnesota, the Osage, and the Menominee were exempt from this act, no doubt because separate legislation existed governing their enrollment.

3. PRACTICALLY WHITE

1. Hoxie, *A Final Promise*, 180.
2. Leupp, "Indian Lands: Their Administration," 141.
3. Indian Rights Association, *Twenty-Seventh Annual Report, 1919*, 32.
4. Bonnin, Fabens, and Sniffen, *Oklahoma's Poor Rich Indians*, 7.
5. Cohen, *Handbook of Federal Indian Law*, 216.
6. McDonnell, *The Dispossession of the American Indian*, 121.
7. Deloria, *Indians in Unexpected Places*, 151.

8. Office of Indian Affairs, *Indian Land Tenure, Economic Status, and Population Trends*, 7.

9. C. F. Larrabee, acting commissioner to Agents and Superintendents, 6 May 1907, File 73385-1907-127, Tulalip General Services File 127, Indians Competent—Roll of Honour, Central Classified Files 1907-1939, RG 75, NARA-Washington DC [hereafter File 127, Indians Competent].

10. F. E. Leupp to secretary of the interior, 29 January 1908, File 6912-1908-127, Pottawatomi General Services File 127, Indians Competent.

11. Schmeckebier, *The Office of Indian Affairs*, 151.

12. Schmeckebier, *The Office of Indian Affairs*, 148.

13. C. F. Hauke to [applicant], 15 January 1910, box 6, Seneca General Services File 127, Indians Competent.

14. R. G. Valentine to D. M. Carr, superintendent Yakima School, 10 September 1912, Yakima General Services File 127, Indians Competent.

15. For a discussion of "political competency" as applied to Native Americans see Basson, "Challenging Boundaries and Belongings," 158-61.

16. Cohen, *Handbook of Federal Indian Law*, 167.

17. It also conveyed a particular set of legal rights about land, which meant it sometimes had little to do with the personal attributes. Felix Cohen gives the example of "Charles Curtis, who, though he became Senator and Vice President of the United States, remained all his life an incompetent Indian, incapable of disposing of his trust property by deed or devise, without securing the approval of the Secretary of the Interior." In addition, in some times and places, the restrictions on alienation of lands imposed by competency ran "with the land and [were] not personal to the allottee" which meant that people could be given a fee patent for some sections of their land while other sections remained restricted. Cohen, *Handbook of Federal Indian Law*, 167, 226.

18. U.S. Congress, Senate, *Rights of Mixed Blood Indians*; U.S. Congress, House, *Confirming Title of Mixed-Blood Indians to Lands*; U.S. Congress, Senate, *Title of Mixed-Blood Indians to Their Lands*.

19. Leupp, *The Indian and His Problem*, 344.

20. McDonnell, *The Dispossession of the American Indian*, 105.

21. See Harmon, "American Indians and Land Monopolies in the Gilded Age," 113-14.

22. C. F. Hauke, chief clerk, to Mr. Julian H. Fleming, 12 October 1917, File 85832-1917-127, Pottawatomi General Services File 127, Indians Competent; Simpson, *Mohawkus Interruptus*, 7.

23. [Applicants] to Cato Sells, 14 February 1918, C. F. Hauk to Ira C. Deaver, 11 January 1918, Supt. Seneca School and Agency to commissioner of Indian Affairs,

10 December 1917, File 113704–17–127, Seneca General Services File 127, Indians Competent.

24. Stremlau, *Sustaining the Cherokee Family*, 201.

25. Confidential report on [applicant] by Cody Gray, M.D, n.d., box 6, Applications for Certificates of Competency, 1945–1965, Osage Agency, RG 75 NARA–Fort Worth.

26. Indian Rights Association, *Twenty-Seventh Annual Report*, 31.

27. Benj. Mossinau, Acting U.S. Agent to commissioner of Indian Affairs, 20 May 1908, box 1, Records Relating to Application for Removal of Restrictions on Cherokee Allotments, 1906–1908, Records Concerning the Removals and Restrictions on Land Sales and Certificates of Competency, Records of the Land Division, RG 75, NARA–Washington DC.

28. C. F. Hauke to [applicant], n.d.; Ira C. Deaver to the commissioner of Indian Affairs, 31 October, 1917; J. M. Stewart to [applicant], 21 January 1937 and [applicant] to commissioner of Indian Affairs, 10 May 1938, box 8, Seneca General Services File 127, Indians Competent.

29. Report of commissioner of Indian Affairs Cato Sells, October 15, 1917, quoted in Washburn, *The American Indian and the United States*, 868–69.

30. Schmeckebier, *The Office of Indian Affairs*, 154.

31. Cohen, *Handbook of Federal Indian Law*, 26.

32. U.S. Congress, House, *Cancellation of Patents in Fee Simple to Indians*; U.S. Congress, House, *Cancellation of Certain Fee Simple Patents Issued to Indians*; U.S. Congress, Senate, *Cancellation of Certain Fee Simple Patents Issued to Indians*.

33. Report of commissioner of Indian Affairs, 1917, quoted in Washburn, *The American Indian*, 867.

34. Sells, "The 'First Americans' as Loyal Citizens," 524.

35. C. F. Hauke, acting commissioner of Indian Affairs, to the secretary of the interior, 2 April 1919, and Cato Sells to [applicant], 24 May 1918, Cheyenne and Arapaho General Services File 127, Indians Competent.

36. Acting chief clerk to John W. Shafer, 9 July 1919, File 52031–1919–127, Digger General Services File 127, Indians Competent.

37. Indian Rights Association, *Twenty-Seventh Annual Report*, 30.

38. U.S. Congress, House, *Indians of the United States, Field Investigation*, 18.

39. U.S. Congress, House, *Reorganizing the Indian Service*, 2.

40. Office of Indian Affairs, *Indian Land Tenure*, 6.

41. Cohen, *Handbook of Federal Indian Law*, 448–49; U.S. Congress, House, *Reorganizing the Indian Service*, 2.

42. Although, by contrast, the Kaw Nation were also subject to special legislation in 1924 which extended the period of restriction to those who had not yet been declared competency (the report said there were only 21 such people out of 420

living on the reservation) because oil had been discovered on the reservation and it was "well known that many of the Kaw Indians are incompetent to manage their own business affairs." U.S. Congress, Senate, *To Authorize the Extension of the Period of Restriction Against Alienation on the Homestead Allotments*, 1924.

43. A Petition to the Honourable the President of the United States [received in the Office of Indian Affairs on 2 January 1917], Cheyenne and Arapaho General Services File 127, Indians Competent.

44. Richard H. Harper to C. F. Larrabee, 15 August 1907, Charles E. Shell to C. F. Larrabee, 11 July 1907, Francis E. Leupp to secretary of the interior, 28 August 1907, Francis E. Leupp to superintendent of Cheyenne and Arapaho Agency, 3 September 1907, Francis E. Leupp to secretary of interior, 29 January 1908, Cheyenne and Arapaho General Services File 127, Indians Competent.

45. Charles E. Shell to commissioner of Indian Affairs, 3 March 1909, Cheyenne and Arapaho General Services File 127, Indians Competent.

46. Charles E. Shell to commissioner of Indian Affairs, 18 August 1909, Cheyenne and Arapaho General Services File 127, Indians Competent.

47. Charles E. Shell to commissioner of Indian Affairs, 18 October 1909, F. H. Abbott, acting commissioner to F. E. Farrell, 16 April 1913, Cheyenne and Arapaho General Services File 127, Indians Competent.

48. Donald J. Berthrong, "Legacies of the Dawes Act," 43–44.

49. A Petition to the Honourable the President of the United States [received in the Office of Indian Affairs on 2 January 1917], Cheyenne and Arapaho General Services File 127, Indians Competent.

50. E. B. Meritt to Mr. O. M. McPherson, 12 January 1917, Cheyenne and Arapaho General Services File 127, Indians Competent.

51. O. M. McPherson to Franklin K. Lane, 4 February 1917, Cheyenne and Arapaho General Services File 127, Indians Competent.

52. 19 January 1917, E485, Journal of Cheyenne and Arapaho Competency Board, Jan–Feb 1917, RG 75, NARA–Washington DC.

53. 19 January 1917, E485 Journal of Cheyenne and Arapaho Competency Board, Jan–Feb 1917.

54. Leupp, "Indian Lands: Their Administration," 141.

55. Berthrong, "Legacies of the Dawes Act," 44–45.

56. Franklin K. Lane to the President, 26 March 1917, Cheyenne and Arapaho General Services File 127, Indians Competent.

57. McDonnell, "Land Policy on the Omaha Reservation," 405. In a longer study, McDonnell argued that the Indian Office, in particular Commissioners McLaughlin and Lane, members of the first Competency Commission created in 1915, also forced Indians into accepting patents. McDonnell, *The Dispossession of the American Indian*, 98.

58. Application for a Certificate of Competency, 15 March 1914, box 6, Seneca General Services File 127, Indians Competent.

59. Application for a Certificate of Competency, 10 February 1915, box 7, Seneca General Services File 127, Indians Competent.

60. Application for a Certificate of Competency, 29 May 1915, box 7, Seneca General Services File 127, Indians Competent.

61. Chang, *The Color of the Land*, 127–28.

62. [Applicant] to Cato Sells, 22 September 1919; E. B. Meritt to [Applicant], 4 May 1920 and Carl F. Mayer to Cato Sells, 6 October 1919, File 81553-19–127, Seneca General Services File 127, Indians Competent.

63. Deloria, *Indians in Unexpected Places*, 151–82.

64. C. L. Ellis, special Indian agent and member of Quapaw Competency Commission to Mr. E. P. Holcombe, chief supervisor, U.S. Indian Service, Denver Colorado, 19 December 1910, box 5, Seneca General Services File 127, Indians Competent.

65. Interview with Hazel Lohah Harper, Vol. 46, T-253, Doris Duke Collection, 1–5.

66. Gertrude Bonnin to President Wilson, 29 November 1918, General Services File 53 Enrollment—Citizenship—Degree of Indian Blood, box 22196347, 1918, Central Classified Files 1907–1939, RG 75, NARA-Washington DC.

67. Memorial from delegates from the Cherokee, Choctaw, Creek, and Seminole Nations of Indians, *Congressional Record,* 45th cong., 2nd sess. (22 April 1878), 2711.

68. Interview with Joseph Rogers (Delaware), Vol. 31, T-572-1, Doris Duke Collection, 11.

69. Interview with Clarence King (Ottawa), Vol. 49, T-443-1, Doris Duke Collection, 6–7.

70. Ross Swimmer, Former Principal Chief, Cherokee Nation of Oklahoma, "Firsthand Accounts," 181.

71. Leupp, "Indian Lands: Their Administration," 142.

72. *Congressional Record*, 65th cong. 2st sess., 1923–1924, 844. According to Felix Cohen, during the assimilation period Native American people could have become citizens either by being subject to some early treaties, special statutes or acts which naturalized members of certain tribes, being allotted, or no longer living with the tribe under the 1887 Dawes Act, by being an Indian woman who married a citizen under legislation passed in 1888, through competency (under the Burke Act of 1906, or by being an Indian man who enlisted to fight in World War I in legislation passed in 1919). Cohen, *Handbook of Federal Indian Law,* 153–54. As we see in the case of August A. Breuninger discussed in the introduction, it was not always so simple.

73. *Congressional Record*, 65th cong. 2st sess., 1923–1924, 854.

74. "An Act to authorize the Secretary of the Interior to issue certificates of citizenship to Indians," 43 Stat. 253, 68th cong. 1st sess., 1924, Chap 233.
75. For a comparative discussion of the mechanics by which Indigenous peoples were dispossessed from their lands in colonies around the Pacific, see Banner, *Possessing the Pacific*.

4. THE SAME OLD DEAL

1. [Applicant] to commissioner of Indian Affairs, 25 February 1939, box 1, E616 Applications and Other Records Relating to Registrations Under the Indian Reorganization Act of 1934, 1935–42, RG 75, NARA–Washington DC [hereafter E616, Applications].
2. Indian Reorganization Act, 1934, 48 Stat. 984, 25 U.S. C. 461, quoted in Cohen, *Handbook of Federal Law*, 5.
3. Circular No. 3134, John Collier to superintendents, "Enrollment under the Indian Reorganization Act," 7 March 1936, box 1, E616, Applications.
4. Wolfe, *Traces of History*, 197.
5. Sen. Rept. No. 1080, 73d cong., 2d sess. (May 10, 1934), quoted in Cohen, *Handbook of Federal Law*, 84.
6. Nash, LaFarge, and Ryan, *The New Day for the Indians*, 4.
7. Philp, "John Collier and the Controversy over the Wheeler–Howard Bill," 174.
8. Collier, "A Birdseye View of Indian Policy," 11.
9. Collier, "A Birdseye View of Indian Policy," 14.
10. Rusco, "The Indian Reorganization Act and Indian Self-Government," 49; Reinhardt, "A Crude Replacement," para. 5.
11. Quoted in Schwartz, "Red Atlantis Revisited," 521.
12. Quoted in Deloria and Lytle, *The Nations Within*, 133.
13. Brown, *Injun Joe's Ghost*, 181.
14. *Congressional Record*, 73d cong., 2d sess., 1934, 11725–6.
15. U.S. Congress, House, *Hearings Before the Committee on Indian Affairs*, 22.
16. Kelly, "The Indian Reorganization Act," 297.
17. U.S. Congress, House, *Conference Report on Indian Lands and Resources, to accompany S.3645*, 8. See Rusco, *A Fateful Time*, 268–69.
18. U.S. Senate Committee on Indian Affairs, *Hearings Before the Committee on Indian Affairs, Second Session on S.2755 and S.3645*, 263–64.
19. *Congressional Record*, 73d cong., 2d sess., 1934, 9270–1.
20. *Congressional Record*, 73d cong., 2d sess., 1934, 11734.
21. F. H. Daiker to [Applicant], 24 July 1936, box 1, E616, Applications.
22. J. M. Stewart, director of lands, Department of the Interior to [Applicant], n.d., box 11, E616, Applications.

23. Memorandum, June 18, 1938. Meeting of Enrollment Committee, June 3, 1938, box 3, E616, Applications.

24. O. H. Lipps to commissioner of Indian Affairs, 28 July 1937, box 16, E616, Applications.

25. Form letter 7602 from John Collier, n.d., box 1, E616, Applications.

26. Form letter 7602 from John Collier, n.d., box 1, E616, Applications.

27. Form letter 7602 from John Collier, n.d., box 1, E616, Applications.

28. Form letter 7602 from John Collier, n.d., box 1, E616, Applications.

29. Memorandum, Meeting of Enrollment Committee, 18 June 1938, box 3, E616, Applications.

30. Application for Registration as an Indian, box 1, E616, Applications.

31. List of Pending Cases, box 1, E616, Applications.

32. Attorney to chief of department, Office of Indian Affairs, 29 August 1938; E. J. Armstrong for the commissioner to attorney, 26 October 1938, Memo from Indian Organization, 21 June 1938, box 1, E616, Applications.

33. Indian Organization Memorandum, 21 June 1938, box 1, E616, Applications.

34. D. E. Murphy for commissioner of Indian Affairs to [Applicant], 28 June 1940; [Applicant's father] to [Applicant], n.d., box 1, E616, Applications.

35. E. E. McNeill, superintendent, Rocky Boy's Agency, Montana to Commissioner of Indian Affairs, 20 February 1942, box 1, E616, Applications.

36. Fred H. Daiker to Mr. O. M. Boggess, 26 November 1938, box 2, E616, Applications.

37. Henry Roe Cloud to commissioner of Indian Affairs, 11 November 1937; J. M. Stewart, Director of Lands, Memorandum for Mr. Daiker, 30 August 1937; William Zimmerman Jr. to J. E. Balmer, Supt. Turtle Mountain Agency, 13 September 1937; O. H. Lipps to Commissioner of Indian Affairs, 28 July 1937, box 16, E616, Applications.

38. F. H. Daiker, assistant to the commissioner of Indian Affairs, to [Applicant's acquaintance], 9 April 1937, box 1, E616, Applications.

39. F. H. Daiker to [Applicant], 21 June 1938, box 1, E616, Applications.

40. Chairman, Committee on Enrollment under Section 19, Memorandum to the Commissioner, 6 July 1936, box 3, E616 Applications and Other Records Relating to Registrations Under the Indian Reorganization Act of 1934, RG 75, NARA–Washington DC.

41. John Collier, "Memorandum: Registration as an 'Indian' in Accordance with Section 19, Indian Reorganization Act," 22 September 1936, box 3, E616, Applications.

42. Spruhan, "Indian as Race/Indian as Political Status," 30.

43. Spruhan, "Indian as Race/Indian as Political Status," 31.

44. Spruhan, "Indian as Race/Indian as Political Status," 32.

45. At least one woman (for a reason that unfortunately went unrecorded) was given special attention—she was examined and measured by Dr. W. Montague Cobb of

Howard University, and Aleš Hrdlička, whose work at White Earth is described in chapter 1, and her results were forwarded to Seltzer for his opinion. Fred H. Daiker, assistant to commissioner, to Dr. Carl C. Seltzer, Physical Anthropologist, Peabody Museum, Harvard University, 18 April 1940; commissioner of Indian Affairs to Dr. Aleš Hrdlička, curator of Physical Anthropology, National Museum, Washington 1 April 1940, box 1, Folder 'S', E616, Applications.

46. Sider, *Lumbee Indian Histories*, xv–xvi. See also Oakley, *Keeping the Circle*.

47. Lowery, *Lumbee Indians in the Jim Crow South*, 3.

48. "The Problem of Illegitimacy," box 15, E616, Applications (emphasis in original).

49. "The Problem of Illegitimacy."

50. "The Problem of Illegitimacy."

51. "The Problem of Illegitimacy."

52. Carl C. Seltzer, "Racial Diagnosis," box 13, E616, Applications.

53. "Genealogical Chart with Racial Diagnoses," box 15, E616, Applications.

54. Lowery, *Lumbee Indians in the Jim Crow South*, 140.

55. Cohen, *On the Drafting of Tribal Constitutions*, 173.

56. Gover, *Tribal Constitutionalism*, 114, 124–25.

57. Nash, LaFarge, and Ryan, *The New Day for the Indians*, 36. The view that the divide between Indians of mixed and full descent was cultural not blood-based has been echoed by scholars who have examined the workings of the New Deal on individual reservations, thus it was not always the case that "full bloods [were] opposed . . . and mixed bloods [were] supportive," as Wilcomb E. Washburn concluded as early as 1984. Washburn, "A Fifty-Year Perspective on the Indian Reorganization Act," 282. On Pine Ridge reservation in 1934 and 1935, for example, according to Akim D. Reinhardt, there was "a longstanding political dispute with cultural overtones between Oglalas. On one side were people [who] had tended to hold onto their lands after allotment and generally rejected those aspects of American culture that clashed with their own. They have occasionally been called 'traditionals,' 'full bloods,' or 'treaty Indians.' They tended to oppose the IRA. On the other side were those known as 'progressives' for their tendency to refute pre-conquest Lakota culture and embrace American ways, or as 'mixed bloods,' since most (but certainly not all) of them had mixed Euro-American/indigenous ancestry." Reinhardt, "A Crude Replacement," para. 34. Paul C. Rosier's study of the Blackfeet Nation also emphasizes the importance of the noting the different ways people of mixed and full descent approached economic development in understanding that nation's reaction and negotiation with the Collier administration. Rosier, *Rebirth of the Blackfeet Nation*, 56, 64, 83, 97. Philp's collection of writings and speeches about the workings of the 1934 act tells a similar story. "Tribal factionalism made it difficult to administer the IRA," Philp summarizes. "Internal disunity was caused by wide variations

in acculturation, mixed-versus full-blood rivalry, and religious and cultural differences." Philp, "Introduction," in *Indian Self-Rule*, 19. Graham D. Taylor used data from forty-four reservations between 1930 and 1933 from the Bureau of the Census Works Administration and the National Resources Board to catalogue the "patterns of assimilation or acculturation" that, he argues, affected each nation's response to the New Deal. He identifies three leading factors: the "extent of white intermarriage with the Indian group, based on the percentage of mixed-blood members," the extent of exposure to white education, and the extent to which tribal lands had been alienated. He asserts that a "basic division characteristic of all the Indians of the Northern Plains and Northwest [existed] between mixed-bloods and full-bloods." Taylor, *The New Deal and American Indian Tribalism*, 42–43, 50.

58. O. H. Lipps to commissioner of Indian Affairs, 28 July 1937, box 16, E616, Applications.

59. [Applicant] to the commissioner of Indian Affairs, 9 August 1937, box 1, E616, Applications.

60. [Applicant] to Mrs. Franklin D. Roosevelt, 13 September 1937, box 1, E616, Applications.

61. [Applicant] to Indian Bureau, 29 May 1937, F. H. Daiker to [Applicant], 7 July 1937, box 1, E616, Applications.

62. F. H. Daiker to [Applicant], 24 July 1936, box 1, E616, Applications.

63. Folder 892, box 12, E616, Applications.

64. Testimony given before "Members of the Siouian Investigating Commission and Mr. E. B. Sampson, Mr. James E. Bell and Mr. James E. Chavis, a committee representing the Indians of Robeson County, box 13, E616, Applications.

65. F. H. Daiker assistant to commissioner of Indian Affairs to [Applicant's acquaintance], 9 December 1938, box 1, E616, Applications.

66. [Applicant] to commissioner of Indian Affairs, 17 February 1939, box 1, E616, Applications.

5. COLORED

1. "Warning. To be attached to the backs of birth or death certificates of those believed to be incorrectly recorded as to color or race." Copy in Clerks Correspondence (A. T. Shields), Rockbridge County Court Records, box 1, Library of Virginia [hereafter Clerk's Correspondence (A. T. Shields).] The Rockbridge County Circuit Court still exists and, in giving permission for this image to be used, would like to emphasize that it no longer engages in such practices.

2. "During the first half of the twentieth century, then, the Monacans were an utterly powerless people," writes Samuel R. Cook. Cook, "The Monacan Indian Nation," 98.

3. Mandell, "The Saga of Sarah Muckamugg," 72, and "Shifting Boundaries of Race and Ethnicity," 466–501.

4. Saunt, Krauthamer, Miles, Naylor, and Sturm, "Rethinking Race and Culture in the Early South," 401. "If all Americans could map their genealogies back to 1500," writes Claudio Saunt, "millions would find that they are enmeshed in a tangled web of African, European, and native peoples. Too often, we stand at the crown of a branching family tree and trace our ancestors back to a single trunk of sturdy and supposedly pure stock . . . A more revealing exercise would place us at the base of the tree and follow the branches of our ancestors back in time as they divide and sub-divide, finally encompassing . . . all other forebears, African and Indian alike. . . . The revelation might persuade Americans to abandon the idea of race altogether." Saunt, *Black, White, and Indian,* 29.

5. Forbes, "The Manipulation of Race, Caste, and Identity," 5. See also Green, "Who's Who," 93–110; Higginbotham Jr. and Kopytoff, "Racial Purity and Inter-racial Sex"; Hollinger,"Amalgamation and Hypodescent," 1363–90; Nash, "The Hidden History of Mestizo America."

6. Hollinger, "Amalgamation and Hypodescent," 1368.

7. Sturm, *Blood Politics,* 188.

8. Forbes, "Undercounting Native Americans," 2.

9. Dippie, *The Vanishing American,* 250–51.

10. Peggy Pascoe's work on antimiscegenation laws shows that Native Americans were hardly ever targeted in anti-interracial marriage statutes, which were mostly directed at African Americans. Pascoe, "Race, Gender, and Intercultural Relations," 5–18; "Miscegenation Law, Court Cases, and Ideologies of 'Race,'" 44–69; "Race, Gender, and the Privileges of Property," 215–30.

11. Wolfe, "Land, Labor, and Difference."

12. Miles, *Ties that Bind,* xv.

13. For a discussion of Virginia's early attempts to regulate racial boundaries see Brown, *Good Wives, Nasty Wenches, and Anxious Patriarchs.*

14. Coleman, *That the Blood Stay Pure,* 121. The most comprehensive account of the Virginian Indians and their "racial integrity" is Rountree's *Pocahontas's People,* 219–68. Other important studies include: Coleman, *That the Blood Stay Pure*; Endo, "'The Word 'Mixed' without the 'Indian' Would Be Better," 92–107; Smith, *Managing White Supremacy*; Sherman, "The Last Stand," 69–82; Wallenstein, *Tell The Court I Love My Wife,* 137–41; and Dorr, "Arm in Arm," 143–66.

15. Smith, *Managing White Supremacy,* 4.

16. Anglo-Saxon Clubs of America, *Anglo-Saxon Clubs of America.*

17. Copy of 1924 act reprinted in Bureau of Vital Statistics, State Board of Health, Richmond, Va, *Eugenics in Relation to the New Family*; Smith, *Managing White*

Supremacy, 87–88. The control of intermarriage in Virginia has a well-documented history. See Higginbotham and Kopytoff, "Racial Purity and Interracial Sex"; Smits, "Abominable Mixture," 157–92; Wadlington, "The *Loving* Case," 1189–223; and Wallenstein, "Race, Marriage and the Law of Freedom," 371–437.

18. For more on this see Maillard, "The Pocahontas Exception," 351–86.

19. Smith, *Managing White Supremacy*, 88. See Bair, "Remapping the Black/White Body," 399–419, for a fascinating description of the involvement of the Black political community from outside the state.

20. W. A. Plecker to H. D. Kissenger, 17 May 1939, box 56, MSS 7284, John Powell Papers, Alderman Library, University of Virginia, Charlottesville. [Hereafter John Powell Papers.]

21. Walter A. Plecker to Matthew K. Sniffen, 27 June 1925, reel 42, *Indian Rights Association Papers, 1864–1973* (Glen Rock, NJ: Microfilming Corporation of America, 1975).

22. Smith, *Managing White Supremacy*, 99; Bureau of Vital Statistics, *Eugenics in Relation to the New Family*, 11.

23. W. A. Plecker to the clerks of Rockbridge, Amherst and Augusta Counties, 28 April 1924, Clerk's Correspondence (A. T. Shields).

24. W. A. Plecker to physicians of Virginia, June 1924 and W. A. Plecker to Mr. V. W. Davis, 13 May 1924, Clerk's Correspondence (A. T. Shields).

25. Letter from W. A. Plecker, 11 July 1924 and 15 August 1924, Clerk's Correspondence (A. T. Shields). See also W. A. Plecker to [midwife], 23 November 1925, Clerk's Correspondence (A. T. Shields).

26. Letter from W. A. Plecker, 9 March 1944, box 56, John Powell Papers.

27. Letter from state registrar, 30 April 1924, box 56, John Powell Papers.

28. Letter from W. A. Plecker, 22 October 1929, Clerks Correspondence (A. T. Shields).

29. Tucker, Bronson, Satterfield and Mays, Attorneys to W. A. Plecker, 1 October 1942, box 56, John Powell Papers.

30. Letter from W. A. Plecker, 9 October 1930, Clerks Correspondence (A. T. Shields).

31. W. A. Plecker to William E. Bradby, 2 February 1942, box 56, John Powell Papers.

32. Letter from W. A. Plecker, 11 June 1904, box 56, John Powell Papers.

33. Letter from W. A. Plecker, 3 February 1943, box 56, John Powell Papers.

34. Letter from W. A. Plecker, 10 March 1943. In another letter Plecker reiterated: "'Mixed' is not a desirable term, but in an emergency it might be accepted with the understanding that it always means colored and cannot be interpreted as 'Mixed Indian,' which is what they would try to do." W. A. Plecker to Dr. Algerd Powell, 30 March 1943, box 56, John Powell Papers.

35. There is some evidence that Jim Crow laws directly prompted at least one Virginian Indian nation to begin promoting their Indian status. George H. Marston, a white resident of Charles City County, told Plecker that he had

"never heard of a drop of Indian blood being in Charles City County until [a] 'Jim Crow' law was passed. As soon as that was passed, they had a big fish fry on the Chickahominy River at Osborne, and . . . on that day [they] organized as Indians." "A Statement as to the Origins of the So-called 'Indians' of Charles City County, as Given by Mr. George H. Marston, brother of Mr. E. H. Marston, both of whom have lived in Charles City County all of their lives in February 1925," undated typescript, box 56, John Powell Papers.

36. Letter from W. A. Plecker, 6 October 1930, Clerks Correspondence (A. T. Shields). Plecker retaliated by passing on the family name to the superintendent of schools in the relevant county, no doubt in the hope that the children would be ejected from their white school. A lack of written evidence that the family were colored was no deterrent; Plecker simply advised that "it is necessary to judge them upon the appearance of individual members of their family, even though other individuals are apparently white, according to Mendel's law." Letter from W. A. Plecker, 6 October 1930, Clerks Correspondence (A. T. Shields).

37. Letter from W. A. Plecker, 3 March 1942, box 56, John Powell Papers.

38. Letter from W. A. Plecker, 7 January 1930, Clerks Correspondence (A. T. Shields).

39. Letter from W. A. Plecker, 10 October 1930, Clerks Correspondence (A. T. Shields).

40. W. A. Plecker to A. T. Shields, 17 October 1930, Clerks Correspondence (A. T. Shields).

41. W. A. Plecker to Ernest S. Cox, 9 August 1924, box 56, John Powell Papers.

42. *Richmond Times-Dispatch*, 26 March 1925, cutting in box 56, John Powell Papers; *Richmond News-Leader*, 22 July 1925, 4, cutting in box 56, John Powell Papers.

43. Letter from W. A. Plecker, 7 November 1924, box 43, E. Lee Trinkle Executive Papers, 1922–26, Accession Number 21567b, Library of Virginia, Richmond. [Hereafter E. Lee Trinkle Executive Papers.]

44. W. A. Plecker to A. T. Shields, 17 October 1930, Clerks Correspondence (A. T. Shields).

45. Rountree, "Ethnicity among the 'Citizen' Indians of Tidewater Virginia," 199.

46. W. A. Plecker to A. T. Shields, 26 September 1935, Clerks Correspondence (A. T. Shields).

47. "Inter Office Information" from Jim to Ken, 14 January 1947, James R. Coates Papers, Accession 31577, Personal Papers Collection, Library of Virginia, Richmond. [Hereafter James R. Coates Papers.] See also Rountree, *Pocahontas's People*, 231, 267.

48. W. A. Plecker to J. R. Tucker, 8 October 1942, box 56, John Powell Papers.

49. *Richmond Times-Dispatch*, 29 January 1929, cutting in box 56, John Powell Papers.

50. W. A. Plecker to Senator J. Griswold Webb, 3 March 1926, box 56, John Powell Papers.

51. Unreferenced, undated newspaper article in James R. Coates Papers.
52. Endo, "The Word 'Mixed' without the 'Indian' Would Be Better," 95–98.
53. E. P. Bradby to Matthew K. Sniffen, 6 July 1925, reel 42, *Indian Rights Association Papers*. The Chickahominy Indians–Eastern Division Inc. were a band of about forty people who formed in the early nineteenth century and had incorporated themselves in order to try to achieve some kind of legal status.
54. Norman Cassell to "Whom it may concern," 10 October 1905, James R. Coates Papers.
55. Rev. E. D. Gooch to "Whom it may concern," 24 April 1945; Vice President, Goddin and Cayton Inc., Distributors of Standard Replacement Parts, 11 April 1945; V. W. Fox, Dealer in General Merchandise, to James R. Coates, 28 May 1945, James R. Coates Papers.
56. Local Registrar to W. A. Plecker, 28 July 1923, box 56, John Powell Papers.
57. Anonymous to W. A. Plecker, 13 November 1930; W. A. Plecker to Hon. R. M. Irby, Supt. Of Schools, 19 November 1930; W. A. Plecker to Mr. Turner McDowell, Clerk of the Circuit Court, 27 September 1937, Clerks Correspondence (A. T. Shields).
58. W. A. Plecker to A. T. Shields, 1 May 1925, Clerks Correspondence (A. T. Shields).
59. Letter from W. A. Plecker, 10 March 1934, box 56, John Powell Papers.
60. Letter from W. A. Plecker, 11 June 1930, box 56, John Powell Papers.
61. Letter from W. A. Plecker, 21 July 1943, box 56, John Powell Papers.
62. Atha Sorrells v. A. T. Shields, Petition for Mandamus, Circuit Court of Rockbridge, enclosed with Henry Holt to John Powell, 17 November 1924, box 56, John Powell Papers.
63. W. A. Plecker to Mr. V. W. Davis, 14 January 1932, Clerks Correspondence (A. T. Shields); *Richmond Times-Dispatch*, 20 November 1924, cutting in box 56, John Powell Papers.
64. Attorney, Lexington VA to Hon. E. Lee Trinkle, 20 November 1924, box 43, E. Lee Trinkle Executive Papers.
65. W. A. Plecker to A. T. Shields, 9 May 1925, Clerks Correspondence (A. T. Shields).
66. E. H. Anderson, Secy, Virginia Post No. 1 Anglo-Saxon Clubs of America, to E. Lee Trinkle, 17 April 1924, box 43, E. Lee Trinkle Executive Papers.
67. E. Lee Trinkle to E. P. Bradby, 1 December 1925, box 43, E. Lee Trinkle Executive Papers.
68. E. Lee Trinkle to W. A. Plecker, 1 December 1925, box 43, E. Lee Trinkle Executive Papers.
69. E. Lee Trinkle to W. A. Plecker, 4 December 1925, box 43, E. Lee Trinkle Executive Papers.
70. *Richmond Times-Dispatch*, 12 November 1925, cutting in box 56, John Powell Papers; Letter from W. A. Plecker, 19 November 1925, E. Lee Trinkle Executive Papers.

71. Wallenstein, *Tell the Court I Love My Wife*, 141.
72. *Virginia Health Bulletin* 22, no. 8 (August 1930): n.p.
73. W. A. Plecker to John Powell, 13 October 1942, box 56, John Powell Papers.
74. *Indian Truth* 3, no. 4 (April 1926): 2.
75. W. A. Plecker, "Vital Statistics," *Virginia Health Bulletin* 18 (1926): 304.
76. W. A. Plecker to Mr. M. A. Taff, Director, Division of Public Health Statistics, New Orleans, 8 February 1945, box 56, John Powell Papers.
77. W. A. Plecker to Mr. R. N. Anderson, Supt., Russell County School Board, 31 July 1924, box 56, John Powell Papers.
78. F. G. Speck to M. K. Sniffen, 7 May 1925, and enclosures, reel 42, *Indian Rights Association Papers*.
79. *Indian Truth* 2, no. 6 (June 1925): 3.
80. Walter A. Plecker to Matthew K. Sniffen, 27 June 1925, reel 42, *Indian Rights Association Papers*.
81. *Richmond News-Leader*, 2 July 1925, 1.
82. Nelson to Sniffen, 3 August 1925, reel 42, *Indian Rights Association Papers*.
83. E. P. Bradby to M. K. Sniffen, 23 September 1925, reel 42, *Indian Rights Association Papers*.
84. Speck to Virginia Chief, 27 October 1925, reel 42, *Indian Rights Association Papers*.
85. Speck to Virginia Chief, 27 October 1925, Sniffen to Speck, 29 October 1925, reel 42, *Indian Rights Association Papers*.
86. Speck to Sniffen, 17 February 1928, reel 42, *Indian Rights Association Papers*.
87. *Richmond Times-Dispatch*, 31 March 1925; *Richmond News-Leader*, 2 April 1925, 8, 26.
88. Bair, "Remapping the Black/White Body."
89. W. A. Plecker to L. G. Moffatt, 21 April 1943, box 56, John Powell Papers.
90. *Richmond Times-Dispatch*, 15 August 1925. As Daylanne K. English has argued, eugenics was such a salient discourse that, "in some form [it] can (and often does) show up on almost anyone's ideological map between 1890 and 1940." English, *Unnatural Selections*, 2.
91. *Norfolk Journal and Guide*, 19 September 1925.
92. W. A. Plecker to John Collier, 6 April 1943, box 56, John Powell Papers.
93. John S. Fulton, MD, to Plecker, n.d., John Powell Papers.
94. For a discussion of the history and intricacies of federal recognition, see Kopotek, *Recognition Odysseys* and Quinn Jr., "Federal Acknowledgment of American Indian Tribes," 331–64, and "Federal Acknowledgment of American Indian Tribes: Authority, Judicial Interposition, and 25 C.F.R.," 37–69.
95. Donaldson, *Extra Census Bulletin*, 7.
96. Donaldson, *Extra Census Bulletin,* 9.

97. Secretary of the Interior to Hon. Homer P. Snyder, chairman, Committee on Indian Affairs, House of Representatives, n.d., E591, Correspondence, Reports and Related Records Concerning Eastern Cherokee Enrollments, 1907–16, RG 75, NARA–Washington DC [hereafter E591, Eastern Cherokee Enrollments].

98. Mattie Russell, "William Holland Thomas: White Chief of the North Carolina Cherokees" (PhD diss., Duke University, 1947), quoted in Weeks, "The Eastern Cherokee and the New Deal," 304; Gulick, "Language and Passive Resistance among the Eastern Cherokees," 61–62.

99. Joseph W. Howell, *Brief on Behalf of the Eastern Band of Cherokees of North Carolina. In the Matter of the Enrollment of the Members of the Eastern Band of Cherokees of North Carolina, Under the Act of Congress Approved June 4, 1924 (43 Stat. 376)* (Washington DC: Press of Byron S. Adams, 1929), 9, included as part of E603 Records of Land Office, Enrollment Records, Records Relating to the Enrollment of Eastern Cherokee, RG 75, NARA–Washington DC.

100. John G. Welch, Joseph A. Saunooke, and Chas L. Davis to Applicants for Enrollment with Eastern Band of Cherokee Indians, 21 October 1910, E591, Eastern Cherokee Enrollments.

101. C. F. Hauke, second assistant commissioner, to Charles L. Davis, 15 December 1910; Charles Davis to applicants for enrollment with Eastern Band of Cherokee Indians, 20 December 1910; Eastern Band of Cherokee Indians, Council Proceedings, 9 October, 1913, E591, Eastern Cherokee Enrollments.

102. Fred A. Baker, "Final Report on Enrollment of Eastern Band of Cherokee Indians of North Carolina," submitted to the commissioner of Indian Affairs, 1 December 1928, 4 E597 Applications and Related Records, 1925–1928, Records of the Eastern Cherokee Enrolling Commission, RG 75, NARA–Washington DC.

103. Howell, *Brief on Behalf of the Eastern Band of Cherokees of North Carolina*, 18–19.

104. Howell, *Brief on Behalf of the Eastern Band of Cherokees of North Carolina*, 24–25.

105. See, for example, the testimony and decisions contained in E589 Guion Miller Report and Exhibits, 1908–1910, Records of the Land Office, RG 75, NARA–Washington DC.

106. Osburn, "The 'Identified Full-Bloods' in Mississippi," 423–47.

107. In the 1970s the Mashpee Wampanoags had to defend accusations that they were "more" African American than American Indian when they filed a lawsuit asking for the return of ancestral land. Carrilo, "Identity as Idiom," 511–45.

108. Rountree, "Ethnicity among the 'Citizen' Indians of Tidewater Virginia," 201.

109. Gover, *Tribal Constitutionalism*, 76n45.

CONCLUSION

1. Moreton-Robinson, *The White Possessive*, xxiii–xxiv.

2. Cohen, *Handbook of Federal Indian Law*, 3–4.

3. "Current Comments by the Editor-General," *Quarterly Journal of the Society of American Indians* 2., no. 1 (January-March 1914): 3–4.
4. *Report of the Commissioner to the Five Civilized Tribes to the Secretary of the Interior, 1912*, 6.
5. *Report of the Commissioner to the Five Civilized Tribes to the Secretary of the Interior, 1910*, 6.
6. Gover, *Tribal Constitutionalism*, 112. For a discussion of how one nation, the Navajo, arrived at a definition of tribal membership that uses blood quantum, see Spruhan, "The Origins, Current Status, and Future Prospects of Blood Quantum."
7. Banivanua Mar, *Decolonisation and the Pacific*, 77.
8. Lowery, *Lumbee Indians in the Jim Crow South*, xi.
9. Stremlau, *Sustaining the Cherokee Family*, 13.

BIBLIOGRAPHY

ARCHIVES AND MANUSCRIPT MATERIALS

Alderman Library, University of Virginia, Charlottesville. MSS 7284, John Powell Papers.

Library of Virginia, Richmond. Clerk's Correspondence (A. T. Shields), Rockbridge County Court Records; James R. Coates Papers, Accession 31577; E. Lee Trinkle Executive Papers, 1922–26, Accession Number 21567b.

National Archives and Records Administration—Great Lakes Region, Chicago. RG 75: White Earth Reservation Records: E1293 Records of Special Agent John H. Hinton, Correspondence, 1910–1914. Chippewa Commission Records: E1297 Correspondence, 1889–1900; E1298 Letters Sent by the Chairman, 1893–1900; E1300, Letters Sent by the Chairman to the Secretary of the Interior, May–December 1892; E1303 Proceedings in Enrollment Cases, 1897–1899. RG 118: Records Related to the White Earth Cases, 1911–1919.

National Archives and Records Administration—Southwest Region, Fort Worth. RG 75: E57 J. W. Howell, Report Relating to the Enrollment of Citizens and Freedmen of the Five Civilized Tribes, 1909; E58A Transcripts of Testimony Given to W. C. Pollock, Five Civilized Tribes Agency, 1910–1911; E65A Records of the Chief Clerk of the Cherokee Enrollment Division, 1900–1901; E74 Applications for Enrollment Through Intermarriage, Records Relating to Cherokee Citizenship; E90B1 Dockets of Special Enrollment Cases, Muskogee, 1905–1907; Applications for Certificates of Competency, 1945–1965, Osage Agency.

National Archives and Records Administration—Washington DC. RG 75: Central Classified Files 1907–1939: General Services File 53, Enrollment—Citizenship—Degree of Indian Blood; General Services File 127, Indians Competent—Roll of Honour; E96 Letters Sent "Land"; E485 Journal of Cheyenne and Arapaho

Competency Board, Jan–Feb 1917; Records of the Land Division, Records Concerning the Removals and Restrictions on Land Sales and Certificates of Competency, Records Relating to Application for Removal of Restrictions on Cherokee Allotments, 1906–08; E589 Records of the Land Office, Guion Miller Report and Exhibits, 1908–1910; E591 Correspondence, Reports and Related Records Concerning Eastern Cherokee Enrollments, 1907–16; E597 Applications and Related Records, 1925–1928, Records of the Eastern Cherokee Enrolling Commission; E603 Records of Land Office, Enrollment Records, Records Relating to Enrollment of Eastern Cherokee. E616 Applications and Other Records Relating to Registrations Under the Indian Reorganization Act of 1934, 1935–42.

National Library of Australia, Canberra. Collier, John. "A Birdseye View of Indian Policy: Historic and Contemporary (Submitted to the Sub-Committee of the Appropriation Committee of the House of Representatives, December 30, 1935, upon request of Representative Marion Zioncheck, of Washington)," unpublished typescript.

Oklahoma Historical Society, Oklahoma City. Letters and Documents Relating to Citizenship in the Creek Nation, 1896–1910; Choctaw National Record and Other Documents.

Washington State University Libraries, Manuscripts, Archives and Special Collections, Pullman, Washington State. Papers of Lucullus Virgil McWhorter, 1845–1945.

Western History Collections, University of Oklahoma, Norman, Oklahoma. Doris Duke Collection; Indian Pioneer Papers.

PUBLISHED WORKS

Adams, Charles E. *Assault on a Culture: The Anishinaabeg of the Great Lakes and the Dynamics of Change*. Bloomington IN: Xlibris, 2013.

Allen, Chadwick. "Blood (and) Memory." *American Literature* 71, no. 10 (March 1991): 93–116.

Anderson, Warwick. *The Cultivation of Whiteness: Science, Health, and Racial Destiny in Australia*. Carlton South: Melbourne University Press, 2002.

Anglo-Saxon Clubs of America. *Anglo-Saxon Clubs of America*. Richmond VA: National Executive Committee, 1923.

Armstrong, S. C. *Report of a Trip Made in Behalf of The Indian Rights Association to some Indian Reservations of the Southwest by S. C. Armstrong, Principal of Hampton School, Va*. Philadelphia: Office of the IRA, 1884.

Aubert, Guillaume. "'The Blood of France': Race and Purity of Blood in the French Atlantic World Author." *William and Mary Quarterly* 61, no. 3 (July 2004): 439–78.

Bair, Barbara. "Remapping the Black/White Body: Sexuality, Nationalism, and Biracial Antimiscegenation Activism in 1920s Virginia." In *Sex/Love/Race: Crossing*

Boundaries in North American History, ed. Martha Hodes, 399–419. New York: New York University Press, 1999.

Baker, Lee D. *Anthropology and the Racial Politics of Culture*. Durham NC: Duke University Press, 2010.

Banivanua Mar, Tracey. *Decolonisation and the Pacific: Indigenous Globalisation and the Ends of Empire*. Cambridge UK: Cambridge University Press, 2016.

Banner, Stuart. *Possessing the Pacific: Land, Settlers, and Indigenous People from Australia to Alaska*. Cambridge MA: Harvard University Press, 2007.

Barker, Joanne. "IndianTM USA." *Wičazo Ša Review* 18, no. 1 (Spring 2003): 25–79.

Basson, Lauren L. "Challenging Boundaries and Belongings: 'Mixed Blood' Allotment Disputes at the Turn of the Twentieth Century." In *Boundaries and Belonging: States and Societies in the Struggle to Shape Identities and Local Practices*, ed. Joel S. Migdal, 151–76. New York: Cambridge University Press, 2004.

————. *White Enough to Be American: Race Mixing, Indigenous People, and the Boundaries of State and Nation*. Chapel Hill: University of North Carolina Press, 2008.

Beaulieu, David L. "Curly Hair and Big Feet: Physical Anthropology and the Implementation of Land Allotment on the White Earth Chippewa Reservation." *American Indian Quarterly* 8, no. 4 (1984): 281–314.

Beresford, Quentin, and Paul Omagi. *Our State of Mind: Racial Planning and the Stolen Generation*. Fremantle, Western Australia: Fremantle Arts Centre Press, 1998.

Berthrong, Donald J. "Legacies of the Dawes Act: Bureaucrats and Land Thieves at the Cheyenne–Arapaho Agencies of Oklahoma." In *The Plains Indians of the Twentieth Century*, ed. Peter Iverson, 31–54. Norman: University of Oklahoma Press, 1985.

Beverley, Robert. *The History and Present State of Virginia*, ed. Louis B. Wright. Charlottesville: University Press of Virginia, 1968 [1705].

Bieder, Robert E. "The Representations of Indian Bodies in Nineteenth-Century American Anthropology." *American Indian Quarterly* 20, no. 2 (Spring 1996): 165–79.

Biolsi, Thomas. "The Birth of the Reservation: Making the Modern Individual among the Lakota." *American Ethnologist* 22, no. 1 (1995): 28–53.

Birch, Tony. "A Mabo Blood Test?" *Australasian Journal of Anthropology* 6, nos. 1–2 (1995): 32–42.

Bizzaro, Resa Crane. "Shooting Our Last Arrow: Developing a Rhetoric of Identity for Unenrolled American Indians." *College English* 67, no. 1 (September 2004): 61–74.

Bohaker, Heidi. "'Nindoodemag': The Significance of Algonquian Kinship Networks in the Eastern Great Lakes Region, 1600–1701." *William and Mary Quarterly* 63, no. 1 (2006): 23–52.

Bokovoy, Matthew F. *The San Diego Fairs and Southwestern Memory, 1880–1940*. Albuquerque: University of New Mexico Press, 2005.

Bonnin, Gertrude, Charles H. Fabens, and Matthew K. Sniffen. *Oklahoma's Poor Rich Indians: An Orgy of Graft and Exploitation of the Five Civilized Tribes—Legalized Robbery*. Philadelphia: IRA, 1924.

Bragi, David Arv. *Invisible Indians: Mixed-Blood Native Americans Who Are Not Enrolled in Federally Recognized Tribes*. Tucson AZ: Grail Media, 2005.

Brooks, James F. "Confounding the Color Line: Indian–Black Relations in Historical and Anthropological Perspective." *American Indian Quarterly* 22, nos. 1–2 (Winter–Spring 1998): 125–33.

Brown, Harry J. *Injun Joe's Ghost: The Indian Mixed-Blood in American Writing*. Columbia: University of Missouri Press, 2004.

Brown, Kathleen M. *Good Wives, Nasty Wenches, and Anxious Patriarchs: Gender, Race, and Power in Colonial Virginia*. Chapel Hill: University of North Carolina Press, 1996.

Brownell, Margo S. "Who Is an Indian? Searching for an Answer to the Question at the Core of Federal Indian Law." *University of Michigan Journal of Law Reform* 34, nos. 1–2 (2000–2001): 275–320.

Brownlie, Robin Jarvis. *A Fatherly Eye: Indian Agents, Government Power, and Aboriginal Resistance in Ontario, 1918–1939*. Don Mills, ON: Oxford University Press, 2003.

Bureau of Vital Statistics, State Board of Health. *Eugenics in Relation to the New Family and the Law on Racial Integrity*. Richmond VA: David Bottom, Supt. Public Printing, 1924.

Burton, Jeffrey. *Indian Territory and the United States, 1866–1906: Courts, Government, and the Movement for Oklahoma Statehood*. Norman: University of Oklahoma Press, 1995.

Cahill, Cathleen C. *Federal Fathers and Mothers: A Social History of the United States Indian Service, 1869–1933*. Chapel Hill: University of North Carolina Press, 2011.

Carrilo, Jo. "Identity as Idiom: *Mashpee* Reconsidered." *Indiana Law Review* 28 (1994–1995): 511–45.

Carroll, Charles. *The Tempter of Eve, or, The Criminality of Man's Social, Political, and Religious Equality with the Negro, and the Amalgamation to which these Crimes Inevitably Lead*. St. Louis MO: The Adamic Publishing Co., 1902.

Carter, Kent. *The Dawes Commission and the Allotment of the Five Civilized Tribes, 1893–1914*. Orem UT: Ancestry.com, 1999.

———. "Snakes & Scribes: The Dawes Commission and the Enrollment of the Creeks."' *Prologue* 29, no. 1 (1997), http://www.archives.gov/publications/prologue/1997/spring/dawes-commission-1.html, accessed February 16, 2007.

———. "Wantabes and Outalucks: Searching for Indian Ancestors in Federal Records." U.S. National Archives and Records Administration, http//www.archives.gov/genealogy/heritage/native-american/ancestor-search.html, accessed November 17, 2007.

Chang, David A. Y. O. "Where Will the Nation Be at Home?: Race, Nationalisms, and Emigration Movements in the Creek Nation." In *Crossing Waters, Crossing Worlds: The African Diaspora in Indian Country*, ed. Tiya Miles and Sharon P. Holland, 80–99. Durham NC: Duke University Press, 2006.

———. *The Color of the Land: Race, Nation, and the Politics of Land Ownership in Oklahoma, 1832–1929*. Chapel Hill: University of North Carolina Press, 2011.

Chaplin, Joyce E. "Natural Philosophy and an Early Racial Idiom in North America: Comparing English and Indian Bodies." *William and Mary Quarterly* 54, no. 1 (January 1997): 229–52.

Churchill, Ward. "The Crucible of American Indian Identity: Native Tradition versus Colonial Imposition in Postconquest North America." In *Contemporary Native American Cultural Issues*, ed. Duane Champagne, 39–68. Walnut Creek CA: AltaMira Press, 1999.

Clark, Jennifer. *Aborigines & Activism: Race, Aborigines, and the Coming of the Sixties to Australia*. Crawley: UWA Publishing, 2008.

Cohen, Felix S. *Handbook of Federal Indian Law*. Washington DC: United States Department of the Interior, 1945.

———. *On the Drafting of Tribal Constitutions*. Ed. David E. Wilkins. Norman: University of Oklahoma Press, 2006.

Coleman, Arica L. *That the Blood Stay Pure: African Americans, Native Americans, and the Predicament of Race and Identity in Virginia*. Bloomington: Indiana University Press, 2013.

Commission to the Five Civilized Tribes. *Report of the Commission to the Five Civilized Tribes, 20 November 1894*, published as Senate Mis. Doc. No. 24, 53d cong. 3d sess. 1894.

———. *Annual Report of the Commission to the Five Civilized Tribes in the Indian Territory to the Secretary of the Interior, 1896*. Washington DC: Government Printing Office, 1896.

———. *Annual Report of the Commission to the Five Civilized Tribes in the Indian Territory to the Secretary of the Interior, 1898*. Washington DC: Government Printing Office, 1898.

———. *Sixth Annual Report of the Commission to the Five Civilized Tribes to the Secretary of the Interior, 1899*, published as part of the *Annual Report of the Commissioner of Indian Affairs, 1899*, 56th cong., 1st sess, H.doc 5, Part II.

———. *Report of the Commission to the Five Civilized Tribes to the Secretary of the Interior for the Year ended June 30, 1905*. Washington DC: Government Printing Office, 1905.

———. *Report of the Commission to the Five Civilized Tribes to the Secretary of the Interior for the Fiscal year ended June 30, 1907*. Washington DC: Government Printing Office, 1907.

————. *Report of the Commissioner to the Five Civilized Tribes to the Secretary of the Interior for the Fiscal Year Ended June 30 1908.* Washington DC: Government Printing Office, 1908.

————. *Report of the Commissioner to the Five Civilized Tribes to the Secretary of the Interior for the Fiscal Year Ended June 30, 1909.* Washington DC: Government Printing Office, 1909.

————. *Report of the Commissioner to the Five Civilized Tribes to the Secretary of the Interior for the Fiscal Year Ended June 30 1910.* Washington DC: Government Printing Office, 1910.

————. *Report of the Commissioner to the Five Civilized Tribes to the Secretary of the Interior for the Fiscal Year Ended June 30 1912.* Washington DC: Government Printing Office, 1912.

————. *Report of the Commissioner to the Five Civilized Tribes to the Secretary of the Interior, 1913.* Washington DC: Government Printing Office, 1913.

————. *Report of the Superintendent for the Five Civilized Tribes of Oklahoma to the Secretary of the Interior for the Fiscal Year ended June 30 1916.* Washington DC: Government Printing Office, 1917.

Cook, Samuel R. "The Monacan Indian Nation: Asserting Tribal Sovereignty in the Absence of Federal Recognition." *Wíčazo Ša Review* 17, no. 2 (Autumn 2002): 91–116.

Corntassel, Jeff J. "Who Is Indigenous?" 'Peoplehood" and Ethnonationalist Approaches to Rearticulating Indigenous Identity." *Nationalism and Ethnic Politics* 9, no. 1 (Spring 2003): 75–100.

Crum, Steven. "The Idea of an Indian College or University in Twentieth Century America before the Formation of the Navajo Community College in 1968." *Tribal College: Journal of American Indian Higher Education* 1, no. 1 (1989): 20–23.

Debo, Angie. *And Still the Waters Run: The Betrayal of the Five Civilized Tribes.* Princeton NJ: Princeton University Press, 1991 [1940].

Deer, Sarah, and Cecilia Knapp. "Muscogee Constitutional Jurisprudence: Vhakv Em Pvtakv (The Carpet Under the Law)." *Tulsa Law Review* 49 (2013–2014): 125–81.

Deloria, Philip J. *Playing Indian.* New Haven CT: Yale University Press, 1998.

————. *Indians in Unexpected Places.* Lawrence: University Press of Kansas, 2004.

Deloria, Vine, Jr., and Clifford M. Lytle. *The Nations Within: The Past and Future of American Indian Sovereignty.* Austin: University of Texas Press, 1998.

Dennison, Jean. *Constituting a Twenty-First-Century Osage Nation.* Chapel Hill: University of North Carolina Press, 2012.

————. "The Logic of Recognition: Debating Osage Nation Citizenship in the Twenty-First Century." *American Indian Quarterly* 38, no. 1 (Winter 2014): 1–35.

Denson, Andrew. *Demanding the Cherokee Nation: Indian Autonomy and American Culture, 1830–1900.* Lincoln: University of Nebraska Press, 2004.

Dickson-Gilmore, E. J. "*Iati-Onkwehonwe*: Blood Quantum, Membership, and the Politics of Exclusion in Kahnawake." *Citizenship Studies* 3, no. 1 (1999): 27–43.

Dippie, Brian W. *The Vanishing American: White Attitudes and U.S. Indian Policy.* Lawrence: University Press of Kansas, 1982.

Doerfler, Jill. *Those Who Belong: Identity, Family, Blood, and Citizenship among the White Earth Anishinaabeg.* East Lansing: Michigan State University Press, 2015.

Donaldson, Thomas. *Extra Census Bulletin: Indians. Eastern Band of Cherokees of North Carolina.* Washington DC: United States Census Printing Office, 1892.

Dorr, Lisa Lindquist. "Arm in Arm: Gender, Eugenics, and Virginia's Racial Integrity Acts of the 1920s." *Journal of Women's History* 11, no. 1 (1999): 143–66.

Dusenberry, Verne. "Waiting for a Day That Never Comes: The Dispossessed Métis of Montana." *The Magazine of Western History* 6 (1958). Reprinted in *The New Peoples: Being and Becoming Métis in North America,* ed. Jacqueline Peterson and Jennifer S. H. Brown, 119–36. Manitoba: University of Manitoba Press, 1989.

Ellinghaus, Katherine. *Taking Assimilation to Heart: Marriages of White Women and Indigenous Men in Australia and North America, 1880s–1930s.* Lincoln: University of Nebraska Press, 2006.

Endo, Mika. "The Word 'Mixed' without the 'Indian' Would Be Better." *Native South* 7 (2014): 92–107.

English, Daylanne K. *Unnatural Selections: Eugenics in American Modernism and the Harlem Renaissance.* Chapel Hill: University of North Carolina Press, 2004.

Forbes, Jack D. *Africans and Native Americans: The Language of Race and the Evolution of Red-Black Peoples.* 2nd ed. Urbana: University of Illinois Press, 1993.

———. "Basic Concepts for Understanding Native History and Culture." In *Native American Voices: A Reader,* ed. Susan Lobo and Steve Talbot, 28–40. New York: Longman, 1998.

———. "The Manipulation of Race, Caste, and Identity: Classifying Afroamericans, Native Americans, and Red-Black People." *Journal of Ethnic Studies* 17, no. 4 (1990): 1–51.

———. "Undercounting Native Americans: The 1980 Census and the Manipulation of Racial Identity in the United States." *Wíčazo Ša Review* 6, no. 1 (Spring 1990): 2–26.

Foster, Martha Harrows. *We Know Who We Are: Métis Identity in a Montana Community.* Norman: University of Oklahoma Press, 2006.

Fritz, Henry E. "The Last Hurrah of Christian Humanitarian Indian Reform: The Board of Indian Commissioners, 1909–1918." *Western Historical Quarterly* (April 1985): 147–62.

Gardiner-Garden, John. *Current Brief No. 10: Defining Aboriginality in Australia.* Canberra: Department of the Parliamentary Library, 2003.

Garroutte, Eva Marie. "The Racial Formation of American Indians: Negotiating Legitimate Identities within Tribal and Federal Law." *American Indian Quarterly* 25, no. 2 (2001): 224–39.

———. *Real Indians: Identity and the Survival of Native America*. Berkeley: University of California Press, 2003.

Genetin-Pilawa, C. Joseph. *Crooked Paths to Allotment: The Fight over Federal Indian Policy after the Civil War*. Chapel Hill: University of North Carolina Press, 2012.

Goldberg, Carole. "Members Only: Designing Citizenship Requirements for Indian Nations." In *American Indian Constitutional Reform and the Rebuilding of Native Nations*, ed. Eric D. Lemont, 107–43. Austin: University of Texas Press, 2006.

Gonzales, Angela A. "Racial Legibility: The Federal Census and the (Trans)Formation of 'Black' and 'Indian' Identity, 1790–1920." In *IndiVisible: African-Native American Lives in the Americas*, ed. Gabrielle Tayac, 57–68. Washington DC: National Museum of the American Indian, 2009.

Gould, L. Scott. "Mixing Bodies and Beliefs: The Predicament of Tribes." *Columbia Law Review* 101 (2001): 702–72.

Gover, Kirsty. *Tribal Constitutionalism: States, Tribes, and the Governance of Membership*. New York: Oxford University Press, 2010.

Grande, Sandy, Timothy San Pedro, and Sweeney Windchief. "Indigenous Peoples and Identity in the 21st Century: Remembering, Reclaiming, and Regenerating." In *Multicultural Perspectives on Race, Ethnicity, and Identity*, ed. D. Koslow and L. Salett, 105–22. Washington DC: NASA Press, 2015.

Graybill, Andrew R. *The Red and the White: A Family Saga of the American West*. New York: Liveright, 2013.

Green, Keneisha M. "Who's Who: Exploring the Discrepancy between the Methods of Defining African Americans and Native Americans." *American Indian Law Review* 31 (2006–7): 93–110.

Grinde, Donald A., Jr., and Quintard Taylor. "Red vs. Black: Conflict and Accommodation in the Post–Civil War Indian Territory, 1865–1907." *American Indian Quarterly* 8, no. 3 (Summer 1984): 211–29.

Gross, Ariela J. *What Blood Won't Tell: A History of Race on Trial in America*. Cambridge MA: Harvard University Press, 2008.

Gulick, John. "Language and Passive Resistance among the Eastern Cherokees." *Ethnohistory* 5, no. 1 (1958): 60–81.

Hagan, William T. "Full Blood, Mixed Blood, Generic and Ersatz: The Problem of Indian Identity." *Arizona and the West* 27 no. 4 (Winter 1985): 309–26.

Hamill, James F. "Show Me Your CDIB: Blood Quantum and Indian Identity among Indian People of Oklahoma." *American Behavioral Scientist* 47, no. 3 (November 2003): 267–82.

Hanson, K. C. "Blood and Purity in Leviticus and Revelation." *Listening: Journal of Religion and Culture* 28 (1993): 215–30.

Harmon, Alexandra. "When Is an Indian Not an Indian?: The Friends of the Indian and the Problem of Indian Identity." *Journal of Ethnic Studies* 18, no. 2 (Summer 1990): 95–123.

———. "American Indians and Land Monopolies in the Gilded Age." *Journal of American History* 90, no. 1 (June 2003): 106–33.

Harring, Sidney L. "Crazy Snake and the Creek Struggle for Sovereignty: The Native American Legal Culture and American Law." *American Journal of Legal History* 34 (1990): 365–80.

Higginbotham, A. Leon Jr., and Barbara K. Kopytoff. "Racial Purity and Interracial Sex in the Law of Colonial and Antebellum Virginia." *Georgetown Law Journal* 77, no. 6 (August 1989): 1967–2029.

Hinsley, Curtis M. *Savages and Scientists: The Smithsonian Institution and the Development of American Anthropology, 1846–1910.* Washington DC: Smithsonian Institution Press, 1981.

Hollinger, David A. "Amalgamation and Hypodescent: The Question of Ethnoracial Mixture in the History of the United States." *American Historical Review* 108, no. 5 (2003): 1363–90.

Holm, Tom. "Indian Lobbyists: Cherokee Opposition to the Allotment of Tribal Lands." *American Indian Quarterly* 5, no. 2 (May 1979): 115–34.

Hosmer, Brian C. "Reflections on Indian Cultural 'Brokers': Reginald Oshkosh, Mitchell Oshkenaniew, and the Politics of Menominee Lumbering." *Ethnohistory* 44, no. 3 (1997): 493–509.

Hoxie, Frederick E. *A Final Promise: The Campaign to Assimilate the Indians, 1880–1920.* Lincoln: University of Nebraska Press, 1984.

Hubner, Brian Edward. "'This Is the Whiteman's Law': Aboriginal Resistance, Bureaucratic Change, and the Census of Canada, 1830–2006." *Archival Science* 7, no. 3 (September 2007): 195–206.

Hrdlička, Aleš. "Physical Anthropology of the Lenape or Delawares, and of the Eastern Indians in General." *Bureau of American Ethnology Bulletin* 62, Serial Set vol. no. 7088, session vol. no. 134, 64th cong., 1st sess., H.Doc. 854 (1916).

Hyde, Anne F. "The Blue Flower and the Account Book: Writing a History of Mixed-Blood Americans." *Pacific Historical Review* 85, no. 1 (February 2016): 1–22.

———. *Empires, Nations, and Families: A New History of the North American West, 1800–1860.* New York: HarperCollins, 2011.

Indian Rights Association. *Eighteenth Annual Report, 1900.* Philadelphia: Office of the Indian Rights Association, 1901.

———. *Twenty-Third Annual Report, 1905.* Philadelphia: Office of the Indian Rights Association, 1906.

———. *Twenty-Seventh Annual Report, 1919.* Philadelphia: Indian Rights Association, 1919.

———. *Twenty-Eighth Annual Report, 1920.* Philadelphia: Office of the Indian Rights Association, 1920.

———. *Forty-Eighth Annual Report, 1930.* Philadelphia: Office of the Indian Rights Association, 1931.

———. *Indian Rights Association Papers, 1864–1973.* Glen Rock NJ: Microfilming Corporation of America, 1975.

Ingersoll, Thomas N. *To Intermix with Our White Brothers: Indian Mixed Bloods in the United States from Earliest Times to the Indian Removals.* Albuquerque: University of New Mexico Press, 2005.

Jaimes, M. Annette. "Federal Indian Identification Policy: A Usurpation of Indigenous Sovereignty in North America." In *The State of Native America: Genocide, Colonization, and Resistance,* ed. M. Annette Jaimes, 123–38. Boston: South End Press, 1992.

Jenks, Albert Ernest. *Indian–White Amalgamation: An Anthropometric Study.* Studies in the Social Sciences 6. Minneapolis: Bulletin of the University of Minnesota, 1916.

Johnson, Christopher H., Bernhard Jussen, David Warren Sabean, and Simon Teuscher, eds. *Blood and Kinship: Matter for Metaphor from Ancient Rome to the Present.* New York: Berghahn Books, 2013.

Kauanui, J. Kēhaulani. *Hawaiian Blood: Colonialism and the Politics of Sovereignty and Indigeneity.* Durham NC: Duke University Press, 2008.

Kelly, Lawrence C. "The Indian Reorganization Act: The Dream and the Reality." *Pacific Historical Review* 44, no. 3 (August 1975): 291–312.

Kopotek, Brian. *Recognition Odysseys: Indigeneity, Race, and Federal Tribal Recognition Policy in Three Louisiana Indian Communities.* Durham NC: Duke University Press, 2011.

LaVelle, John P. "The General Allotment Act 'Eligibility' Hoax: Distortions of Law, Policy, and History in Derogation of Indian Tribes." *Wičazo Ša Review* 14, no. 1 (1999): 251–302.

Lawrence, Bonita. "Gender, Race, and the Regulation of Native Identity in Canada and the United States: An Overview." *Hypatia* 18, no. 2 (2003): 3–31.

———. *"Real" Indians and Others: Mixed-Blood Urban Native Peoples and Indigenous Nationhood.* Lincoln: University of Nebraska Press, 2004.

Leupp, Francis E. *The Indian and His Problem.* New York: Charles Scribner's Sons, 1910.

———. "Indian Lands: Their Administration with Reference to Present and Future Use." *Annals of the Academy of Political and Social Science* 33, no. 3 (May 1909): 136–46.

Limerick, Patricia. *The Legacy of Conquest: The Unbroken Past of the American West.* New York: W. W. Norton & Company, 1987.

Linke, Uli. *Blood and Nation: The European Aesthetics of Race*. Philadelphia: University of Pennsylvania Press, 1999.

Littlefield, Daniel F. Jr., and Lonnie E. Underhill. "The 'Crazy Snake Uprising' of 1909: A Red, Black, or White Affair?" *Journal of the Southwest* 20, no. 4 (Winter 1978): 307–24.

Lovett, Laura L. " 'African and Cherokee by Choice': Race and Resistance under Legalized Segregation." *American Indian Quarterly* 22, nos. 1–2 (Winter–Spring 1998): 203–29.

Lowery, Malinda Maynor. *Lumbee Indians in the Jim Crow South: Race, Identity, and the Making of a Nation*. Chapel Hill: University of North Carolina Press, 2010.

Lyons, Scott Richard. *X-Marks: Native Signatures of Assent*. Minneapolis: University of Minnesota Press, 2010.

Maillard, Kevin Noble. "The Pocahontas Exception: The Exemption of American Indian Ancestry from Racial Purity Law." *Michigan Journal of Race and Law* 12 (2006–7): 351–86.

Malcomson, Scott C. *One Drop of Blood: The American Misadventure of Race*. New York: Farrar Straus Giroux, 2000.

Mandell, Daniel R. "The Saga of Sarah Muckamugg: Indian and African American Intermarriage in Colonial New England." In *Sex, Love, Race: Crossing Boundaries in North American History*, ed. Martha Hodes, 72–90. New York: New York University Press, 1999.

———. "Shifting Boundaries of Race and Ethnicity: Indian–Black Intermarriage in Southern New England, 1760–1880." *Journal of American History* 85, no. 2 (1998): 466–501.

Martínez, María Elena. "The Black Blood of New Spain: Limpieza de Sangre, Racial Violence, and Gendered Power in Early Colonial Mexico." *William and Mary Quarterly* 61, no. 3 (July 2004): 479–520.

May, Katja. *African Americans and Native Americans in the Creek and Cherokee Nations, 1830s–1920s*. New York: Garland Publishing, 1996.

McCorquodale, John. "The Legal Classification of Race in Australia." *Aboriginal History* 10, no. 1 (1986): 7–24.

McDonald, Dedra S. "Intimacy and Empire: Indian-African Interaction in Spanish Colonial New Mexico, 1500–1800." *American Indian Quarterly* 22, nos. 1/2 (Winter–Spring 1998): 134–56.

McDonnell, Janet A. *The Dispossession of the American Indian, 1887–1934*. Bloomington: Indiana University Press, 1991.

———. "Land Policy on the Omaha Reservation: Competency Commissions and Forced Fee Patents." *Nebraska History* 63, no. 3 (Fall 1982): 399–411.

McDonnell, Michael. *Masters of Empire: Great Lakes Indians and the Making of America*. New York: Hill & Wang, 2015.

McGregor, Russell. *Imagined Destinies: Aboriginal Australians and the Doomed Race Theory, 1880–1939.* Carlton South, Victoria: Melbourne University Press, 1997.

McLaughlin, William G. *After the Trail of Tears: The Cherokees' Struggle for Sovereignty, 1839–1880.* Chapel Hill: University of North Carolina Press, 1993.

McMullen, Ann. "Blood and Culture: Negotiating Race in Twentieth-Century Native New England." In *Confounding the Color Line: The Indian–Black Experience in North America,* ed. James. F. Brooks, 261–91. Lincoln: University of Nebraska Press, 2002.

McNally, Michael D. *Ojibwe Singers: Hymns, Grief, and a Native Culture in Motion.* St. Paul: Minnesota Historical Society Press, 2009.

Meyer, Melissa L. "American Indian Blood Quantum Requirements: Blood Is Thicker Than Family." In *Over the Edge: Remapping the American West,* ed. Valerie J. Matsumoto and Blake Allmendinger, 231–49. Berkeley: University of California Press, 1999.

———. "Race and Identity in Indian Country." *Ethnohistory* 51, no. 4 (2004): 799–803.

———. *Thicker Than Water: The Origins of Blood as Symbol and Ritual.* New York: Routledge, 2005.

———. *The White Earth Tragedy: Ethnicity and Dispossession at a Minnesota Anishinaabe Reservation, 1889–1920.* Lincoln: University of Nebraska Press, 1994.

Micco, Melinda. "'Blood and Money': The Case of Seminole Freedmen and Seminole Indians in Oklahoma." In *Crossing Waters, Crossing Worlds: The African Diaspora in Indian Country,* ed. Tiya Miles and Sharon P. Holland, 121–44. Durham NC: Duke University Press, 2006.

Mihesuah, Devon A. "American Indian History as a Field of Study." In *Indigenizing the Academy: Transforming Scholarship and Empowering Communities,* ed. Devon Abbott Mihesuah and Angela Cavender Wilson, 143–59. Lincoln: University of Nebraska Press, 2004.

———. "American Indian Identities: Issues of Individual Choice and Development." In *Contemporary Native American Cultural Issues,* ed. Duane Champagne, 13–38. Walnut Creek CA: AltaMira Press, 1999

Miles, Tiya. *Ties That Bind: The Story of an Afro-Cherokee Family in Slavery and Freedom.* Berkeley: University of California Press, 2005.

Miles, Tiya, and Sharon P. Holland, ed. *Crossing Waters, Crossing Worlds: The African Diaspora in Indian Country.* Durham NC: Duke University Press, 2006.

Miller, Bruce Granville. *Invisible Indigenes: The Politics of Nonrecognition.* Lincoln: University of Nebraska Press, 2003.

Miller, Cary. *Ogimaag: Anishinaabeg Leadership, 1760–1845.* Lincoln: University of Nebraska Press, 2010.

Miller, Mark. *Claiming Tribal Identity: The Five Tribes and the Politics of Federal Acknowledgment.* Norman: University of Oklahoma Press, 2013.

Million, Dian. *Therapeutic Nations: Healing in an Age of Indigenous Human Rights.* Tucson: University of Arizona Press, 2013.

Moorehead, Warren K. *Our National Problem: The Sad Condition of the Oklahoma Indians.* Privately Published, 1913.

Moran, Anthony. "White Australia, Settler Nationalism, and Aboriginal Assimilation." *Australian Journal of Politics and History* 51, no. 2 (2005): 168–93.

Moreton-Robinson, Aileen. *The White Possessive: Property, Power, and Indigenous Sovereignty.* Minneapolis: University of Minnesota Press, 2015.

Morse, Rev. Jedidiah. *A Report to the Secretary of War of the United States on Indian Affairs, Comprising a Narrative of a Tour Performed In the Summer of 1820, Under a Commission from the President of the United States, for the Purpose of Ascertaining, for the Use of the Government, the Actual State of the Indian Tribes in Our Country.* New Haven CT: S. Converse, 1822.

Moses, A. Dirk, ed. *Genocide and Settler Society: Frontier Violence and Stolen Indigenous Children in Australian History.* New York: Berghan Books, 2004.

Mulroy, Kevin. "Mixed Race in the Seminole Nation." *Ethnohistory* 58, no. 1 (Winter 2011): 113–41.

Murphy, Lucy Eldersveld. *Great Lakes Creoles: A French-Indian Community on the Northern Borderlands, Prairie du Chien, 1750–1860.* New York: Cambridge University Press, 2014.

Nagel, Joanne. *American Indian Ethnic Renewal: Red Power and the Resurgence of Identity and Culture.* New York: Oxford University Press, 1996.

Nash, Gary B. "The Hidden History of Mestizo America." *Journal of American History* 82, no. 3 (1995): 941–64.

Nash, Jay B., Oliver LaFarge, and W. Carson Ryan, eds. *The New Day for the Indians: A Survey of the Working of the Indian Reorganization Act.* New York: Academy Press, 1938.

Naylor, Celia E. *African Cherokees in Indian Territory: From Chattel to Citizens.* Chapel Hill: University of North Carolina Press, 2008.

Oakley, Christopher Arris. *Keeping the Circle: American Indian Identity in Eastern North Carolina, 1885–2004.* Lincoln: University of Nebraska Press, 2005.

Office of Indian Affairs. *Indian Land Tenure, Economic Status, and Population Trends,* Part 10 of the Report on Land Planning. Washington DC: Government Printing Office, 1935.

Olsen, James S., and Raymond Wilson. *Native Americans in the Twentieth Century.* Urbana: University of Illinois Press, 1986.

Osburn, Katherine M. B. "'Any Sane Person': Race, Rights, and Tribal Sovereignty in the Construction of the Dawes Rolls for the Choctaw Nation." *Journal of the Gilded Age and Progressive Era* 9, no. 4 (October 2010): 451–71.

———. "The 'Identified Full-Bloods' in Mississippi: Race and Choctaw Identity, 1898–1918." *Ethnohistory* 56, no. 3 (Summer 2009): 423–47.

Otis, Elwell S. *The Indian Question*. New York: Sheldon and Company, 1878.

Parker, Arthur C. "Current Comments by the Editor-General." *Quarterly Journal of the Society of American Indians* 2, no. 1 (January–March 1914): 3–4.

Pascoe, Peggy. "Miscegenation Law, Court Cases, and Ideologies of 'Race' in Twentieth-Century America." *Journal of American History* 83, no. 1 (1996): 44–69.

———. "Race, Gender, and Intercultural Relations: The Case of Interracial Marriage." *Frontiers* 22, no. 1 (1991): 5–18.

———. "Race, Gender, and the Privileges of Property: On the Significance of Miscegenation Law in the U.S. West." In *Over the Edge: Remapping the American West*, ed. Valerie J. Matsumoto and Blake Allmendinger, 215–30. Berkeley: University of California Press, 1999.

Perdue, Theda. *"Mixed Blood" Indians: Racial Construction in the Early South*. Mercer University Lamar Memorial Lectures 45. Athens: University of Georgia Press, 2003.

———. "Race and Culture: Writing the Ethnohistory of the Early South." *Ethnohistory* 51, no. 4 (2004): 701–23.

Penn, William S., ed. *As We Are Now: Mixblood Essays on Race and Identity*. Berkeley: University of California Press, 1997.

Peterson, Jacqueline. "Prelude to Red River: A Social Portrait of the Great Lakes Metis." *Ethnohistory* 25, no. 1 (1978): 41–67.

Peterson, Jacqueline, and Jennifer S. H. Brown, eds. *The New Peoples: Being and Becoming Métis in North America*. Winnipeg: University of Manitoba Press, 1985.

Philp, Kenneth R. "John Collier and the Controversy over the Wheeler–Howard Bill." In *Indian-White Relations: A Persistent Paradox*, ed. Jane F. Smith and Robert M. Kvasnicka, 171–206. Washington DC: Howard University Press, 1976.

———. *John Collier's Crusade for Indian Reform, 1920–1954*. Tucson: University of Arizona Press, 1977.

———, ed. *Indian Self-Rule: First-Hand Accounts of Indian-White Relations from Roosevelt to Reagan*. Salt Lake City UT: Howe Brothers, 1986.

Plecker, W. A. "Vital Statistics." *Virginia Health Bulletin* 18 (1926).

Porter, Robert P., and Carroll D. Wright. *Extra Census Bulletin. The Five Civilized Tribes in Indian Territory: The Cherokee, Chickasaw, Choctaw, Creek, and Seminole Nations*. Washington DC: United States Census Printing Office, 1890.

"Qualifications of Applicants." Code of Federal Regulations Title 43, pt. 2531.1 (1887).

Quinn, William W., Jr. "Federal Acknowledgment of American Indian Tribes: Authority, Judicial Interposition and 25 C.F.R." *American Indian Law Review* 17, no. 1 (1992): 37–69.

———. "Federal Acknowledgment of American Indian Tribes: The Historical Development of a Legal Concept." *American Journal of Legal History* 34, no. 4 (October 1990): 331–64.

Raibmon, Paige. *Authentic Indians: Episodes of Encounter from the Late Nineteenth-Century Northwest Coast.* Durham NC: Duke University Press, 2005.

Ray, S. Alan. "A Race or a Nation?: Cherokee National Identity and the Status of Freedmen's Descendants." *Michigan Journal of Race and Law* 12 (Spring 2006–7): 387–463.

Reddy, Marlita A., ed. *Statistical Record of Native North Americans.* Detroit MI: Gale Research Inc., 1993.

Reinhardt, Akim D. "A Crude Replacement: The Indian New Deal, Indirect Colonialism, and Pine Ridge Reservation." *Journal of Colonialism and Colonial History* 6, no. 1 (2005): n.p. Available through http://muse.uq.edu.au, accessed September 21, 2010.

Rountree, Helen C. "Ethnicity Among the 'Citizen' Indians of Tidewater Virginia, 1800–1930." In *Strategies for Survival: American Indians in the Eastern United States*, ed. Frank W. Porter III, 173–209. New York: Greenwood Press, 1986.

———. *Pocahontas's People: The Powhatan Indians of Virginia through Four Centuries.* Norman: University of Oklahoma Press, 1990.

Rosier, Paul C. *Rebirth of the Blackfeet Nation, 1912–1954.* Lincoln: University of Nebraska Press, 2001.

Rowse, Tim. "Indigenous Heterogeneity." *Australian Historical Studies* 45, no. 3 (2014): 297–310.

Rowse, Tim, and Len Smith. "The Limits of 'Elimination' in the Politics of Population." *Australian Historical Studies* 41, no. 10 (2010): 90–106.

Rusco, Elmer. *A Fateful Time: The Background and Legislative History of the Indian Reorganization Act.* Reno: University of Nevada Press, 2000.

———. "The Indian Reorganization Act and Indian Self-Government." In *American Indian Constitutional Reform and the Rebuilding of Nations*, ed. Eric D. Lemont, 49–82. Austin: University of Texas Press, 2006.

Russell, Steve. "The Racial Paradoxes of Tribal Citizenship." *American Studies* 46, nos. 3–4 (Fall–Winter 2005): 163–85.

Russell-Wood, A. J. R. *Slavery and Freedom in Colonial Brazil.* Oxford: Oneworld Publications, 2002.

Salesa, Damon. *Racial Crossings: Race, Intermarriage, and the Victorian British Empire.* Oxford: Oxford University Press, 1991.

Saunt, Claudio. *Black, White, and Indian: Race and the Unmaking of an American Family.* New York: Oxford University Press, 2005.

———. "'The English Has Now a Mind to Make Slaves of Them All': Creeks, Seminoles, and the Problem of Slavery." In *Confounding the Color Line: The Indian–Black*

Experience in North America, ed. James F. Brooks, 47–75. Lincoln: University of Nebraska Press, 2002.

Saunt, Claudio, Barbara Krauthamer, Tiya Miles, Celia E. Naylor, and Circe Sturm. "Rethinking Race and Culture in the Early South." *Ethnohistory* 53, no. 2 (2006): 399–405.

Schmeckebier, Laurence F. *The Office of Indian Affairs: Its History, Activities, and Organization*. Baltimore MD: Johns Hopkins University Press, 1927.

Schreier, Jesse T. "Indian or Freedman?: Enrollment, Race, and Identity in the Choctaw Nation, 1896–1907." *Western Historical Quarterly* 42, no. 4 (Winter 2011): 458–79.

Schwartz, E. A. "Red Atlantis Revisited: Community and Culture in the Writings of John Collier." *American Indian Quarterly* 18, no. 4 (Autumn 1994): 507–31.

Sells, Cato. "The 'First Americans' as Loyal Citizens." *American Review of Reviews* (May 1918): 523–24.

Shannon, A. H. *The Negro in Washington: A Study in Race Amalgamation*. New York: Walter Neale, 1930.

Sherman, Richard B. "'The Last Stand': The Fight for Racial Integrity in Virginia in the 1920s." *Journal of Southern History* 54, no. 1 (February 1988): 69–82.

Shoemaker, Nancy. *American Indian Population Recovery in the Twentieth Century*. Albuquerque: University of New Mexico Press, 1999.

Sider, Gerald M. *Lumbee Indian Histories: Race, Ethnicity, and Indian Identity in the Southern United States*. New York: Cambridge University Press, 1993.

Simpson, Audra. *Mohawk Interruptus: Political Life across the Borders of Settler States*. Durham NC: Duke University Press, 2014.

———. "On Ethnographic Refusal: Indigeneity, 'Voice', and Colonial Citizenship." *Junctures* 9 (December 2007): 67–80.

———. "Paths toward a Mohawk Nation: Narratives of Citizenship and Nationhood in Kahnawake." In *Political Theory and the Rights of Indigenous Peoples*, ed. Duncan Ivison, Paul Patton, and Will Sanders, 113–36. Cambridge UK: Cambridge University Press, 2000.

Smith, J. Douglas. *Managing White Supremacy: Race, Politics, and Citizenship in Jim Crow Virginia*. Chapel Hill: University of North Carolina Press, 2002.

Smithers, Gregory D. *The Cherokee Diaspora: An Indigenous History of Migration, Resettlement, and Identity*. New Haven CT: Yale University Press, 2015.

———. "The Dark Side of Anti-Racism: 'Half-Breeds' and the Anthropology of Aleš Hrdlička." *Transnational Subjects* 1, no. 1 (2011): 65–88.

Smits, David D. "'Abominable Mixture': Toward the Repudiation of Anglo-Indian Intermarriage in Seventeenth-Century Virginia." *Virginia Magazine of History and Biography* 95, no. 2 (April 1987): 157–92.

────. "'Squaw Men,' 'Half-Breeds,' and Amalgamators: Late Nineteenth-Century Anglo-American Attitudes toward Indian-White Race-Mixing." *American Indian Culture and Research Journal* 15, no. 3 (1991): 29–61.

Snelgrove, Corey, Rita Kaur Dhamoon, and Jeff Corntassel. "Unsettling Settler Colonialism: The Discourse and Politics of Settlers, and Solidarity with Indigenous Nations." *Decolonization: Indigeneity, Education & Society* 3, no. 2 (2014): 1–32.

Snipp, C. Matthew. "An Overview of American Indian Populations." In *American Indian Nations: Yesterday, Today, and Tomorrow*, ed. George Horse Capture, Duane Champagne, and Chandler Jackson, 38–48. Walnut Creek CA: Altamira Press, 2007.

────. "Who Are American Indians?" Some Observations about the Perils and Pitfalls of Data for Race and Ethnicity." *Population Research and Policy Review* 5 (1986): 237–52.

Sober, Nancy Hope. *The Intruders: The Illegal Residents of the Cherokee Nation, 1866–1907.* Ponca City OK: Cherokee Books, 1991.

Spear, Jennifer M. "'Clean of blood, without stain or mixture': Blood, Race, and Sexuality in Spanish Louisiana." In *A Centre of Wonders: The Body in Early America*, ed. Janet Moore Lindman and Michele Lise Tarter, 95–108. Ithaca NY: Cornell University Press, 2001.

Spencer, Frank. "Aleš Hrdlička, M.D., 1869–1943: A Chronicle of the Life and World of an American Physical Anthropologist." PhD diss., University of Michigan, 1979.

Spruhan, Paul. "Indian as Race/Indian as Political Status: Implementation of the Half-Blood Requirement under the Indian Reorganization Act, 1934–45." *Rutgers Race and The Law Review* 8, no. 1 (2006): 27–49.

────. "A Legal History of Blood Quantum in Federal Indian Law to 1935." *South Dakota Law Review* 51, no. 1 (2006): 1–50.

────. "The Origins, Current Status, and Future Prospects of Blood Quantum as the Definition of Membership in the Navajo Nation." *Tribal Law Journal* 8 (2007–8): 1–17.

Stark, Heidi Kiiwetinepineskiik. "Marked by Fire: Anishinaabe Articulations of Nationhood in Treaty Making with the United States and Canada." *American Indian Quarterly* 36, no. 2 (Spring 2012): 119–49.

Stocking, George Jr. "The Turn-of-the-Century Concept of Race." *Modernism/Modernity* 1, no. 1 (1994): 4–16.

Stoler, Ann Laura. *Along the Archival Grain: Epistemic Anxieties and Colonial Common Sense.* Princeton NJ: Princeton University Press, 2009.

Stremlau, Rose. *Sustaining the Cherokee Family: Kinship and the Allotment of an Indigenous Nation.* Chapel Hill: University of North Carolina Press, 2011.

Strong, Pauline Turner, and Barrik Van Winkle. "'Indian Blood': Reflections on the Reckoning and Refiguring of Native North American Identity." *Cultural Anthropology* 11, no. 4 (1996): 547–76.

Sturm, Circe. *Blood Politics: Race, Culture, and Identity in the Cherokee Nation.* Berkeley: University of California Press, 2002.

———. "Blood Politics, Racial Classification, and Cherokee National Identity: The Trials and Tribulations of the Cherokee Freedmen." In *Confounding the Color Line: The Indian-Black Experience in North America,* ed. James. F. Brooks, 223–57. Lincoln: University of Nebraska Press, 2002.

Sweet, John Wood, *Bodies Politic: Negotiating Race in the American North, 1730–1830.* Baltimore MD: Johns Hopkins University Press, 2003.

Swimmer, Ross, Former Principal Chief, Cherokee Nation of Oklahoma. "Firsthand Accounts: Membership and Citizenship." In *American Indian Constitutional Reform and the Rebuilding of Native Nations,* ed. Eric D. Lemont, 166–83. Austin: University of Texas Press, 2006.

Tallbear, Kimberley. "DNA and Native American Identity." In *IndiVisible: African-Native American Lives in the Americas,* ed. Gabrielle Tayac, 69–76. Washington DC: National Museum of the American Indian, 2009.

———. "The Political Economy of Tribal Citizenship in the United States." *Aboriginal Policy Studies* 1, no. 3 (2011): 72.

Taylor, Graham D. *The New Deal and American Indian Tribalism: The Administration of the Indian Reorganization Act, 1934–45.* Lincoln: University of Nebraska Press, 1980.

Treuer, Anton. *Warrior Nation: A History of the Red Lake Ojibwe.* St. Paul: Minnesota Historical Society Press, 2015.

Trosper, Ronald L. "Native American Boundary Maintenance: The Flathead Indian Reservation, Montana, 1860–1970." *Ethnicity* 3 (1976): 256–74.

U.S. Census Bureau. *Statistics of the Indian Population—Number, Tribes, Sex, Age, Fecundity, and Vitality.* Washington DC: Department of Commerce and Bureau of the Census, 1910.

U.S. Congress. *Congressional Record.* 45th cong., 2d sess., 1878.

———. *Congressional Record.* 65th cong., 1 sess., Rec. 841, 1923–24.

———. *Congressional Record.* 73rd cong., 2d sess., 1934.

U.S. Congress. House. *Annual Report of the Commissioner of Indian Affairs, 1888.* Washington DC: Government Printing Office, 1889.

———. *Annual Report of the Commissioner of Indian Affairs. 1890.* Washington DC: Government Printing Office, 1891.

———. *Final Report of the United States Chippewa Commission, 26 December 1889, Presidential message on relief of Chippewa Indians of Minnesota.* 51st cong., 1 sess., 1890.

———. *Annual Report of the Commissioner of Indian Affairs, 1892*. Washington DC: Government Printing Office, 1892.

———. *Annual Report of the Commissioner of Indian Affairs, 1895*. Washington DC: Government Printing Office, 1896.

———. *Confirming Title of Mixed-Blood Indians to Lands*. House Rpt. 2276, 54th cong., 1 sess., 1896.

———. *An Act for the Protection of the People of the Indian Territory, and for other purposes*, 30 Stat., 495. Chapter 517, 55th cong., 2d sess., 1898.

———. *Annual Report of the Commissioner of Indian Affairs, 1905*. Washington DC: Government Printing Office, 1905.

———. *Report in the Matter of the Investigation of the White Earth Reservation* 62nd cong., 3d sess. Washington DC: Government Printing Office, 1913.

———. *An Act Making Appropriations for the Current and Contingent Expenses of the Bureau of Indian Affairs, for fulfilling treaty stipulations with various Indian tribes, and for other purposes, for the fiscal year ending June 30, 1920*. 66th cong., 1 sess., 1919.

———. *Indians of the United States, Field Investigation*, House Rpt. 1133, 66th cong, 3d sess., 1920.

———. *Reorganizing the Indian Service*, House Rpt. 1189, 66th cong., 3d sess., 1921.

———. *Cancellation of Patents in Fee Simple to Indians for Allotments held in trust by the United States*. 69th cong., 2d sess., 1927.

———. *Cancellation of Certain Fee Simple Patents Issued to Indians for Allotments Without Their Consent*. 71st cong., 2d sess., 1931.

———. *Hearings Before the Committee on Indian Affairs*, 73d cong., 2d sess. Washington DC: Government Printing Office, 1934.

———. *Conference Report on Indian Lands and Resources, to accompany S.3645*, House Rpt. 2049, 73rd cong, 2d sess., 1934.

U.S. Congress. Senate. *Report of the Commission Appointed to Negotiate with the Five Civilized Tribes of Indians Known as the Dawes Commission, December 5, 1895*, Sen. Doc. No. 12, 54th cong., 1 sess. Washington DC: Government Printing Office, 1895.

———. *Argument Made By Judge McKennon Before the Committee on Indian Affairs of the House of Representatives Relative to the Condition of Affairs in the Indian Territory Together with Other Papers*. Sen. Doc. 182. 54th cong., 1 sess., 1896.

———. *Rights of Mixed Blood Indians*. Sen. Rpt. 969, 54th cong., 1 sess., 1896.

———. *Title of Mixed-Blood Indians to Their Lands*. Sen. Rpt. 7, 55th cong., 1 sess., 1897.

———. *Protest of Keetoowah Cherokees*, Senate Doc. 333, 56th cong. 1 sess., 1900.

———. *Rights of Mississippi Choctaws in the Choctaw Nation. Memorial of the full-blood Mississippi Choctaws relative to their rights in the Choctaw Nation*, Senate Doc. 319, 57th cong., 1 sess., 1902.

———. *Allotting Indian lands in Indian Territory. Petition praying for an investigation by Congress of the conduct and actions of the "Dawes Commission" in allotting Indian lands in the Indian Territory*, Senate Doc. 260, 58th cong., 2d sess., 1904.

———. *Letter from Albert J. Lee, Remonstrating Against the Passage of an Amendment to the Bill (H.R.5976) to Provide for the Final Disposition of the Five Civilized Tribes in the Indian Territory, March 31, 1906*, Protest to Passage of Amendment to H.R. 5976, Sen. Doc No. 301, 59th cong., 1 sess., April 3, 1906.

———. *Condition of Indian Affairs in Wisconsin: Hearings before the Committee on Indian Affairs, United States Senate, on Senate resolution no. 263*, 61st cong., 2d sess., 1910.

———. *Memorial from the Keetoowah Society on Behalf of the Cherokee Indians Relative to lands of Cherokee Indians which are to be allotted to children*, Senate Doc. No. 816, 61st cong, 3d sess., 1911.

———. *To Authorize the Extension of the Period of Restriction Against Alienation on the Homestead Allotments made to the Members of the Kansas or Kaw Tribe of Indians in Oklahoma*, Senate Rpt. 433, 68th cong., 1 sess., 1924.

———. *Cancellation of Certain Fee Simple Patents Issued to Indians for Allotments Without Their Consent*. 71st cong., 3d sess., 1931.

U.S. Senate Committee on Indian Affairs. *Hearings Before the Committee on Indian Affairs, Second Session on S.2755 and S.3645 A Bill to Grant to Indians Living Under Federal Tutelage the Freedom to Organize*, Part 2, 73rd cong., 2d sess., 1934. Washington DC: Government Printing Office, 1934.

———. *Thomasina E. Jordan Indian Tribes of Virginia Federal Recognition Act: Hearing before the Committee on Indian Affairs*. 107th cong., 2d. sess. Washington DC: Government Printing Office, 2003.

———. Committee on Indian Affairs. *To extend federal recognition to the Chickahominy Indian Tribe, the Chickahominy Indian Tribe-Eastern Division, the Upper Mattaponi Tribe, the Rappahannock Tribe, Inc., the Monacan Indian Nation, and the Nansemond Indian Tribe: Report (to accompany S. 1423)*. Washington DC: Government Printing Office, 2004.

United States v. First National Bank of Detroit, Minnesota, No 873, Supreme Court of the United States, 234 U.S. 245, 1914.

United States v. Nichols-Chisholm Lumber Company, No 874, Supreme Court of the United States, 34 S. Ct. 846, 1914.

United States v. Nichols-Chisholm Lumber Company, No 875, Supreme Court of the United States, 58 L. Ed. 1298, 1914.

Unrau, William E. *Mixed Bloods and Tribal Dissolution: Charles Curtis and the Quest for Indian Identity*. Lawrence: University of Kansas Press, 1989.

Upham, Warren. "Holmes Anniversary Volume: Anthropological Essays Presented to William Henry Holmes in Honor of His Seventieth Birthday, December 1, 1916." *Minnesota History Bulletin* 2, No. 3 (August 1917): 181–83

Van Kirk, Sylvia. *Many Tender Ties: Women in Fur-Trade Society, 1670–1870*. Norman: University of Oklahoma Press, 1983.

Van Riper, Paul P. "The American Administrative State: Wilson and the Founders." In *A Centennial History of the American Administrative State*, ed. Ralph Clark Chandler, 3–36. New York: The Free Press, 1987.

Vezina v. United States et al, No. 4725 Circuit Court of Appeals, Eighth Circuit, 245 F. 411, 1917.

Villazor, Rose Cuison. "Blood Quantum Land Laws and the Race versus Political Identity Dilemma." *California Law Review* 96, no. 3 (2008): 801–37.

Villella, Peter B. " 'Pure and Noble Indians, Untainted by Inferior Idolatrous Races': Native Elites and the Discourse of Blood Purity in Late Colonial Mexico." *Hispanic American Historical Review* 91, no. 4 (2011): 633–63.

Vizenor, Gerald. "American Indian Art and Literature Today: Survivance and Tragic Wisdom." *Museum International* 62, no. 3 (September 2010): 41–51.

——, ed. *Survivance: Narratives of Native Presence*. Lincoln: University of Nebraska Press, 2008.

Vizenor, Gerald, and Jill Doerfler. *The White Earth Nation: Ratification of a Native Democratic Constitution*. Lincoln: University of Nebraska Press, 2012.

Wadlington, Walter. "The *Loving* Case: Virginia's Anti-Miscegenation Statue in Historical Perspective." *Virginia Law Review* 52, no. 6 (October 1966): 1189–223.

Wallenstein, Peter. "Race, Marriage, and the Law of Freedom: Alabama and Virginia, 1860s-1960s." *Chicago-Kent Law Review* 70, no. 2 (1994): 371–437.

——. *Tell The Court I Love My Wife: Race, Marriage, and the Law—An American History*. New York: Palgrave MacMillan, 2002.

Wanhalla, Angela. "The Politics of 'Periodical Counting': Race, Place, and Identity in Southern New Zealand." In *Making Settler Colonial Space: Perspectives on Race, Place, and Identity*, ed. Tracey Banivanua Mar and Penelope Edmonds, 198–217. London: Palgrave Macmillan, 2010.

Washburn, Wilcomb E. *The American Indian and the United States: A Documentary History*. New York: Random House, 1973.

——. "A Fifty-Year Perspective on the Indian Reorganization Act." *American Anthropologist* 86, no. 2 (June 1984): 279–89.

Weaver, Hilary N. "Indigenous Identity: What Is It, and Who *Really* Has It?" *American Indian Quarterly* 25, no. 2 (2001): 240–55.

Weeks, Charles J. "The Eastern Cherokee and the New Deal." *North Carolina Historical Review* 53 (July 1976): 303–19.

Wilson, Terry P. "Blood Quantum: Native American Mixed Bloods." In *Racially Mixed People in America*, ed. Maria P. P. Root, 108–25. Newbury Park CA: Sage Publications, 1992.

Witgen, Michael. *An Infinity of Nations: How the Native New World Shaped Early North America*. Philadelphia: University of Pennsylvania Press, 2012.

———. "The Rituals of Possession: Native Identity and the Invention of Empire in Seventeenth-Century Western North America." *Ethnohistory* 54, no. 4 (Fall 2007): 639–68.

Wolfe, Patrick. "Land, Labor, and Difference: Elementary Structures of Race." *American Historical Review* 106, no. 3 (June 2001): 1866–905.

———. "Settler Colonialism and the Elimination of the Native." *Journal of Genocide Research* 8, no. 4 (December 2006): 387–409.

———. *Settler Colonialism and the Transformation of Anthropology: The Politics and Poetics of an Ethnographic Event*. London: Cassell, 1999.

———. *Traces of History: Elementary Structures of Race*. London: Verso, 2016.

Yarborough, Fay A. "'Dis Land Which Jines Dat of Ole Master's': The Meaning of Citizenship for the Choctaw Freedpeople." In *Civil War Wests: Testing the Limits of the United States*, ed. Adam Arenson and Andrew R. Graybill, 224–41. Berkeley: University of California Press, 2015.

———. *Race and the Cherokee Nation: Sovereignty in the Nineteenth Century*. Philadelphia: University of Pennsylvania Press, 2008.

Zellar, Gary. *African Creeks: Estelvste and the Creek Nation*. Norman: University of Oklahoma Press, 2007.

Zissu, Erik. *Blood Matters: Five Civilized Tribes and the Search for Unity in the Twentieth Century*. New York: Routledge, 2001.

Page numbers in italic indicate illustrations.

allotments (*cont.*)
   Dawes Commission and, 24–26,
      27–30, 32, 34, 35–39, 41–44, 116–17,
      133n66, 138–39n24; education and
      schools regarding, xx, 41, 55–56, 57,
      58, 61, 62–64, 142n80, 150n57; fee
      patents and certificates for, 13, 16,
      45–59, *48*, 59–60, 63–64, 143n17;
      gender and, xvi–xvii, 10, 56; graft-
      ers and intruders regarding, xxiv,
      16, 19, 24–26, 40–42, 61; intermar-
      riage and, 4–5, 10, 11, 28, 56, 81, 94;
      investigations concerning, 13–14,
      15, 16–17, 20–21; laws and legisla-
      tion regarding, 16, 21, 40, 46–47,
      50–53, 55, 72, 115; negotiations for,
      xix, 4, 15, 22, 25, 37, 43; residency
      as requirement for, 7–8, 10–11, 34,
      135n36; resistance and, xix, 26, 38–
      39; taxes for, 35, 40, 46, 54, 59, 66,
      68; tribal rolls and, 25–27, 30–31,
      34–36, 37–38, 40, 42–44, 71–72. *See
      also* competency; General Allot-
      ment Act of 1887; lands
amalgamation, 19, 109, 129–31n48. *See
   also* biological absorption
American Review of Reviews (Sells), 58
Amherst County (VA), 98, 100–101
ancestry: assumptions and prejudices
   regarding, 27–28, 59, 115–17; biology
   and "science" regarding, 11, 17–20,
   82–83, 86–87, *87*; censuses and, xxiii–
   xxiv, 109–10; children and, 23, 32–36,
   42–43, 98–100; citizenship and, 28–
   29, 32–34, 40, 43, 53, 58; competency
   and, 40, 53–55, 58, 64–65; court cases
   and lawsuits regarding, 17–20, 104–
   5, 156n107; enrollments and tribal
   memberships regarding, 10, 11, 28,
   32–36, 42–43, 71; intermarriage and

miscegenation concerning, 28, 36, 86,
   92–95, 97–99, 130n48, 151n4, 151n110;
   land allotments and, xxiii–xxiv, 10–11,
   17, 27–29, 77–78, 138n16, 156n107;
   mothers and, 16, 23, 32–34, 35–36, 43;
   "one-drop rule" and, xiii, 92–95, 96,
   126n11; racial integrity concerning,
   91–100, 102–6; racism and segregation concerning, 92–100; registration
   under IRA and, 77–81, *79*, 84–85, 86
"Anglo-Saxon Club of America," 95–
   96, 105
Anishinaabeg: anthropometry and
   eugenics regarding, 18–19, 136n64;
   Burke Act and, 13, 46–47, 51;
   censuses for, 3, 5–6, 6–7, 9, 12;
   competency and, xix–xx, 12–13, 16,
   20, 22, 46, 51, 55, 59; enrollments
   and tribal memberships for, xix,
   1–2, 4–10, 11, 12, 17, 22; ethnographic refusal and survivance by,
   12, 22; identities and status of, 1–4,
   6–7, 9–12, 14–22; land allotments
   for, xix, 1, 3–8, 10–22; negotiations
   and resistance concerning, xix, 4,
   7–8, 15, 22; tribal rolls for, 5–6,
   11, 13, 14–16, 17, 21; usage of term,
   133n1. *See also* Chippewas; White
   Earth Reservation
annuities, 6, 10, 77, 135n36. *See also*
   Chickasaw Annuity Roll of 1878
anthropologists: amalgamation and,
   129n48; regarding blood and Indianness, xiii, xvii–xviii, 17–19, 102,
   110, 111; examinations, investigations, and studies by, 13–14, 17–19,
   82–87, *87*; as sympathizers, 107–8
anthropology, xvii–xviii, 17–19,
   82, 83–84, 85, 130n48. *See also*
   anthropometry

anthropometry, 71, 82–83, 85–87, *87*, 90. *See also* anthropology; "science"

applicants: for certificates and licenses, 104; competency and fee patents, 46–47, 51, 65–66, 67–68; for enrollments and tribal memberships, 2, 6–7, 9, 10–11, 29–36, 71–72, 76–78, 82–84, 88, 89–90, 111–13, 134n28, 135n36; for land allotments, 10–11, 71–72, 89, 135n36; for registration under IRA, 76–78, 80–82, 84–86. *See also* claimants

applications, xviii, xxx; citizenship, 34; competency and fee patents, 13, 16, 46–47, 51–57, 58, 64, 67–68; enrollments and tribal memberships, 23–24, 25, 29, 71–72, 75–76, 90, 117, 137n1; marriage certificates and licenses, 102; for registration under IRA, 76–80, *79*, 82, 85, 86

archaeologists, 13–14, 116–17

Armstrong, S. C., 27

assimilation: acculturation regarding, 77–78, 90; biological absorption and amalgamation concerning, xxi–xxiii, 112, 128–29n43, 129–31n48; blood and, xiv–xvii, xviii–xxiii, xxvii–xxx, 46–47, 50, 71, 90–95, 129n46; blood quantum and, xiv–xvii, xviii–xxiii, 46–47, 71, 92, 115–19, 128n41, 129n46; competency and, 45–47; elimination and genocide regarding, xxi–xxiii, xxvii, 28–29, 128–29n43; Wheeler-Howard Act and, xii, xx, 70, 72–75. *See also* colonialism; Dawes Act; General Allotment Act of 1887; Indian New Deal; Indian Reorganization Act

Atha Sorrells v. A. T. Shields, 104

attorney generals, 15, 106; assistant, enrollments and tribal memberships, 7–8, 11, 23, 34; representative, land allotments and, 14

Australia, xii, xxi–xxii, xxvii, 125n1, 128n43, 132n62, 133n66

babies. *See* birth certificates

Bair, Barbara, 152n19

Baker, Lee D., xiii

"Baker Roll," 112

Banivanua Mar, Tracey, 118

Barker, Joanne, xxvii

beliefs. *See* prejudices

benefits. *See* resources

Berthrong, Donald J., 63

Beverley, Robert, 129–30n48

biological absorption, xxi–xxii, 128–29n43, 130n48. *See also* amalgamation

biology, xvii, 4, 11, 127n23. *See also* "science"

Biolsi, Thomas, 132–33n66

birth certificates, xviii, xxi, 91, 98–100, 103, 106, 108, 109, 150n1

Bixby, Tams, 37

Bizzaro, Resa Crane, 131n53

Blackfeet. *See* Siksikas

Blackness, xx, 94, 95, 96

Blacks. *See* African Americans; freedmen; "Negroes"

blood: acculturation concerning, xiii–xiv, xvii–xviii, 11–12, 71–72, 74–75, 117, 118, 149–50n57; anthropologists and anthropology regarding, xiii, xvii–xviii, 17–19, 102, 110, 111; assimilation and, xiv–xvii, xviii–xxiv, xxvii–xxx, 46–47, 50, 90–95, 115–19, 129n46; assumptions and prejudices regarding, xvi, 116–17;

blood (*cont.*)
authenticity and characteristics concerning, xii–xiv, 2, 82–83, 86–87, *87*, 111–13, 116–17, 126n8; biology and, 4, 11; censuses and, 6–7, 26–27, 110; citizenship and, 28–29, 30, 31–34, 36, 40, 43, 53, 58, 68–69; competency and, 40, 44, 46–47, 50, 53–55, 56, 57–58, 63, 67–69; constitutions and governments concerning, 22, 86, 88, 117; court cases regarding, 17–18, 104–5; early colonialism and, xiv, xv; intermarriage and miscegenation concerning, 36, 92–95, 113; laws and, xi–xii, xiv, 15, 26, 32, 46, 55, 94, 95, 102, 152–53n35; legislation and, xii, xv, 21, 40, 42, 46–47, 53, 74, 94, 95, 96, 102, 115; "one-drop rule" and, xiii, 92–95, 96, 100; racial integrity regarding, xvi–xviii, xx–xxi, xxiv, 91–92, 95–97, 100, 102, 104–6, 107, 110, 116–17, 139n24; racism and segregation concerning, 92–95, 100; registration under IRA and, 76–79, *79*, 84, 85–86; "science" and, xv, xvii, xix, 4, 17–18, 82–83, 86, 119; settler colonialism and, xv–xvi, xviii, xx, xxi–xxiii, xxiv–xxx, 26, 94, 132n62; tribal revenues and, 137n8. *See also* blood quantum
blood quantum: allotment and land, xi, xiv–xvii, xv, xviii–xxiii, 46, 68–69, 115–19, 128n41, 129n46; assumptions and prejudices regarding, xvi, 111, 113, 116, 118–19, 126n8; censuses and, 26–27; citizenship and, 31–36; competency and, 44, 46–47, 54, 58, 67–69; constitutions and governments concerning, 111, 113, 117–18,

119; early colonialism and, xv, 127n17, 128n30; laws and legislation concerning, 21, 46–47, 74, 115; registration under IRA and, xx, 71–72, 74–75, *78*, 78–79, 80, 88; settler colonialism regarding, xv–xvi, xx, xxi–xxiii, xxvii–xxviii, 69, 128n41
Blood Roll, 21, 28–29
Bloom, Leonard, 111
Board of Indian Commissioners, 13–14, 41. *See also* Office of Indian Affairs
Boas, Franz, xvii
Bohaker, Heidi, 3
Bokovoy, Matthew F., 18, 136n64
Bonnin, Gertrude. *See* Zitkála-Šá
Boomers. *See* intruders
Bradby, E. P., 102, 105, 108
Breckinridge, Commissioner, 138n24
Breuninger, August A., xxiv–xxv, xxvi, 131n54, 146n72
Brown, Harry J., 74
Brown, Kathleen M., 151n13
Brownlie, Robin, 133n66
Bruner, Joseph, 73–74
bulletins, 110–11
Burch, Marsden C., 14
Bureau of Ethnology and the Census, 109–10
Bureau of the Census, 150n57. *See also* censuses
Bureau of Vital Statistics, 91, 95, 96–100, 101, 103, 151n17. *See also* Racial Integrity Act
Burke, Charles, 51, 57
Burke Act, 13, 46–47, 51, 146n72
Bushyhead, Chief, 34
Byrd, William, 129–30n48

Cahill, Cathleen, xvi, 128n31
California. *See* Hoopa Valley Agency

Choctaws (*cont.*)
history of, 24, 35, 93; intermarriage and miscegenation regarding, 36–37, 93, 130n48; Mississippi Choctaws, 84, 113; registration under IRA and, 80, 82, 89; resistance, 67; revenues of, 137n8; status of, 38, 67, 113. *See also* Five Tribes
Churchill, Ward, 129n46
CIA. *See* Commissioner of Indian Affairs
circuit court, Rockbridge County, 150n1
circulars, 51, 58
citizenship: enrollments and tribal memberships regarding, xxiv–xxv, 23, 25–26, 28–38, 42–44, 131n54; ethnographic refusal and resistance concerning, xxviii, 26, 36–38; land allotments and, xxv, 22, 25–26, 28, 37–38, 47, 53, 68–69, 146n72; laws, legislation, and statutes regarding, 36–37, 40, 42, 47, 51, 53, 69, 146n72; tribal rolls and, 26, 28–36, 37–38, 40, 42–44, 47
claimants: competency, 67–68; enrollments and tribal memberships, 6–7, 8–9, 38, 67, 70, 74–75; land allotments, xxiii–xxiv, 4–5, 10, 16–17, 67, 138–39n24; registration under IRA and, 76, 78. *See also* applicants
Clapp, Moses E., 13. *See also* riders
Clark, Jennifer, 133n66
classification, racial: ancestry and blood, xvi–xvii, xviii–xxi, xxiv, 17–19, 91–95, 110; anthropology and anthropometry regarding, xvii–xviii, 17–19, 83–87, *87*, 90; identities and status, xv–xviii, xxiv, 91–92, 94–95; racism and, 92–101, 103. *See also* race; racial integrity

Cloud, Henry Roe, 81–82
coal, 137n8
Coates, James R., 101, 102–3
Cobb, W. Montague, 148–49n45
Code of Federal Regulations (CFR), xi–xii
Cohen, Felix S., 53, 143n17, 146n72
Coleman, Arica L., 95, 151n14
College of William and Mary, 105
Collier, John, 49, 70, 72–74, 76–77, 84–85, 86, 109, 149n57
colonialism, 73; blood and blood quantum regarding, xviii, xx, xxi–xxiii, xxiv–xxx, 26, 94, 119, 132n62; citizenship and, xxiv–xxv, 69; early, xiv, xv–xvi, 128n30; enrollments and tribal memberships regarding, xx, xxv–xxvii, xxviii–xxix; identities and status concerning, xxi–xxiii, xxiv–xxix, 26–27, 94; sovereignty and, xxiv, xxvii–xxviii, 26; unwritten ideas for, xv–xvi, 128n30
Commissioner of Indian Affairs (CIA): biology and culture concerning, 83–84; citizenship and, xxv, 1–2, 36, 37, 47, 125–26n2, 131n54; competency and fee patents concerning, xxii–xxiii, 13, 16, 49, 51–58, 60–61, 63, 145n57; "Declaration of Policy" by, 57–59, 60, 67; enrollments and tribal memberships concerning, xxv, 1–2, 6–7, 9, 10, 11, 14, 37, 77, 83–84, 89–90; identities and status regarding, 1–2, 10, 11, 37, 89–90, 125–26n2; incompetency and, 65–66; intermarriage, 36, 140n52; land allotments and, 10–11, 13, 14, 16, 37, 47, 49, 51–53, 57–59, 65–66, 89; lawsuits against, 131n54; leases and, 13, 49,

Dawes Commission: enrollments and tribal memberships concerning, 23–24, 25–26, 28–38, 42–44, 117, 137n1; ethnographic refusals and resistance concerning, 26, 36–40, 133n66; land allotments and, 24–26, 27–28, 30, 35–39, 40–44, 116–17, 138–39n24; negotiations and, 25, 37, 39, 43, 140n61; testimonies and, 138–39n24, 141n71; tribal governments and, 24, 25–26, 35, 38, 39–40, 117, 141n71. *See also* Five Tribes; General Allotment Act of 1887; Indian Territory

death certificates, 91, 99, 150n1

"Declaration of Policy," 57–59, 60, 67

defendants, 15, 20, 136n55

Delawares, 67

Deloria, Philip, 50, 66

Deloria, Vine, Jr., 73

Dennison, Jean, xxvii

Denson, Andrew, 138n16

descendants. *See* ancestry

Dhamoon, Rita, 132n62

Dippie, Brian W., 93–94

discrimination. *See* racism; segregation

district courts, 14, 21

Doerfler, Jill, 7, 11–12

DOI. *See* United States Department of the Interior

Dorr, Lisa Lindquist, 151n14

Dusenberry, Verne, 131n53

Eastern Band of Cherokees, 92, 110–14

education, 55, 62–64, 78, 150n57. *See also* schools

elimination. *See* amalgamation; biological absorption; genocide

Ellis, C. L., 66

Endo, Mika, 151n14

enfranchisement, 133n66. *See also* competency

English, Daylanne K., 155n90

enrollment: activism and resistance concerning, xix, 26, 36–38, 111–13; ancestry and, 9–10, 28, 32–36, 42–43; anthropometry and anthropology regarding, 17–19; applications for, 23–24, 25, 29, 90, 117, 137n1; biology and "science" concerning, xv, 4, 17; censuses and, 6–8, 9–10, 12, 37; citizenship and, 23, 28–36; court cases and hearings for, 7–9, 12, 17, 37; laws and, xix, 32, 33–34; legislation and, 7–8, 23, 36–37, 142n89; mistakes and omissions concerning, 29, 30–31, 32–34, 35–36, 43, 138n24; negotiations and, xix, 4, 7, 22, 37, 43; registration under IRA and, 76–77, 80–82; residency as requirement for, 7–8, 32–33, 34; settler colonialism and, xv–xvi, xviii–xix, xxv–xxvi, 24–26; testimonies and, 22, 131n54, 138n24. *See also* memberships, tribal; rolls, tribal

"equitable box," 23, 43

Estabrook, Arthur H., 114. See also *Mongrel Virginians*

ethnographic refusal, xxvii–xxix, 12, 22, 54, 92, 132–33nn64–66. *See also* activists; resistance, acts of

eugenicists, xvii, 18–19, 136n64

eugenics, xvii, 18, 97–98, 109, 155n90

Eugenics in Relation to the New Family and the Law on Racial Integrity (Bureau of Vital Statistics), 97, 109, 151n17

Europeans, xii–xiii, xiii–xiv, 2–3, 24, 151n4. *See also* whites

exploitation. *See* fraud

Fabens, Charles H., 40–41, 49

General Allotment Act of 1887: blood and blood quantum as criteria for, xi–xii, xv–xvi, xix–xx, xxii–xxiii, xxx, 43–44, 129n46; Burke Act and, 13, 46–47, 51; detribalization and displacement through, xix–xx, xxii–xxiii, 128n41; "Indian problem" and, 72; settler colonialism and, xxv, xxvii; trust period for, xix–xx, 13, 40, 46, 50, 51. See also assimilation; Dawes Act

Genetin-Pilawa, C. Joseph, xviii

genocide, xxi–xxiii, 28–29, 128–29n43, 132n62

George Gustav Heye Center. See National Museum of the American Indian

Gonzales, Angela A., xv

Gover, Kirsty, 88, 118

governments, tribal: Dawes Commission and, 24, 25–26, 35, 38, 39–40, 117; Indian Reorganization Act and, 72–73, 74–75; sovereignty and, xxviii–xix, 39–40, 117–19, 132n64; testimonies and, 141n71

grafters, xxiv, 16, 19, 40–42

Grande, Sandy, xxix

Grant, Ulysses S., 37

Grayson family, 35, 139n41

Great Lakes, 2, 134n8

Gross, Ariela J., xv

Hall, D. S., 6, 8, 9, 134n28, 135n36. See also Chippewa Commission

Harjo, Chitto. See Crazy Snake

Harmon, Alexandra, 54

Harper family, 66

Hartness, Ben, 42

Harvard University, 84

Haskell Institute, 55, 63, 105

Hastings, William Wirt, 138–39n24

Haudenosaunee, 132n64

Hawaiian Homes Commission Act of 1921 (HHCA), xxvii, 128n41

Hayden, Carl Trumbull, 69

headmen. See chiefs, tribal; leaders, tribal

hearings, xxx, 7–9, 12. See also court cases; trials

HHCA. See Hawaiian Homes Commission Act of 1921

Higginbotham, A. Leon, 152n17

Hinton, John, 14, 16, 17

Hitler, Adolf, 109

Hollinger, David A., 93

Holt, Judge, 104–5

Hoopa Valley Agency, 81

Howard University, 148–49n45

Howell, Joseph W., 23, 31, 33–34, 43, 112–13, 139n33

Hoxie, Frederick E., 45

Hrdlička, Aleš, 17–18, 19, 85, 136n64, 149n45

Hubner, Brian Edward, 133n66

Hyde, Anne F., xxvi

hypodescent. See "one-drop rule"

identity: biology and "science" regarding, 17–19, 85, 127n23; censuses for, xv, 97; fluidity of, xxvi–xxvii, 2, 12, 17, 21–22, 70–71, 118–19; intermarriage and, 37; racial integrity concerning, 92, 96–97, 101–2; settler colonialism and, xxi, xxvii–xxix; tribal rolls and, xxvi–xxvii, 17, 21, 29; usage of term, 118–19, 125n1. See also Indianness; status

illegitimacy, 85

incompetency, 53, 62, 64, 65–66, 143n17, 145n42. See also competency

Indian Appropriation acts, 12–13, 44, 51, 128n31, 142n89

*Indian Land Tenure, Economic Status,
and Population Trends* (Office of
Indian Affairs), xxv–xxvi
Indianness: blood and blood quantum
regarding, xi–xiii, 3, 15, 46, 74, 90,
94, 96, 102, 105, 110–11, 113, 116–19;
blood and culture regarding, 12, 17,
21–22, 74–75, 117–18; registration
under IRA and, 82; reservations
and, 90. *See also* identity; status
Indian New Deal: acculturation and
assimilation regarding, 70–74,
83–84, 86, 90, 116, 149–50n57;
anthropometry and anthropology
concerning, 82–87, *87*; enrollments
and tribal memberships regarding,
70–73, 74, 82–84, 88–90; land
allotments and claims concerning, 71–72, 89, 149n57, 150n57; for
registration under IRA and, 76–82,
79, 84–87, *87*; Wheeler-Howard Act
and, xii, xx, 70. *See also* assimilation; Indian Reorganization Act
"Indian problem," xxii–xxiii, 27, 47,
53–54, 68–69, 72, 74
Indian Reorganization Act (IRA):
assimilation and culture regarding,
xii, 70–75, 77–78; enrollments and
tribal memberships regarding,
xii, 70–72, 74, 75–77, 80–82; land
allotments and, xii, 71–72, 77, 81;
registration under IRA and, 76–82,
79, 84–87, *87*; Section 19 and, xii,
71, 74, 75–76, 89; Wheeler-Howard
Act as, xii, xx, 70. *See also* assimilation; Indian New Deal; nations
Indian Rights Association (IRA):
competency and, 13, 47, 49, 56, 58;
racial integrity regarding, 97, 102,
106, 107–8

Indian Territory: Cheyenne and Arapahos in, 60–65; enrollments and
tribal memberships in, xviii–xx,
23–24, 25–26, 28–36, 36–38, 43–44,
117, 139n33; land allotments for,
xviii–xx, 23–26, 27–28, 31, 34–36,
37–39, 43–44, 117; schools in, 41,
142n80; tribal governments in,
39–40, 117, 141n71. *See also* Dawes
Commission; Five Tribes
Indian Truth, 106, 107–8
Indian University, 131n54
Indigenous peoples: Aboriginal Australians as, xii, xxi–xxii, 133n66;
ethnographic refusal and resistance
by, xxvii–xxviii, 119, 132–33n66;
lands and, 147n75; settler colonialism and, xxi, 132n62; usage of term,
125n1. *See also* Native Americans
intermarriage: amalgamation and
biological absorption regarding,
19, 130n48; benefits, funds, and
resources through, 3, 4, 11, 81; citizenship through, 32, 36–37, 146n72;
enrollments and tribal memberships concerning, 28, 36–37, 112–13;
Indian New Deal and, 73, 150n57;
kinship relationships through, 3,
134n8; land allotments and claims
through, 4–5, 10, 11, 28; laws,
legislation, and statutes regarding,
36–37, 104–5, 140n52, 151n10; registration under IRA and, 81–82, 86.
See also amalgamation; biological
absorption; miscegenation
interviews, 34, 35, 36, 42, 61, 62–64,
66, 67–68, 132n65, 139n24
intruders, xxiv, 24–26
IRA. *See* Indian Reorganization Act;
Indian Rights Association

Lyons, Scott Richard, xxvi, xxix
Lytle, Clifford J., 73

Māori, 133n66
marriage certificates, xxi, 96, 98, 99,
102, 103–4, 109
marriages. *See* intermarriage
Marston, George H., 152–53n35
Mashpee Wampanoags, 156n107
May-zhuck-ke-ge-shig, Chief, 8
McDonnell, Janet A., 49, 64, 145n57
McDougle, Ivan E., 114. See also *Mongrel Virginians*
McIntosh, Jobe, 35
McKennon, Commissioner, 33, 141n71
McLaughlin, Commissioner, 145n57
McLaughlin, William G., 25
McMullen Ann, xvii
McPherson, O. M., 62
memberships, tribal: applicants and
claimants for, xxiii–xxiv, 2, 21,
70–72, 74–76, 88, 111–13, 135n36;
biology and "science" concerning,
xv, 4, 17; censuses and, 5–6, 37–38;
citizenship and, 22, 23–24, 25–26,
36–38, 42, 44; laws and legislation
regarding, xi–xii, 36–37, 74; negotiations and resistance concerning,
xxvii–xxix, 4, 37–38, 88–89,
111–13; registration under IRA and,
76–77, 81–82; residency as requirement for, 11, 71, 76–77, 88; settler
colonialism and, xx, xxv–xxvi,
xxviii–xxix, 25–26; sovereignty and,
xxviii–xxix, 117–18, 157n6. *See also*
enrollments; rolls, tribal
Menominees, xxv, 115, 131n54, 142n89
Meritt, E. B., xxv, 61, 131n8
Métis, xiv, 2–3, 131n53, 134n8
Meyer, Melissa L., xv, 6

Michigan, 7, 84
Mihesuah, Devon A., xxix
Miles, Tiya, 28–29, 93, 94
Mille Lacs Band, 5–6
Miller, Bruce Granville, xxi
Miller, Cary, 3
Miller, Mark, 142n88
Million, Dian, xxix
mines, 65–66, 137n8
Minnesota. *See* Anishinaabeg; Chippewas; Red Lake Reservation;
University of Minnesota; White
Earth Reservation
miscegenation, 92–95, 113, 130n48,
151n10. *See also* intermarriage
Mississippi Choctaws, 84, 113
"mixed bloods": activism and resistance
concerning, 88–89; assumptions,
prejudices, and tropes concerning,
xii–xiii, 38, 73–74, 83–84, 86, 116–17,
118–19, 149n57; Burke Act and, 13,
46–47, 51; citizenship of, xxiv–xxv,
53, 69, 131n54; competency and,
xix–xx, 46–47, 50, 51, 53–58, 59–60,
64–65, 67–69; constitutions and
governments regarding, 88, 117;
enrollments and tribal memberships
of, xv, xxii–xxvii, 46–47, 50, 57, 70–
72, 115, 117, 131n54; land allotments
for, xxii, 50, 53–58, 67–69, 71–72,
115, 116–17; landlessness and poverty
of, xxv–xxvi; laws and legislation
regarding, 46–47, 50–51, 53, 115, 125–
26n2; populations of, xxiii, 131n51;
racial classification of, xiv, xv, 53, 59,
71–72, 73–75, 86; registration under
IRA and, 75–82, 79, 84, 86, 88–90,
91; settler colonialism and, xxi–xxiii,
xxiv–xxvii; tribal rolls and, 71–72, 75,
88, 89; usage of term, 118–19

Monacans, xxi, 97–98, 100, 150n2
Mongrel Virginians (Estabrook and McDougle), 91, 114
Montana, 22, 75–76, 81–82, 131n53. *See also* Métis
Moorehead, Warren K., 13–14, 17, 41
Moreton-Robinson, Aileen, 115
Morgan, Thomas, 125–26n2, 134n28
Morse, Jedidiah, 130n48
mothers, 2, 10, 14, 16, 23, 32–34, 35–36, 40, 43, 80, 81, 82, 99, 100, 103. *See also* gender
"mulattoes," xiv, 99–100, 103, 109
Mulroy, Kevin, 29
Muscogees. *See* Creeks; Five Tribes

names: on censuses, 88, 132–33n66; for competency, fee patents, and leases, 51–53, 54, 58, 60, 61, 65; on tribal rolls, 29–31, 33, 35–36, 37, 77, 88, 132n66; racial integrity, 99, 101
National Archives, 43
National Association for the Advancement of Colored People, 108–9
National Resources Board, 150n57
nations: enrollments and tribal memberships for, xxviii–xxix, 117–18; sovereignty and, xxiv, xxviii–xxix, 117–18; usage of term, 125n1. *See also* Anishinaabeg, Blackfeet, Cherokees, Cheyenne and Arapahos, Chickahominy peoples, Chickasaws, Chippewa-Crees, Choctaws, Creeks, Delawares, Eastern Band of Cherokees, Five Tribes, Haudenosaunee, Kansas peoples, Kaws, Lakotas, Lumbees, Mashpee Wampanoags, Menominees, Mississippi Choctaws, Monacans, Navajos, Oglalas, Omahas, Osages, Ottawas, Pamunkeys,

Pueblos, Quapaws, Rappahannocks, Seminoles, Wyandottes
Native Americans: ethnographic refusal and resistance by, xxviii, xxix, 119; settler colonialism and, xviii, xx, xxi, xxiii, xxvii–xxix; usage of term, 125n1. *See also* nations
naturalization, xxv
Navajos, 157n6
Naylor, Celia E., 93
Nebraska. *See* Omahas
Needle, Commissioner, 33, 138n24
"Negroes," xxiii, 30, 33, 38, 86, 90, 91, 99, 101, 103, 104, 106, 107, 108–9. *See also* African Americans; freedmen
Nelson, George L., 107–8
neo-Lamarckism, xvii
The New Day for The Indians, 88–89
New Mexico. *See* Pueblos
newspapers, 103, 105, 108, 109
New Zealand, 133n66
Ngāi Tahu, 133n66
nindoodemag. See kinship
9/11 attacks, 129n46
Norfolk Journal and Guide, 109
North Carolina, 34, 84–86. *See also* Eastern Band of Cherokees
North Dakota, 76, 81, 89. *See also* Chippewa-Crees
numbers, roll, 80–81

Oakball, Jenny, 39
Office of Indian Affairs (OIA): anthropometry and anthropology concerning, xvii–xviii, 17–18, 82–83, 85; Chippewa Commission and, 1–2, 3–12, 15, 17, 21, 134n28, 135n36; competency and fee patents

concerning, 13–14, 41, 45–47, 49–57, 58–59, 60–61, 63, 68–69, 145n57; Dawes Commission and, 25, 43; employees of, xvi–xvii, 76, 88–89, 128n31; enrollments and tribal memberships concerning, xvi–xviii, xxv–xxvi, 1–2, 9–10, 42–43, 44, 71, 82–84, 88–90; identities and status concerning, 70, 76, 81–82, 88–89; incompetency and, 53, 66; "Indian problem" and, xxii–xxiii, 47; land allotments and, 13–14, 45–47, 50–57, 60–61, 71, 89; racial integrity concerning, 109–10; registration under IRA and, 70, 71, 75, 76–77, 79, 79–82, 83, 84, 85, 89, 90. *See also* Commissioner of Indian Affairs; Dawes Commission; General Allotment Act of 1887

Oglalas, 149n57

OIA. *See* Office of Indian Affairs

oil, 56, 60, 144–45n42

Ojibwes. *See* Anishinaabeg; White Earth Reservation

Oklahoma: Cheyenne and Arapahos, 60–65; Five Tribes, 24, 25, 26, 41, 42; Quapaws, 55–56, 56–57, 65–66; Union Agency, 42. *See also* Cherokees; Chickasaws, Choctaws, Creek; Five Tribes; Indian Territory; Seminole

Omahas, 60, 64

"one-drop rule," xiii, 92–95, 96

Oochalata, Chief, 37

opposition, acts of. *See* activists; resistance, acts of

Oregon, 52–53

Osages, xxvii, 56, 59, 60, 66, 142n89

Osborne VA, 153n35

Osburn, Katherine M. B., 38, 113

Otis, Elwell S., 130n48

Ottawas, 67–68

Pacific Ocean, 147n75

pamphlets, 49, 72, 88–89, 97, 109, 131n54

Pamunkeys, xxi, 97, 100, 105, 114

Parker, Arthur Caswell, 116–17

Pascoe, Peggy, 151n10

paternalism, 50, 95. *See also* gender

Peabody Museum of Archaeology and Ethnology, 84

Perry family, 33–34, 139n35

Philp, Kenneth R., 72, 149–50n57

Pine Ridge Indian Reservation, 149n57

Plecker, Walter Ashby, 95, 97–110, 152–53nn34–36

Pocahontas, 96, 112

Pocahontas Exception, 96–97

policies. *See* assimilation; competency; Dawes Act; "Declaration of Policy"; foreign policy; General Allotment Act of 1887; Indian New Deal; Indian Reorganization Act (IRA)

politics, 2, 6–7, 9, 73–74

populations: African Americans, xxiii, 86, 106–7, 110, 131n51; Eastern Band of Cherokees, 112; Five Tribes, 43–44; Native Americans, xxiii, 26, 43–44, 86, 91–92, 106–7, 110, 131n51; Indian Territory, 43–44; "mixed bloods," xxiii, 86, 118–19, 131n51; Virginia, 97–98, 106–7, 110; whites, xxiii, 86, 106–7, 131n51

Porter, Pleasant, 36

post–Civil War Reconstruction. *See* Reconstruction Era

Pottawatomi Reservation, 54

poverty, xxv–xxvi

Powell, John, 106

Powell, Ranson J., 18–19
properties. *See* allotments, land; lands
Pueblos, 60, 72, 73, 84

Quapaw Competency Commission, 65
Quapaw Agency, 55, 66
Quapaws, 55–56, 56–57, 65–66
Quarterly Journal of the Society of American Indians, 116
Quinn, William W., 155n94

race: biology and "science" concerning, xv, 17–19, 71–72, 82–85, 127n23; blood and blood quantum for defining, xiv, xv–xvii, 74–75, 91–95, 118–19; Racial Integrity Act and, xxi, 91, 95–96, 101–2, 104–6, 108, 109, 151n17
racial integrity: blood, and 91–92, 95–100, 102–6, 107–8, 110; Bureau of Vital Statistics and, 91, 95, 96–100, 101, 103, 151n17; Racial Integrity Act and, 95–96, 101–2, 104–6, 108, 109, 151n17; racism and, 92–101, 103, 107
Racial Integrity Act, 95–96, 101–2, 104–6, 108, 109. *See also* Bureau of Vital Statistics; racial integrity
Rappahannocks, xxi, 97, 100, 107–8
Reconstruction Era, 24
Reddy, Marlita A., 131n51
Red Lake Reservation, 3
Reinhardt, Akim D., 149n57
reservations: citizenship and, xxv, 68–69, 131n54; competency and fee patents concerning, 49, 51, 52–55, 58–59, 60, 64, 68–69, 144–45n42; land allotments and, xv, xxv, 49, 52–53, 58–59, 60, 68–69, 115, 117; residency on, 71, 74, 76–77, 80, 88; Rosebud Reservation, 132–33n66.

See also lands; White Earth Reservation
residency: of Anishinabeg, 7–8, 9–11, 135n36; for Five Tribes, 31–32, 34; on reservations, 7–8, 9–11, 71, 74, 76–77, 80, 88
resistance, acts of: enrollments and tribal memberships, xix, 26, 36–38, 88–89, 111–13; racial integrity to, 100–102, 108–10. *See also* activists; ethnographic refusals
resources: through intermarriage, 3, 4, 11; through status, 6, 10, 28; registration under IRA and, 71–72, 75, 81, 115
Rice, Commissioner, 5–6, 8
Richmond News-Leader, 105, 108
Richmond Times-Dispatch, 105, 108
Richmond VA, 105, 108
riders, Clapp, 12–13, 14, 15
rituals, 45
robberies. *See* fraud
Robeson County (NC), 84–85
Rockbridge County (VA), 104, 150n1
Rocky Boy's Band of Chippewas. *See* Chippewa-Crees
Rogers, Joseph, 67
Rolfe, John, 96
rolls, tribal: "Baker Roll" as, 112; "Blood Roll" as, 21; citizenship and, 26, 28–36, 37–38, 40, 42–44, 47; "Indian Role" as, 89; land allotments and, xi, 25–27, 30–31, 34–36, 37–38, 40, 42–44, 47; mistakes and omissions concerning, 29, 30–31, 32–34, 35–36, 43, 138n24; names on, 6, 9, 29–31, 35–36, 37, 77, 88; negotiations and, 37, 43; roll numbers for, 80–81. *See also* enrollments; memberships, tribal

Roosevelt, Eleanor, 89
Rosebud Agency. *See* Rosebud Indian Reservation
Rosebud Indian Reservation, 132–33n66
Rosier, Paul C., 149n57
Rountree, Helen C., 101, 114, 151n14
Rowse, Tim, 129n43, 132n62
Russell, Steve, xi
Russell County (VA), 107

sangre pura, xiv
San Pedro, Timothy, xxix
Saunooke, Joseph A., 111
Saunt, Claudio, 93, 139n41, 151n4
"scattered" people, xx, xxvi, 75–78, 82, 86, 89
Schmeckebier, Laurence F., 52
schools: competency and fee patents concerning, xx, 52, 57, 58, 61, 62–64; land allotments and, xx, 41, 57, 58, 61, 62–64, 142n80; racism and segregation in, 98–99, 100–101, 103, 107, 153n36; registration under IRA and, 72, 90. *See also* education
Schreier, Jesse T., 38
"science," xv, xvii–xviii, xix, 4, 17, 18–19, 82–84, 85–86, 119. *See also* anthropometry; biology
Scott, W. W., 62
secretary of the Interior. *See* United States Department of the Interior (DOI)
segregation, 28, 94–96, 98–99, 100–101, 109, 153n36
Sells, Cato, 54, 57–58, 66, 67
Seltzer, Carl C., 84–86, 149n45
Seminoles, xix, 24, 28, 37, 44, 67, 93. *See also* Five Tribes
Shannon, A. H., 130–31n48

Sherman, Richard B., 151n14
Shields, A. T., 104
Shoeboots family, 28–29
Siksikas, 149n57. *See* Blackfeet
Simpson, Audra, xxix, 54, 132nn64–65
Siouans. *See* Lumbees
Sioux. *See* Lakotas
Smith, J. Douglas, 95, 96–97, 151–52n17
Smith, Redbird, 38
Smithers, Gregory D., 19, 25, 34
Smithsonian Institution, xvii, 14, 17–18
Sneed, James P., 34
Snelgrove, Corey, 132n62
Sniffen, Matthew K., 40–41, 49, 97, 107–8
Society of American Indians, 67, 116
Sorrells, Atha, 102, 104
sovereignty: blood and blood quantum regarding, 26, 92, 113, 117–19; ethnographic refusals as assertions of, xxvii–xxix, 92, 132–33nn64–66; settler colonialism and, xxiv, xxvii–xxviii, 26; term usage regarding, 125n1; tribal governments and, xxviii–xix, 39–40, 117–19, 132n64
Spear, Jennifer, xiv
Speck, Frank G., 107–8
Spruhan, Paul, xv, 84, 127n17, 157n6
Stann, Robin, 37
status: blood regarding, xii–xiii, xvi–xvii, xx, xxiii, xxix–xxx, 115–17, 118–19; benefits, funds, and resources through, 6, 10, 28, 71–72, 75, 81, 89–90, 115; biology and "science" regarding, xiii–xiv, xix, 4; censuses for, xv, xxiii–xxiv, 6–7, 12, 26–27, 88, 97, 126n2, 131n51, 132–33n66; children and, 23, 32–34, 98–100; court cases and testimonies

*Standing Up to Colonial Power: The Lives of Henry
Roe and Elizabeth Bender Cloud*
Renya K. Ramirez

*Walking to Magdalena: Personhood and Place in
Tohono O'odham Songs, Sticks, and Stories*
Seth Schermerhorn

To order or obtain more information on these or other University of Nebraska
Press titles, visit nebraskapress.unl.edu.

CPSIA information can be obtained
at www.ICGtesting.com
Printed in the USA
LVHW090708250222
711955LV00002B/2

9 781496 230379